There are two books that have shifted my world entirely: Naomi Klein's *This Changes Everything* and Mark Boyle's *Drinking Molotov Cocktails with Gandhi* – and of the two, Boyle's is by far the most affecting. If you care about the planet, about our place on it, about the devastation that is modern western living, you have to read this book. Read it, think on it, act on it. Only by each of us doing this, can we hope to be the change we need to see in the world. It's terrifying. But it's the truth.

Manda Scott, *Sunday Times* best-selling author of *Boudica* and *Rome*

Mark Boyle's book throws down the gauntlet at the feet of the world as we know it. His challenge to the complicity of all of us – even those of us who work for change and against injustice – in a system that is destroying the planet and most of its species will trouble many. So too will his endorsement of violent methods of resistance alongside the more accepted nonviolent ones. But he asks questions that need answering at every turn – and his call for the climate change generation to replace 'reduce, reuse, recycle' with 'resist, revolt, rewild' strikes a nerve.

Chris Brazier, *New Internationalist*

In a time of quiescence and fossilised orthodoxies, what we need most is honesty about the human predicament. In this thought-provoking book, Mark Boyle challenges us to explore the dark corners we'd all rather look away from.

Paul Kingsnorth, author of *The Wake* and co-founder of the Dark Mountain Project

Mark's new work lays bare and dissects the violence that lies behind the comforts of our industrialised society. He asks some very hard questions of the environmental and social change movements, which we will all need to address if we are to create true social justice and restore the wider web of life.

Graham Burnett, author of *Permaculture: A Beginners Guide* and *The Vegan Book of Permaculture*

DRINKING MOLOTOV COCKTAILS
WITH
GANDHI

MARK BOYLE

PERMANENT PUBLICATIONS

Published by
Permanent Publications
Hyden House Ltd
The Sustainability Centre
East Meon
Hampshire GU32 1HR
United Kingdom
Tel: +44 (0)1730 823 311
Fax: +44 (0)1730 823 322
Email: enquiries@permaculture.co.uk
Web: www.permanentpublications.co.uk

Published under licence in North America by
New Society Publishers, P.O. Box 189, Gabriola Island, BC, Canada V0R 1X0
www.newsociety.com

© 2015 Mark Boyle
The right of Mark Boyle to be identified as the author of this work has been asserted
by him in accordance with the Copyrights, Designs and Patents Act 1988

Designed and typeset by Emma Postill

Cover design by Kirsty Alston

Printed in the UK by CPI Antony Rowe, Chippenham, Wiltshire

All paper from FSC certified mixed sources

FSC
www.fsc.org
MIX
Paper from
responsible sources
FSC® C013604

The Forest Stewardship Council (FSC) is a non-profit
international organisation established to promote the
responsible management of the world's forests. Products
carrying the FSC label are independently certified to assure
consumers that they come from forests that are managed to
meet the social, economic and ecological needs of present
and future generations.

British Library Cataloguing-in-Publication Data
A catalogue record for this book is available from the British Library

ISBN 978 1 85623 243 2

ABOUT THE AUTHOR

Mark Boyle is a business graduate who lived completely without money for three years, and author of the best-selling books, *The Moneyless Man*, and *The Moneyless Manifesto*. He is a director of Streetbank, a charity that enables people across the world to share skills and resources with neighbours. Mark writes for publications as varied as the *Guardian* and *Permaculture* magazine, contributes to international radio and television, and has been featured in major media including *CNN*, the *Telegraph*, *BBC*, the *Huffington Post*, *ABC*, *Mother Jones* and *Metro*. He lives on a smallholding in Ireland.

CONTENTS

INTRODUCTION

THE ROAD TO HEAVEN IS PAVED WITH EFFECTIVE ACTION

It is not desirable to cultivate a respect for the law, so much as for the right. The only obligation which I have a right to assume, is to do at any time what I think is right.

Henry David Thoreau

D ESPITE WHAT A CURSORY GLANCE of this book may suggest, it is by no means An Ode to Violence. Our world is already filled with a quantity and quality of violence its complex web of inhabitants have never before had to endure; it is hardly my longing to encourage others to add to the dark, eerie mist that engulfs us.

Surprisingly, the purpose of what follows is to help us take the difficult first steps towards peace. Not the illusion of peace, that masterpiece of psychological creativity conjured up by those of us who enjoy the privileges and protection our industrial culture offers in return for our allegiance and obedience, and which we fool ourselves into experiencing on a daily basis. What I am searching for is an unrecognisable and long-since forgotten brand of peace. One which is free from the systemic violence that invisibly infiltrates almost every aspect of the ways by which we civilised folk meet our needs and insatiable desires. A type whose essence disrupts our tamed minds and reveals itself as much in the calm tranquillity of an ancient woodland as it conceals itself within the timeless chase between wolf and doe. A peace strangely imbued in a lioness's ferocious defence of her cubs and the trilateral struggles of bear and salmon and stream, all of whose stories and ancestral patterns weave together the majestic fabric of The Whole and keep its harmony from unravelling at the seams. The peace I seek in the pages yet unturned is the peace of The Wild, one free from civilised, urbane notions of violence, nonviolence and pacifism.

Those of us who live in industrial civilisation – which, for reasons I'll elucidate in chapter two, I call The Machine – can quite easily spend our days living what we feel are decent lives. We drop the kids off to school in the car, pick up a cheese croissant with the newspaper at the supermarket, a soy latte at the local café, before going to work for a respected firm. We may even pour our daily energy into helping others, or worthy causes. Along the way we might say hello to a neighbour, greet a teacher, and thank the checkout guy. In the moments in between changing nappies and climbing whatever career ladder we've stepped upon, most of us will enjoy much of what we perceive to be industrial society's exciting and liberating benefits – social media, central heating, cheap foreign holidays, washing machines and other seemingly innocent pleasures – free from many of the restrictive familial, social and religious ties that kept our forbears' communities intact for so long. All very civilised, friendly and rarely with any conscious ill-intent.

Scratch below this thin veneer of conviviality, however, and you soon discover that our way of life is imbued with a level of violence so extreme that, if it were not hidden from us by complex mechanisms, most of us could not cope with the psychological and emotional pain it would arouse. I will serve up a thin slice of this violence – towards the Earth, the Great Web of Life we share it with and, ultimately, ourselves – in chapter two. However, if you want to not only intellectually understand it, but feel it, there are unfortunately no end of options to choose from.

Stand in a clear-cut of an old-growth forest and inhale the profound sadness of what you see before you. Visit the greasy waters of the Gulf of Mexico and ask yourself, from the perspective of the marine life there, if our diets of South American soya, vitamin pills, tropical fruits and plasticised convenience foods are nonviolent. Take a short trip to your nearest factory farm, where the vast majority of your meat, eggs and dairy come from, and ponder whether industrialism speaks well of us, or is the apex of our humanity. Such run-of-the-mill violence, masquerading as progress, isn't only targeted at the non-human realm; what we are doing to the world, we do unto ourselves, in more ways than one.

Go undercover to a sweatshop, where the children who produce our everyday branded fashions work long hours, often with their toilet-breaks and productivity levels enforced by armed military, and contemplate what nonviolence means to you. Speak with the parents of any of the 21,000 children who die of starvation every single day,[1] predominantly in the global South, and ask them if commodity markets and international finance have been beneficial to their previously unique culture. Visualise the means by which the 85 richest people in the world have accumulated more wealth than poorest 3.5 billion,[2] and the impact this has on the latter's daily existence. Talk to traditional craftspeople, whose time-tested skills and holistic approach to life can no longer compete with the brutal efficiency of The Machine – or to the operatives working on the conveyor

belt of homogeneous things who have become as uniform and interchangeable as the cogs of the machine they are committed to – and
inquire if automation and button-pressing has imbued their livelihoods
with meaning and happiness. If you labour under the impression that
phenomena such as these aren't violent, but merely lamentable glitches
of modernity waiting to be ironed out by political scientists, by the end
of this book I aim to make full-spectrum resistance look decidedly
peaceful in comparison.

Either way, all of the above Crimes Against Life are not only
legally protected by the police forces and courtrooms of the state, they
are fundamental to the functioning of what we call normality. We have
created Frankenstein, and made ourselves dependent on his monstrous
ways. Juxtaposed to this, the scattered outbursts of 'counterviolence'[3] by
victims and activists in reaction to this normalised, everyday systemic
violence are handled with a severity that suggests holistic resistance is
considered to be a genuine threat by The Establishment, that entrenched
structure of rich and powerful people who dictate the conditions we live
within. While those who plan their actions meticulously almost always
live to fight another day, those who get caught are made an example of. In
2001, an Earth Liberation Front (ELF) activist called Jeffrey Luers was
sentenced to over 22 years in prison for torching three SUVs – a symbol
of hyper-consumerism to some – at a dealership in the U.S., despite
the fact that the action was carried out at night to ensure that nobody's
life was endangered.[4] To put that in context, the average sentencing for
convictions of rape there is eight years, a fact that encapsulates the values
of a male-dominated, industrial society.

Such severe sentencing as Luers received was only the beginning.
As we will see in chapter five, draconian legislation such as the Animal
Enterprise Terrorism Act (AETA), which in 2006 was signed into U.S.
law by George W. Bush, was introduced in an attempt to crush 'extreme'
organisations such as the ELF, Earth First! and Stop Huntingdon Animal
Cruelty (SHAC), all of whom were potently active in the preceding
decades. The disproportionate nature of the corporate-state coalition's
response to these movements emerged precisely because their tactics –
such as 'ecotage', a type of sabotage targeted specifically at destroyers
of the natural world – produced tangible results and stymied financial
investment in the targeted industries,[5] despite the tiny fraction of activists

willing to risk their liberty. This is hardly surprising. After all, in a world where money dominates the political landscape, the state criminalises and stigmatises those who put their necks on the line to protect Life, while those who want to convert its sacred splendour into cash lap up society's platitudes.

On top of that, it has long since been understood by The Machine that if these fledgling movements' unsanctioned ideas and feral means were to catch the imagination of the many who find its ubiquitous, top-down violence increasingly intolerable, this sometimes illicit and wilder form of activism – if one part of a holistic resistance movement – could pose a serious threat to its modus operandi. Industrial civilisation, after all, fears anything it cannot control or predict, and its inherent need to pacify the populace has its roots in the same worldview that drives it to want to control, domesticate and pacify The Wild, that naturally anarchistic realm of intimacy, wonder and organised chaos and home to all that live according to their own indomitable will. Along with a sustained campaign of propaganda indoctrinating us with the moral righteousness of nonviolent protest, which continues to warn us that violence can never succeed in effecting change (advice governments seem to themselves ignore when waging wars aimed at achieving their own economic and political agendas), laws such as the AETA were intended to nip any such threat in the bud before its successes inspired a movement too developed for those in power to successfully surveil, infiltrate, control or prosecute.

These propaganda campaigns, which are a prerequisite for such legislation, have themselves become increasingly effective at strait-jacketing the outrage people feel towards the injustices of our time. Whenever anything resembling bottom-up violence occurs during demonstrations – from protests against the Iraq War and the Keystone XL pipeline, to Spain's *indignados* and the Occupy movement – both The Establishment and the protesters' spokespeople (who are filtered for their advocacy of nonviolence) go immediately to the corporate media to condemn it, or issue statements of nonviolence, regardless of the circumstances and whether the actions they decry were entirely appropriate. In doing so, they reinforce the notion in the minds of the public that any violence, even holistic self-defence (an idea I explore in chapter four), applied to those who routinely inflict it downwards is always unjust, undemocratic and immoral, without any serious critique or historical analysis. All the while the top-down violence of The Establishment, that most undemocratic of social constructs, continues unabated without question or mention.

This hypocrisy in the corporate-state kleptocracy's attitude towards violence would be laughable if it were not so tragic. Because of industrial civilisation's need to feed its own limitless appetite for ever-shinier tat, it starts resource wars, commits wholesale ecocide, invades and pillages the lands of indigenous people and abuses both humans and non-humans on every conceivable level. But as Derrick Jensen observes, 'violence done by those higher on the hierarchy to those lower is nearly always invisible, that is, unnoticed. When it is noticed, it is *fully rationalised*. Violence done by those lower on the hierarchy to those higher is unthinkable, and when it is done it is regarded with shock, horror, and the fetishization of the victims.'[6] I have emphasised 'fully rationalised' because I believe this is the key: almost all violence done by the state, and their ideological partners in crime, towards Life is understood to be, and accepted as, legitimate by those who are not the victims of their aggression (with a few extreme exceptions, most notably the Iraq War, which some of the population at least voiced opposition to). Yet those the corporate-state coalition inflict violence upon, or those who want to act in solidarity with its victims, do not have the legal or cultural freedom to respond with an act of physical force, whether lesser or greater. As we'll see in chapter one, by using qualifying terms like 'non-state', 'clandestine' and 'nonmilitary', The Establishment define themselves out of the debate and establish a monopoly on violence and terrorism.[7]

How have we arrived at this, and how is it sustained? One of our key problems is the degree to which industrial peoples are separated from the consequences of their economic habits.[8] Marketing executives, aided by the functionality of global currency, markets and military-backed international contracts and trade agreements, are given multi-billion dollar budgets to effectively keep those who produce things – and the processes by which they do so – hidden from those who consume them. Separating producers from consumers through global marketing is a critical task within any multinational business, for executives know that people, by and large, do not want to intentionally cause harm to anything that falls within their parameters for moral consideration.

Not only that, they inject their vacuous brands with surrogate meaning – in a similar fashion to how processed food manufacturers inject artificial flavouring into otherwise unpalatable food – that temporarily satisfies their customers' deep craving for real emotional and physical connection. In doing so, they desensitise those they claim to serve to the pain of their profound loss, and medicate the outrage that would otherwise surge amongst a psychologically and emotionally healthy population.

Public relations companies have an unexpected ally in their clients' endeavours to pull the wool over our eyes: ourselves. Because our society, and the violence enmeshed in it, is so complex, so too are the patterns of what psychologists call 'cognitive dissonance', that tension an individual experiences when holding a certain belief and performing a contradictory action. In order to cope with being exposed to the consequences of our actions, we concoct all sorts of philosophies, defences, self-deceptions and myths about the world and our place within it. We distract ourselves with cheap entertainment, numb ourselves with anti-depressants and addictions, and create elaborate narratives to inconsistently restrict our parameters of moral consideration. Of course, most of this is done subconsciously, which just makes it even more dangerous – and the need to face up to it even more urgent.

In spite of our creativity in manufacturing coping mechanisms that help us deal with the incongruity between our head, heart and hands, many people somehow manage to maintain an honesty with themselves. In defiance of the best efforts of PR gurus at putting a green sheen on operations that are invariably covered in crimson red, people are becoming increasingly aware of what is happening in their name, and funded by their money. Much of it is inescapable: in the Age of the Internet, stories and images depicting the horrors underlying our lifestyles burst through the corporate world's best attempts to control the situation. Its cumulative effect has propelled people from all walks of life into the role of activist of one sort or another, campaigning on whatever cause they feel most drawn towards, in those spare moments they find between trying to pay the mortgage and feeding a family.

Traumatised by the aggression piercing their subconscious routinely, indoctrinated by culturally-controlled notions of nonviolence, guided by an understandable desire to carry the opinions of the mainstream, whilst fearful of any radical change to the industrial system whose products help soothe their own deep wounds, the vast majority of these agents of change take nonviolent and reformist approaches.

Reformism, in contrast to revolutionism, is the belief that incremental changes to the institutions that form the foundations of one's society, and its political and economic systems, can lead to an entirely different form of society. Few people would actually recognise this term, or think of themselves as reformists, but it is a category that sums up almost the entirety of political, ecological and social activism in the early 21st century. Many reformist actions and movements – such as clicktivism (see page 101), green consumerism, lobbying, protesting, aboveground campaigning and education, Transition Towns, permaculture and many social enterprises – can be hugely positive forces for dealing with the mess created by industrialism and capitalism, and they can often excel at generating innovative solutions for what could come next. This is their role, and it is a critically important one.

When it comes to getting right to the heart of the matter, in ways that could lead to an authentic and lasting peace, they are not so hot. Rosa Luxemburg, when speaking about reformism as a means to political change, even went as far as to say that capitalism 'is not overthrown, but is on the contrary strengthened by the development of social reforms'.[9] By doing so, she was sound-biting a largely forgotten criticism of reformism that points out its paradoxical and counterproductive nature: it seeks to overcome a tyrannical or harmful system, whilst simultaneously trying to improve the conditions created by that very same system and hence making it more tolerable to the populace. In effect, well-intentioned reformist measures can inadvertently lessen the likelihood of any meaningful change by keeping the people, in the words of *Pink Floyd* lyricist Roger Waters, 'comfortably numb'. After all, systems only change when enough people within them can no longer tolerate them. Of course, if we are serious about creating just and sustainable societies enlivened with new (or perhaps old) values, it is not merely capitalism, which Luxemburg spoke about, that needs to be overthrown, but also the outdated cultural narratives that act as its philosophical foundations and which infiltrate our experience of the world in a hundred thousand toxic ways.

This reformist response to the convergence of crises facing us is, as we shall see, not only tolerated by the powerful institutions and individuals who have had an enormously disproportionate role in escalating these crises – it is implicitly supported by them. By permitting a carefully chosen range of protest, as a gesture to democracy and liberalism, those who hold political and economic power can control the metanarrative through a corporate media they are in ideological partnership with. Once the public discourse is controlled, these vested interests in business-as-usual can co-create new laws and sentencing guidelines that severely discourage dissent from conscientious people in ways that, when utilised as part of a holistic culture of resistance or towards more revolutionary goals, can be effective in creating deep and tangible change. This is something I will shine a torch on in chapter five.

Despite the admirable dedication that industrialism's inadvertent seamstresses have for trying to sew up that which is nine stitches beyond repair, many I have spoken to (I have engaged a lot in reformist activities myself) in private express deep reservations about its efficacy. More often than not, a reformist's initial passion and enthusiasm for their cause sooner or later turns into either fatigue or cynicism, or both. Held up against the overawing backdrop of personal, social and ecological breakdown, one's efforts can feel futile. Not because they do not make a difference; they always do to some degree, both directly and by laying the practical and psychic groundwork (or if you were to subscribe to Rupert Sheldrake's theories, by creating a morphic field)[10] for others to join them in their endeavours. The reason that our efforts to reform our politico-economic system feel futile is that, on the level of our existence ungoverned by coping mechanisms, we know that we are merely fighting systemic symptoms, and not the root cause of the disease itself. When Henry David Thoreau said that 'there are a thousand hacking at the branches of evil to one who is striking at the root',[11] I am sure he had hoped his words would not ring true so many long years after he penned them by the edge of Walden Pond.

My experiences in life have slowly led me to the conclusion that the institutions of industrialism, capitalism, globalisation – and the Enlightenment and Cartesian stories underpinning their foundations – are so rotten as to be beyond reform. To believe that any of these politico-economic forms, especially when combined, can lead to an ecologically diverse world without extreme systemic violence towards both human and non-human life is magical thinking. We know that as soon as we attempt to put a band aid on any one of the many gaping wounds sliced open by the blades of industry, five more will appear. We find ourselves running up the conveyor belt of industrialism, and no matter how urgently we proceed we seem to recede ever faster. The relentless grind of the cogs of The Machine leave us despairing, hopeless and, eventually, paralysed by a feeling of powerlessness. Not only that, but as I'll explore in chapter two, we are starting to display an uncanny resemblance to these cogs ourselves.

Yet still activists and campaigners continue to hack at the branches of industrialism, capitalism and globalisation, using methods that experience tells us lack the required depth if we are serious about creating peaceful, healthy, meaningful and sustainable societies. In many respects this is entirely understandable, as striking at the roots of our social and ecological problems is a scary and overwhelming thought for most people, there are often no clear paths forward, certainly no guaranteed outcomes and, as with everything in life, the lines of division between reformist and more revolutionary actions are not always black-and-white. Though it is unfortunately the exception and not the rule, reformist efforts can sometimes form the foundations for resistance and revolutionary movements whose aim is to topple the entrenched politico-economic structures that lead us down dark alleyways, and which we all know are never going to change voluntarily.

Take one example, from my own Emerald Isle. It is commonly accepted by historians that *Conradh na Gaeilge* (The Gaelic League), which was created to promote a revival in Gaelic language and culture in Ireland, furnished the Irish Volunteers with a lot of their membership which, a few years later, played an important role in the Easter Rising (an armed insurrection in Ireland in 1916). This, in turn, provided the impetus for Ireland's War of Independence that led to the formation of the Irish Free State. Even Rosa Luxemburg, if she were still alive, would admit that reformist measures can, on rare occasions, lead to the more nuts-and-bolts type change that, in times like these, is so desperately needed. Therefore, as I remind the reader throughout the following chapters, if one feels a strong urge to positively reform any part of our broken system, in their own way and drawing on their own unique gifts, they would be wise to trust that urge as, in the end, what we are called to do is always the best we can do. The rest, as they say, is up to Fate.

Exceptions aside, in the more general sense it has become painfully apparent that our politico-economic institutions need a profound over-haul if we are to create livelihoods and ways of being worth sustaining, yet it is still taboo to talk about what ought to be common sense: that forces such as the global finance industry – that corporate-state coalition driving our most life-threatening ecological and social ailments – are never going to reform themselves to death. Their *raison d'être* is premised on the conversion of our physical, cultural and spiritual commons into cash. For them to stop the strip-mining of our landscapes and mindscapes would be an act of suicide, and is clearly not going to happen voluntarily. This is a sobering thought for those to whom the wanton destruction of the Great Web of Life is an atrocity no less terrible than genocide. For if our rivers and oceans are to once more run clean and teem with sturgeon, cod and great whales, if our skies are to be filled with migratory birds instead of vapour trails, and our lands revitalised with a diversity of flora, fauna and human culture that our generation of anthropological and ecological illiterates (through little fault of our own) cannot even imagine, then death is exactly what needs to fall upon the global finance industry.

Modern society's obsession with reformism and nonviolence is as complex as the phenomena that give rise to it. Most of us – whom Lenin would have called 'the labour aristocracy' – have already made our secret Faustian pact with The Machine. Instead of fighting for more ecologically harmonious and fair models of organising ourselves socially, we spend most of our efforts trying to claw a little more money from the coffers of paymasters who profit splendidly from our sweat, toil and paper-shuffling. So whilst The Establishment are busy inheriting the Earth, those they continuously encourage to be meek settle for a nice office, a pension plan and a holiday in Majorca. In doing so, the middle and working classes of the West condemn the majority of the South to lives dominated by economic exploitation and systemic violence.

Our obedience, of course, has been bought. According to economist Arghiri Emmanuel's theory of 'unequal exchange', our rich Western economies profit to the tune of $6,500bn (and rising) from the global South each year, a complex issue which has regrettably convinced the middle and working classes of the superpowers to align themselves with those who extract that astronomical profit from the poor, instead of acting in solidarity with the poor from those countries which we are pillaging.

As long as we get our 'bread and circuses', translated into the technological age as ready meals and soap operas, it seems that most of us have
no desire to rock the boat. That the boat has an irreparable hole in its hull
doesn't seem to matter.

Others amongst our ranks are already weary of the subconscious and
silent hyper-violence of everyday life, and understandably do not want
more of it. There are also classic historical examples of non-reformist,
violent revolutionaries who became the Orwellian pig they once despised,
and who went on to enact the kinds of violent social policy they once
vehemently opposed. The reasons behind our fixation with nonviolence
and reformism run deeper too. The Wild – that spirit within us which
would not dream of constraining itself with moralistic civilised constructs like violence and nonviolence (a perspective I will qualify in the
final chapter) – has been beaten out of us to precisely the same degree it
has been eradicated from the landscapes that, despite our delusions of
human grandeur, we are still reluctantly immersed in. Because of this,
our actions in the face of brutality are as tame and timid as our neatly
trimmed gardens.

Lurking behind reformist measures is also the feeling that we should
not throw out the baby with the bath water, pretending that the vicious,
hissing gremlin we mistook for our child is actually what we intended
to wash in the first place. While many environmentalists may bemoan
bath water such as smart phones, televisions and aeroplanes (all the while
rationalising arguments for using them themselves) for their social and
ecological consequences, even they want to retain industrial babies such
as dialysis machines, ambulances and the World Wide Web, technologies
that industry-induced expectations and conditions have somehow made
indispensable.

Fantastical thinking such as this is a product of a widespread dearth
of modern economic understanding amongst the general public. Because
of basic modern economic principles such as comparative advantage,
economies of scale and specialised division of labour, three central pillars
of the industrial economy, you cannot just produce some 'good' technologies and not produce the 'bad' ones (and who would decide good
and bad, other than a global marketplace heavily influenced and distorted
by the corporate media, is beyond me). In economic reality, you have to
accept the whole gamut of industrialised products, otherwise many of

these technologies would be exorbitantly expensive even for states to buy, let alone individual people. And as we'll see in chapter two, even those products universally accepted as 'good' – the dialysis machines and ambulances of this world – are predicated on a scale and depth of systemic violence and destructiveness that our technology-addicted culture would not dare to admit.

Even if we could magically tap into some kind of divine wisdom and work out exactly which of these industrial-scale technologies served Life as a whole, and which didn't, that wouldn't be the end of our problems in this respect. In order for this most recent model of human economy to stay upright we need to be producing more and more of *all* of these things, regardless of the fact that the physical elements of the Earth which make them up are rapidly running out. Believing that modern economics is reformable, peaceful and potentially sustainable, however, allows us to feel good about ourselves while still harvesting the fermenting fruits of a system whose symptoms we then perform cognitive gymnastics to rail against.

There are other reasons why we cling to reformism despite its obvious incompetence at deeply addressing the challenges before us. In general, genuinely caring people do not want to taint their code of ethics and morals with things that, in the normal course of affairs, are completely abhorrent. But we've also been indoctrinated with banal pseudo-wisdoms such as 'the ends can never justify the means', and 'the master's tools will never dismantle the master's house'.[12] By believing them, we foolishly limit the array of responses that any social movement, which witnesses injustice or mass destruction and decides to act, has at its disposal to tactics that history constantly reminds us are clearly ineffective by themselves. In my personal experience the whole thing can feel like washing the floor with a dirty mop – you know it is marginally useful at best, counterproductive at worst, but it still makes you feel good about having at least done some cleaning.

A revulsion to violence is admirable and something we desperately need to foster in our communities; as Ward Churchill, a proponent of a diverse approach to social change, notes, 'the desire for a nonviolent and cooperative world is the healthiest of all psychological manifestations'.[13] However, a toleration of extreme systemic violence, or a misguided moralistic commitment to means which experience has taught us are clearly ineffective in resisting and ending it, is far from admirable. If we are serious about peace we need to start making a clear distinction between mindless, egoist violence and what amounts to an appropriate response to a dire situation. Nelson Mandela, a man constantly held up by pacifists as an example of the efficacy of nonviolent civil disobedience despite many of his actions to the contrary, once said that 'for me, nonviolence was not a moral principle but a strategy; there is no moral goodness in using an ineffective weapon'. As Mandela acknowledges, a form of nonviolence which witnesses its own ineffectiveness on a daily basis, yet strives to persist with it out of some individualistic notion of moral purity, isn't nonviolence at all; it is nothing less than violence concealed, masquerading as ethics when at its core is little more than fear and indoctrination.

Our own feelings about violence are deeply inconsistent. We live in a culture where inexplicably punching someone on the street would provoke outrage, and rightly so, yet where the extirpation of a couple of hundred species every single day – which is between 1,000 and 10,000 times the natural extinction rate[14] – due to human activity alone barely raises an eyebrow. A culture whose spirituality has been so abstracted from the living, breathing planet that it considers attacks against the industrial apparatus that is causing this mass extinction as violent, while the purchase of a foamed plastic yoga mat – one of its many toxic offspring – is almost viewed as a step on the path to enlightenment. In chapter one I offer up an alternative perspective, one which challenges everything our culture wants us to believe about what violence is, and what it isn't.

Our inconsistencies don't stop there either. There are some instances when the actions of all except the most stubborn advocates of nonviolence and pacifism – whose narratives, with the help of The Establishment, have colonised almost all movements for social and ecological justice – would betray their moralistic stance. Take self-defence, for example. Few people would argue with Edward Abbey when he said, in an interview with the author of *Green Rage*, Christopher Manes, 'when someone invades your home, you don't respond objectively and reasonably. You strike back with emotion, with rage'.[15]

The right to self-defence, if attacked by an aggressor, is protected by most jurisdictions. In chapter four I'll be taking this right out of what Charles Eisenstein calls 'the Age of Separation' – this millennia-long period within which we've somehow fooled ourselves into thinking that we're separate from the rest of creation – and putting it back where it belongs, in the 'Age of Reunion', a time we are slowly moving into in which we remember that our lives, and our health, are entirely dependent on the Great Web of Life, and where we once again accept our interdependence and deep connection to the world around us.[16] By applying self-defence in this more holistic sense I argue that it could profoundly change the way we respond to The Machine's War on Nature and, by interdependency, to its War on Humanity.

Most people I have spoken to would be morally content to take this one degree further, into an area where the law of most nations is not so clear. Picture this scene. You're walking home one night from the pub, and on a side-road you hear muffled screams mixed with sinister laughter. You quietly tiptoe down, hunch behind a bin, whilst you witness five men viciously gang-raping a woman. One is holding some sort of weapon, though you can't make out quite what it is. They continue to rape the woman one by one, each time saluting each other with a high five before the next man moves in. At your right you see a length of two-by-four, discarded by a nearby business and ready and willing to be upcycled. The streets are virtually empty of other passers-by, and the odds of taking them on yourself successfully are slim. Yet time is of the essence. What do you do?

Of course, if you could reason with the rapists and convince them to stop their attack on the woman, that is your ideal first port of call. And of course, the more compassionate amongst us may even want to help the perpetrators (after they have been stopped), along with the victim of such brutality, to find therapy in the months that follow; after all, psychologically and emotionally healthy men do not rape women. Yet in the heat of the moment, when there is no time for niceties, what are you going to do? Do you scream for others to help, before picking up the weapon and using it in an attempt to stop the detestable violence you are witnessing? Or do you walk on by, understandably frightened by the risks of getting involved, coupled with the ethical dilemma of having to fight violence with more violence, and instead go home and sign a petition to end gang-rape?

We all know that in this example, the last option – walking away – is not a particularly honourable one, and the dignity of resisting injustice against the most incredible odds is something I will explore in chapter six. Both our hearts and instincts usually implore us to intervene with an appropriate level of force to stop a greater, or more unjust violence, happening. Therefore, why is it that, at demonstrations and the like, protesters (especially their spokespeople) express condemnation, instead of respect and gratitude, when some amongst them take what they perceive to be violent action against the purveyors of extreme systemic violence?

The rape example may seem like a severe example to prove a point, but I would argue the opposite: that the violence we are currently inflicting on life on Earth and its inhabitants, as a matter of daily course, is as unquantifiable and ineffably horrible as gang-rape. It could even be said that we are collectively raping the personified planet, Mother Earth. But because this has been so culturally normalised, activities such as recycling, filling the kettle half way and buying 'green' products are considered to be ethical responses. In reality, these minutely small changes, which green capitalists have conned us into believing make a big difference, are akin to a rapist taking a moment to put on a fairly-traded condom before continuing to sexually assault a woman. They are a marginally more ethical way of committing an utterly brutal act.

In Ursula Le Guin's *The Ones Who Walk Away from Omelas*, the story is told of the people of Omelas, a utopian society where happiness and joy abounds amongst its people. Beneath the festivities and delights of everyday life, however, lies a darker reality, one that is only revealed to its children when they come of age and are taken to a basement room. Here the adolescents of Omelas, for the first time, come into contact with a child who is locked up, in serious physical pain and covered in vomit and excrement. Those coming of age realise that their entire way of life, one which they thought could not get much better, was founded upon this one child's suffering, and that if they wanted their way of life to continue, they would have to accept this child's suffering as part of the package. Most of the people, though shocked and disgusted by what they have seen, leave the basement and carry on with their lives, enjoying all that their utopian society had to offer. Yet some – and there were always some – decided to walk away from a world that they had previously loved because they could not accept it, and due to the near total pacification of the general public, almost the entirety of those who read it understand these people to be the honourable ones.

However, one of the more subtle messages hidden within this short story, which is commonly missed, is that those who walk away from Omelas, while admirable to a certain degree, do no more to help the imprisoned child than those who return to, and accept, a way of life that is predicated on the torture of another. Walking away from The Machine is important, whether that be by refusing to buy into its stories, developing a localised and ecologically-sound culture, or reminding people of the tortured child in the basement (all important acts of resistance in and of themselves). But it is no longer good enough by itself.

In chapter seven I make the case that if we are to live lives that are dignified, harmonious, meaningful, joyful and genuinely sustainable, it will involve us embracing both the creative and destructive, which in the way of The Wild are nothing but two words for the same thing. Notions of creation and destruction are illusions. Nothing dies, only transforms, but what it transforms into has important consequences for the world we are a part of.

In The Wild, life is transformed into new life through what sometimes appear to be the violent processes of death, and in doing so adds to the complex diversity and health of the Great Web of Life. In The Machine, life is transformed into pollutants through what appears to be the peaceful processes of progress, and in doing so subtracts from the complex diversity and health of the Great Web of Life.

That said, it is natural that, in facing the challenges ahead of us, some will be called to 'create' solutions (which will 'destroy' previous solutions) in a gentle and healing way, others to do the dirty but necessary work of clearing a space for these new ideas to germinate and flourish within. This could never be any other way, for everyone's core nature lends them to fill different niches in the exquisite dramas of life. Regardless of our particular tendencies, what we absolutely cannot do is to continue to walk away and leave the child locked up and tortured in the basement.

To reiterate what I said at the beginning of this introduction, none of this is a mindless and heartless call to arms, nor a romantic salute to violent resistance. The coming chapters are a plea to everyone who wants peace – one which broadens its parameters to include the Great Web of Life – to unite in solidarity, to respect each other's calling, and to appreciate that everyone has a unique role to play in defending animate Life from both the spirit and the apparatus of The Machine. We need those inadvertently born on the side of the oppressor to come together with those on the other end of the leash; those called to tackle personal violence, such as rape, with those who wish to untie the Gordian knots of capitalism, industrialism and cultural imperialism using all tools at their disposal. We need reformists and revolutionaries, those committed to pacifist or nonviolent means to join forces with those who are willing to engage in a diversity of tactics. We need everyone on the side of Life to unite in its defence against the invasion of The Machine. Contrary to what the propaganda of both the state and advocates of nonviolence would lead you to believe, this sense of solidarity between those fighting injustice in their own way is, as we will see in chapter five, exactly what happened in the African-American Civil Rights Movement in the 1960s.

If we are serious about stopping the destruction of all that is meaningful and beautiful about our world, and the injustices inflicted upon Life, we need to refrain from limiting the range of our resistance to means that are ineffective by themselves. In order to do so we must first develop a more nuanced understanding of violence (which I turn inside out in chapter one), and instead of condemning it outright as some imperfection of Nature, we need to put it back in its appropriate place. For as Slavoj Žižek explains:

> ... to chastise violence outright, to condemn it as 'bad', is an ideo-
> logical operation par excellence, a mystification which collaborates
> in rendering invisible the fundamental forms of social violence. It
> is deeply symptomatic that our Western societies which display such
> sensitivity to different forms of harassment are at the same time
> able to mobilise a multitude of mechanisms destined to render us
> insensitive to the most brutal forms of violence.[17]

Yet condemning violence as bad – regardless of its context, intentions, motivations, triggers or potential long-term results – is exactly what those who attempt to create a more just world persist in doing. Within most popular movements for social and ecological change it has become increasingly fashionable to shun, shout down or expel anyone who does not totally conform to the domesticated, entirely nonviolent ways that those who control these movements demand. Some nonviolent protesters have even been known to inform the police (a profession who have absolutely no problem with violence, as long as it is them doing it out) about fellow protesters they believe to be acting illegally, without a moment's thought about whether the laws these people are breaking are unjust, or if their actions are in defence of The Whole. Regurgitating what The Establishment has indoctrinated them with, it is commonplace for nonviolent extremists to forcefully tell their more feral members that nothing meaningful or worthwhile can be achieved through force or violence.

But this is a myth propagated by those who believe that nonviolence is always the only appropriate means by which we should affect change. History, for a start, has taught us that, in the appropriate context, force and violence can break down the institutionalised barriers to a more beautiful world, a perspective which I detail in chapter five. Not only that. More importantly, it seems as if those who condemn people who take a more diverse approach to political change forget that the entire planet, and their own flesh and bones, would perish in a moment if it were not for the very violence (under the commonly-held definition of it) they seem so morally outraged by. Advocates of nonviolence do not complain when the antibodies in their own bodies violently attack the antigens that pose a serious threat to the health of their whole being. As I will argue in chapter seven, they would be just as wise to desist from complaining when Gaia's human antibodies – activists of all varieties – defend the health of The Whole against the antigen-esque invasions of The Machine using whatever means their skills, tendencies and qualities are suited to.

Sentiments such as these have been expressed innumerable times, long before Žižek's Hegelian ramblings. Henry David Thoreau, a man whose prose and life inspired Mahatma Gandhi in his struggle against British imperialism, once said, 'I do not wish to kill nor to be killed, but I can foresee circumstances in which both these things would be by me unavoidable. We preserve the so-called peace of our community by deeds of petty violence every day.'[18] As long as there are laws and economic systems designed to line the pockets of the few to the utter devastation of the rest of Life, there will be a desperate necessity for people to break them both.

We need to start being honest with ourselves about the violence inherent in industrial civilisation. We need to start being honest about the scale and depth of the ecological, social and personal crises we are encountering today. And we need to start being honest about the time

scales we are working with. To do so, we must put all the options available
to us back on the negotiation table. One of the many arguments this book
puts forward is that if the master created his house with hammers and
monkey-wrenches, then surely those tools can also be used to pull out
nails and loosen the screws they tightened. Or as Derrick Jensen, a man
clearly more in favour of preserving salmon than industrialism, has said
with less subtlety, 'you *can* use the master's high explosives to dismantle
the master's dams'.[19]

There is no shortage of good intentions within all aspects of the
aboveground and underground movements to end ecocide (see page 63),
exploitation and social injustice. Still, we all know that the road to hell is
paved with good intentions. That of course does not mean that the road to
heaven is paved with bad intentions. Rather, the road to something more
beautiful is paved with effective actions; actions that dissolve institutions
so inherently violent that they threaten nothing less than life on Earth.
Inspiring initiatives and radical projects are planted like seeds within
fertile soil every day by social entrepreneurs, activists and change agents of
all varieties, yet few, if any, manage to germinate into the solutions they so
often deserve to be. Why? Because large, commercially-grown trees, not
native to their landscape, are blocking out the sunlight that would allow
these seedlings to take hold, grow and flourish. These monocultural trees
need to come down to allow light in and fresh life to begin, and they need
to come down sooner rather than later.

Considering the severity of what lies before us, humanity would be
wise to make use of the entire spectrum of tools it has at hand with skill
and wisdom, not with hate in its mind towards those who are driving the
destruction, but with love in its heart for all that is worth preserving. We
need everyone following their own calling. For those who feel compelled
to subvert a structurally violent system, Nietzsche's advice to 'beware that,
when fighting monsters, you yourself do not become a monster ... for when
you gaze long into the abyss, the abyss gazes also into you',[20] ought to be
heeded. This struggle against The Machine, that multi-headed monster
of our Age, can certainly be both initiated and sustained by a sense of
deep love and compassion for all that is beautiful. In an open letter to
Marcha, Ernesto 'Che' Guevara, a man not known (despite his mainstream
ubiquity) for an advocacy of reformism and one who sadly didn't always
heed Nietzsche's advice, once expressed such feelings when he wrote that

'at the risk of seeming ridiculous, let me say that the true revolutionary is guided by a great feeling of love. It is impossible to think of a genuine revolutionary lacking this quality'.[21]

If you believe that industrial civilisation is the zenith of human endeavour, if the strength of your connection to the World Wide Web is genuinely more important to you than the depth of your connection to the animate world of Life, or if you cherish your belongings over a sense of belonging, then I would recommend you put this book through your paper shredder now. However, if you have a gnawing sense that life can be richer and more playful than working overtime in industrialism's 'dark Satanic Mills',[22] if you do not believe that we can solve our ecological crises by the same sort of techno-fix mentality and culture that has only proven thus far to intensify them, or if beneath the roar of The Machine you can still hear the cries of an old-growth forest as it is razed to the ground, with its stories and its creatures gone forever, then I would suggest you read on.

Over the course of what follows, I do not dare claim to have all, or even any, of the answers to humanity's burgeoning list of crises. After all, I am merely a white male living on a smallholding on the west coast of Ireland, with barely even any idea of what may be best for the place in which I commune; it would be arrogant, and perhaps even racist, to claim to know what may be the appropriate course of action for the peoples of Africa or Latin America, Ohio or Yorkshire, in defence of their own cultures and lands at any given moment in time.

Instead, I simply argue that if humanity wants to reclaim an ecologically and culturally-rich world, and ways of life meaningful enough to be worth sustaining, then the 'three Rs' of the climate change generation – reduce, reuse, recycle – need a serious upgrade. Currently they are little more than a convenient mantra that fits neatly into the dominant cultural narrative of our time, one which does not threaten the hegemony of The Machine in the slightest. This mantra must take a rapid evolution and become one that looks the crises of our time straight in the eye, doesn't shirk, and resolves to become something altogether more befitting. If we want to emerge from the tragedies engulfing us with both the biosphere and our dignity intact, and to participate fully in the Great Web of Life once again, we must dust the failures of half-hearted reformism (and its resultant fatigue) off ourselves and repeat a new mantra over and over again, until it overcomes the spirit of The Machine which has taken a firm grip of our minds. So what is this mantra, these three Rs of the Age of Reunion, that the chapters which follow wish to inspirit your head, your heart and your hands with?

Resist, revolt, rewild.

CHAPTER ONE

THE PACIFIST'S GUIDE TO VIOLENCE

O pardon me, thou bleeding piece of earth, that I am meek and gentle with these butchers.

William Shakespeare, *Julius Caesar*

O NLY A SATANIC CREATION SUCH as Sauron, the Dark Lord of Mordor from Tolkien's legendarium – or an industrial civilisation – could unabashedly turn a diverse and thriving planet into a landfill of plasticated mediocrity and concrete drudgery within the cosmic blink of an eye. For the sake of cheap furniture, games consoles and fizzy drinks, we have reduced complex woodlands to lumber yards, mountains into quarries, oceans into depleted fish farms and rivers into power stations. Heidegger once poignantly remarked that we have reduced the Great Web of Life to 'a gigantic gasoline station, an energy source for modern technology and industry'.[23]

Yet our unyielding march towards such a Mordorian world took another incremental step in November 2013, with the inauguration of the World Forum on Natural Capital in Edinburgh. Here an eclectic and somewhat peculiar mix of big business, wildlife conservationists, government and environmentalists came together to stick a price tag on nature, that wild realm of wonder and enchantment that the UN now poetically refers to as 'ecosystem services'. The perverse logic underlying this forum goes like this: 'If we price everything nature gives us (wildlife, plants, forests, waterways, pollination, you name it), companies would think twice before destroying them.'[24]

There are many problems with this notion of protecting nature by placing a financial valuation on it, and it raises questions that are as multiple as they are varied. Not least, one must ask why anyone who might cherish a sense of awe about the natural world that we are interconnectedly bound with would want to depreciate their experience of it by something so utterly dull and bureaucratic as finance. But more importantly, how does one quantify a life, indeed fully comprehend its niche within a region and the reliance of other life upon it, or fix a monetary value on an entire habitat or the extinction of a species? If such an audacious feat were possible, who would do the quantifying, and in what ways would their philosophical and subconscious assumptions about the world reveal themselves in their valuations? What wisdom could there possibly be in taking the counsel of anyone who has become so unashamedly arrogant as to think that humans could fully grasp the significance of a certain type of butterfly to a particular landscape, or the role of a 'pest' or 'weed' in the intricate web of life, let alone express this significance with some arbitrary financial figure?

Scientists in the 1970s, with what one would hope to be a generous dash of tongue-in-cheek, took the first steps down this path when they intrepidly endeavoured to put a monetary value on the materials that make up the human body. After totting up the sum of its parts – the heart, the hands, the eyes – on their calculators, they came up with the figure of $12.98.[25] It is not the measly figure here – which adjusted for inflation would come to just over $56 at the time of writing – that is comical in its absurdity, but the audacity that one could reduce any human life to a financial calculation, and that a person's worth is nothing more than the sum of their individual physical parts. Yet it does beg the question: on what logic is it that the valuing of non-human life in such a manner is not only seen to be less ludicrous, but a positive step forward in our protection of the Earth? Why do we seem to abandon this sense of absurdity when it comes to the rest of life on Earth? While advocates of pricing nature often do so with the best of intentions, only those of us religiously indoctrinated by humanism and anthropocentrism could even contemplate making the case for applying such perverted thinking to the rest of life.

But such philosophically bankrupt ideas are not the only issue with this latest in a long line of steps in the wrong direction. This millennia-long crusade, whose speed has intensified since the scientific revolution of the 16th century onwards, took its baby steps the moment we started to perceive ourselves as 'skin-encapsulated egos',[26] separate from all else in a scientifically outdated but persistent Cartesian universe that is inherently hostile towards us. This self-perception has been happening incrementally ever since we first sat around a campfire, separating our world into the safe domestic zone and the dark wilderness outside. Language, number, technology, agriculture and money – amongst others – have all embodied and reinforced this understanding, so much so that it is now hard for most of us to understand, let alone experience, the depth of our interdependence on the rest of life.[27] Within this world we created for ourselves, the unique and ineffable slowly became reduced to generic words, whilst the exquisitely unquantifiable became reduced to cold, hard numbers.

However, this move to explicitly put a price on the priceless represents the reaching of a new low for humanity, and smacks of understandable but blatant desperation (and an admission of defeat) from those who want to protect nature and the future of life on Earth. Such a stance taken by the wildlife conservationists (who, incidentally, suffer from Shifting Baseline Syndrome,[28] a condition I'll diagnose in chapter eight) who attended this forum is hardly the bold vision of environmentalism that Aldo Leopold provoked around the time he wrote *A Sand County Almanac*, in which he said, 'We abuse land because we see it as a commodity belonging to us. When we see land as a community to which we belong, we may begin to use it with love and respect'.[29] It is also indicative of a movement that has either realised the impotence and ineffectiveness of its reformist efforts to date, or is unwilling to take the difficult but effective action that is necessary in order for us to begin healing the deeply rooted diseases afflicting the Earth and its inhabitants today.

There are other issues. Such reformist measures have the greenwash potential to provide a numerical foundation that enables both big business and the state to ethically justify the violent destruction of an ancient rainforest in one place through the planting of a tree-farm in another, an activity now euphemistically known as 'biodiversity offsetting'. Despite the obvious foolishness of such logic, it nonetheless appeals to the corporate-state coalition as it fits perfectly into the current narrative that they have shaped for their own ends. For as Wendell Berry reminds us, 'the global economy is built on the principle that one place can be exploited, even destroyed, for the sake of another place.'

Presumably, within the same scheme of logic, the genocide of one people could be ethically offset if the perpetrators could tot up the monetary cost of all the human lives taken, before the military-industrial-media-pharmaceutical-educational-financial complex use their equations to decide how much to 'invest in protecting – or simply not harming – a group of people somewhere else'.[30] Ronald Reagan once remarked that 'a tree is a tree'[31] when talking about plans to destroy ancient redwood forests and offset the massacre by planting saplings elsewhere. On that basis, one would have to presume that he, and other politicians in his mould, would have no problem if a property developer decided that she was going to bulldoze their mansions in Washington or Westminster on the justification that her company would offset its demolition by building three hundred new houses in some suburb of Philadelphia or Portsmouth.

Perhaps the biggest problem of all with this, however, lies in less highfalutin places. The irony was not lost on Nick Dearden, director of the World Development Movement, when at this forum it was an investment professional, and not a wildlife conservationist, who said to him in realistic business terms that 'once you put a price on nature in order to protect something, you will find someone will pay that price in order to destroy it'.[32] The price that is placed on any habitat will rarely, if ever, be enough to dissuade industry, and the exorbitant wealth it possesses, from absolutely ravaging it. Few of even the most enlightened ecologists, in the unlikely event of being consulted on the matter, would dare to suggest to the business world that the depth of life in our thin and rapidly eroding topsoil is worth more financially than industry is willing to pay for the huge reserves of minerals and fossil fuels that lie below it. Neil Evernden makes the point that:

> ... applying monetary evaluation to nature is dangerous to start with, just because it encourages a comparison between the uses of each mountain. As soon as its worth is greater as tin cans than as scenery, the case for the mountain vanishes. But, more important, monetary evaluation distracts us from the fact that the values at issue are not economic in the first place.[33]

Let us not kid ourselves, there are corporations begging their ideological partners in government to turn mountains into tin cans. Take this morning's newspaper headlines as just one example. British Prime Minister David Cameron, at the behest of his friends in the City, says he is 'going all out for shale',[34] despite well-founded ecological and human health concerns about the processes involved – known as fracking – in extracting this gas for human use.

Perhaps some of you believe that hydraulic fracturing of the Earth is a positive step: more jobs, more money for local people, and increased energy to fuel more financial growth. All of the assumptions behind these perceived gains could be counter-argued, referring to the short-term and insult-to-the-human-soul nature of the jobs created, the children'spocket-money levels of financial return for those most harmfully and critically affected, and the fundamental unsustainability of infinite economic growth. That, however, is not my point – for now.

For reasons which will become clear later, the first question we must ask ourselves – before we can even begin to contemplate what an appropriate response to the ecological destruction and social injustice confronting us may look like – is an unusual one. It is this: do we understand processes such as fracking to be violent? In a similar vein, is the flat-packing of rainforest at the rate of one hectare per minute, or the clear-cutting of old-growth forests (or any forest for that matter), an act of violence? What about the annihilation of genuinely sustainable and meaningful livelihoods – and the social fabric they once held together – all of which have been replaced by jobs in call centres, sales offices and on the conveyor belts of industrialism? Let us not forget the homogenisation of the world's diverse cultures into a monoculture, in a pattern that mirrors the brutal reduction of the great diversity of plants and wildlife into fields of monocrops. Are these acts of violence, or not?

What about the *damming* of rivers, and therefore the *damning* of the forests and wilderness areas whose stability, diversity and health is dependent on salmon returning to the place of their birth? Or the gross disparity, and increasing inequality, between the mega-rich and the mega-poor, and all the social implications of that? Or the conversion of our ecological, social and cultural capital, along with our most intimate relationships, into soulless numbers for the sake of the growth imperative inherent in capitalism? The factory farming of animals, the bottom-trawling of the oceans, the looting of the soil? What is it, if anything, that makes the extirpation of the Great Web of Life any less violent than randomly head-butting some innocent reveller boogying in a night club on a drunken Friday night?

Conversely, are non-humans who use force to protect their habitat acting violently? At the Thula Thula Exclusive Private Game Reserve in Zululand, several antelope had been captured for a breeding programme, and were frantically trying to free themselves from their chains. Within hours a herd of elephants burst onto the scene, at which point the matriarch used her trunk to break both the locks and the gate, releasing the antelope. Such solidarity amongst non-humans is surprisingly common, and a little known phenomenon.[35]

Resistance movements are not limited to the human realm either. In the state of Punjab in India, monkeys have resisted human conquest for years by way of property destruction, for which some have been sent to monkey jail (killing monkeys is illegal there) and others illegally shot. Elsewhere in India, elephants have begun to fight back against those who hunt them and destroy their habitat. In two years, elephants killed 130 people in Assam.[36] If such monkey self-defence isn't violence – a perspective I'll qualify a little later – but nothing more sinister than animals protecting that which their lives are dependent upon, then is it the case that their human counterparts are equally justified in protecting their natural habitat with such force?

The answers to these questions are more important than they seem at first glance, as within them lies the potential for us to deal with the injustices around us in a much deeper and more effective way. However, before we can even begin to think about answers to these questions, we first have to explore what we understand by the term violence, the inconsistencies we hold around our views of it and the moral parameters we consider it within. What precisely then – if anything – is violence, this thing that we are told is totally unacceptable by those who use it the most?

VIOLENCE DEBUNKED

Many of us, when asked about our views on violence, vehemently oppose it. It's bad, wrong, an aberration of Nature that just needs to be overcome. That is, only if it is inflicted upwards towards those in positions of power (or their interests), and not downwards by them. This is a perspective that is gaining more widespread understanding the more we realise the precariousness of our predicaments and the forces driving them. In the *Guardian*, Rebecca Solnit writes:

> *If you're poor, the only way you're likely to injure someone is the old traditional way: artisanal violence, we could call it – by hands, by knife, by club, or maybe modern hands-on violence, by gun or by car. But if you're tremendously wealthy, you can practice industrial-scale violence without any manual labor on your own part. You can, say, build a sweatshop factory that will collapse in Bangladesh and kill more people than any hands-on mass murderer ever did,*

or you can calculate risk and benefit about putting poisons or unsafe machines into the world, as manufacturers do every day. If you're the leader of a country, you can declare war and kill by the hundreds of thousands or millions ... But when we talk about violence, we almost always talk about violence from below, not above ... In every arena, we need to look at industrial-scale and systemic violence, not just the hands-on violence of the less powerful.[37]

In many ways Solnit was touching on a sentiment expressed in Bertolt Brecht's *The Threepenny Opera*, where Macheath asks, 'What's picking a lock compared to buying shares? What's breaking into a bank compared to founding one?' To paraphrase Slavoj Žižek, what is the violence that violates the law compared to the violence that takes place within the confines of the law?[38] The difference is, we are expected, *we expect ourselves*, to submit entirely to the systemic abuses of power.

Investigative journalist Will Potter makes a similar point. He recounts a scene from *City of God*, where 'St. Augustine describes Alexander the Great questioning a captured pirate, asking him how he dares to "molest the sea". "How dare you molest the whole world?" the pirate replies. "Because I do it with a little ship only, I am called a thief; you, doing it with a great navy, are called an emperor."' Potter adds that 'regardless of the definition of violence, it is never terrorism if committed by the government.'[39] Max Weber went as far as to define the state as 'a human community that (successfully) claims the monopoly of the legitimate use of physical force within a territory',[40] a perspective whose expression is older than Thrasymacus' assertion of it in Plato's *Republic*.

Regardless of the fact that 'those who deplore violence loudest and most publicly are usually identified with the status quo', people who 'rarely see violence in defence of the status quo in the same light as violence directed against it',[41] our revulsion towards it speaks well of us in many respects. In some circumstances it represents a sense of empathy for others, or perhaps the part of us which, in defiance of the dominant culture's protestations, still remembers that all of our lives exist in a state of interbeing. Despite the voracity of our knee-jerk opposition, whenever we are asked about what the word violence actually means to us, few display even a modicum of clarity on it; and when we think that we do, it rarely stands up to even the gentlest scrutiny.

r

So what exactly is this mysterious thing we call violence? Images that spring to mind when people consider it are the usual suspects: acts of terrorism, murder, human rights abuses, armed robberies, bloody revolutions, sexual assaults, black-clad protesters kicking in corporate windows or something similarly obvious. But is it limited to these types of forms, and is it the case that all of the above, which at a glance seem blatantly violent, are always so once examined under a more holistic lens? Despite some of the greatest minds of our times – philosophers such as Foucault, Arendt, Sartre, Tolstoy, Freud, Hobbes, Girard, Benjamin and Marx, along with politicians as diverse as Gandhi and Hitler – exploring this subject in-depth, each from a different angle, we barely seem closer to having a clear sense of what it is, or a theory of violence that holds up to a close and honest examination of it in all its forms.

What follows aims to take you on a troubling journey from what you are likely to understand violence to encompass now, down a wild and untrodden path that our dominant culture has hoped you would never tread.

A terribly unimaginative, but important place to start this journey is with the dictionary definition, as here is where the popular understanding of the term is best reflected. The *Collins Dictionary* defines violence in a number of ways, one of which is its use in describing the intensification of normal phenomena, such as when we might describe a hurricane as a violent wind. However, the definition that is of relevance to this discussion is 'the exercise or an instance of physical force, usually effecting or intended to effect injuries, destruction, etc'. The *Oxford Dictionary* seconds that, primarily describing it as 'behaviour involving physical force intended to hurt, damage, or kill someone or something'.

Under this commonly accepted understanding, most of what I outlined earlier – the wholesale deforestation, the oil drilling, the hydraulic fracturing and so on that fuels our technological societies – is violent in the extreme, albeit only within moral parameters that are much wider, though more philosophically and scientifically consistent, than those which we seem prepared to employ today. If you consider an animal either a 'someone' or a 'something', then factory farming, pharmaceutical laboratories and industrial-scale slaughterhouses are violent in that they knowingly effect injury (usually involving much cruelty) and eventually death upon the animals that pass through them. If it is fair to say that a forest is 'something' (or from an animist's perspective, perhaps even a 'someone'), then those who clear-cut them are intentionally causing 'destruction' through the use of physical force, in this case by way of bulldozers and chainsaws. Using the definitions prescribed by our most credible dictionaries, these commonplace acts are surely violent, and (as I will argue shortly) those of us who partake in them, however much we try to distance ourselves, are violent through our conscious complicity in their brutality.

At the same time, perhaps it is our common understanding of violence that needs to change, and not the lives of those who are forced to fit into the privileged white man's absurd and civilised conception of peace. For example, it seems reasonable to say that eating, in and of itself, cannot be an inherently violent thing to do. We all have to eat to survive, and doing so plays an integral part in the transformation of life into other forms, and the co-creation of beautifully complex and diverse ecosystems. Yet on the face of it, hunter-gatherers, through their direct connection and intimate relationship with their food, could be seen as an incredibly violent people under the common understanding of the concept of violence, as they will personally use direct physical force to effect injury and take life on a daily basis.

Once you examine their way of life in its entirety, however, it becomes clear that, in generalised terms, their means of acquiring food are the least destructive and injurious known to anthropologists and ecologists. When you consider that in many such societies they took no more life than was necessary, with the minimum of cruelty, the idea of killing a wild animal – who has spent its life roaming the Earth freely and in accordance with its own nature – somehow feels palpably more compassionate in comparison to the superficially nonviolent act of paying a 'food manufacturer' to cage animals in a factory farm for your convenience and ease of conscience.

This is especially the case when you consider that, like every species who fulfils a niche in a delicate ecosystem, the hunter-gatherer's role as predator would often, counterintuitively, allow more life to flourish. It could even be the case that, given their crucial role in a landscape that has evolved with them, the act (or inaction) of not killing certain species could inadvertently lead to the eventual unravelling of a complex and delicate ecological system.

Similarly, I cannot accept that a lioness who also needs to eat to live can be considered violent for killing a hyena for herself and her young, or that an antibody arising naturally in the body is violent for killing an alien bacteria or virus. All of this is simply life, and life is constantly transforming and becoming new life, and in doing so adds to its richness and diversity over time. As George Monbiot so eloquently describes, reintroducing a predator such as the wolf back into its natural habitat creates a trophic cascade – 'processes caused by animals at the top of the food chain, which tumble all the way to the bottom'[42] – and can lead to a remarkably substantial increase in the diversity of the flora and fauna of an entire biome. These timeless cycles of life and death should be celebrated, not stigmatised by the disconnected delusions of urbanites.

I had an experience of this recently. I live on a three-acre small-holding in Ireland, based on permaculture principles and ancient gift culture values, and on it we keep chickens for eggs. One day I went out to clean their coop and found one of them lying there, her head ripped off to the breast, which I eventually deduced to be the work of a mink. Now I did not consider this to be an act of violence by the mink; he needs sustenance to survive after all, and he is a carnivore by nature, and therefore to call him violent for doing so would be a serious defamation of life. That said, the mink is not native to Ireland. The American mink was first recorded in the wilds of Ireland in the 1960s, due to their release from fur farms, places of business whose conditions are such that they would uncontroversially be called violent under even a commonly-held definition of the word. Their release was blamed by the owners of the fur farms on animal rights activists, amidst counter-claims (the validity of claims on both sides has never been conclusively decided) that the owners themselves released them under an insurance scam, and set it up to look like the handiwork of activists, many of whom are fully aware that releasing non-native species into a finely-tuned ecosystem is incredibly problematic.

This presented a problem for me. Taking the life of another creature is not something I would ever do lightly. However, I found myself in a position where if I didn't kill the mink, he would in all likelihood eventually kill all the chickens. Not only that, but because my kind are the American mink's only remaining predator in the ecosystem I inhabit, not killing him would contribute to the wiping out of species who have evolved well with the land here, such as the vole (a female mink with young to feed can wipe out all the voles in her territory in a single year). Therefore, in this instance (and using the understandings of violence that are most widely accepted) is it the action of killing the mink, or – as we will explore shortly – the inaction of letting him run riot in a land he has not yet formed a healthy relationship with, that is the real 'act of violence'?

From a similar but unquestionably more controversial standpoint, is it the case that 'culling' herds of politicians and their corporate bosses should always be considered the violent option? (Utah Philips once famously said, 'The earth is not dying, it is being killed, and those who are killing it have names and addresses'.) Take the U.K.'s former Secretary of State for Environment, Food and Rural Affairs Owen Paterson as an example. When he was in office he was signing off a range of environmental policies – ranging from the bulldozing of ancient woodland for transport projects to the unscientific culling of badgers at a cost of over £4,000 per animal[43] – that could only be described as pathological. Could allowing him to continue to run amok, unchecked within the anthropocentric legal system which his peers created and the limits of his time in office (a lot of harm can be done in five years), instead be considered the violent option?

When you consider that the likes of Paterson have an even less natural role to play in a healthy British ecosystem than the American mink has in an Irish one, what makes culling him and his cronies any less ethical than the mink or the badger? On what grounds do we discriminate? Is it because he is human, one of us? Because he has a higher IQ (allegedly), two legs instead of four, or wears a pinstriped suit? I am by no means suggesting that assassinating or injuring a pathological politician is the right thing to do, though whether or not it is always the wrong thing to do is another question. Most people would have had no problem with such a course of action in relation to another sociopath, Hitler, whose actions differed only in that his brand of hyper-violence was directly aimed at those who fall within our species' and culture's parameters for moral consideration. Instead, I am simply asking why killing the mink feels like the most holistically wise thing to do in the earlier example but why, in another scenario, where a handful of humans are knowingly creating more ecological and social havoc than a hundred thousand mink ever could, it suddenly becomes so unutterable?

Similarly, would destroying the U.S. headquarters of Monsanto – whom many politically astute activists see as one of the most ecologically-damaging corporations on Earth – be the violent option? Or could we start viewing our lack of effective action in stopping them as the truly violent approach? I find it difficult to even whisper these words publicly without incurring the wrath of the strange alliance of pacifists and those in power. Such is the extremity of our conditioning regarding these issues that even the mere posing of these questions will appear heretical to humanists, capitalists and environmentalists alike.

A question we will deal with later will ask whether it is the case that by reintroducing an endangered species, commonly known as the Wild Revolutionary, back into the political landscape we could create the political equivalent of a trophic cascade, eventually leading to a dramatic upsurge in the cultural and socio-diversity of human habitat and the landscapes they are in relationship with? If we are to forge rich and meaningful lives for ourselves, and livelihoods that are harmonious with the Great Web of Life, then our activism and our resistance to The Machine will have to become as wild as the habitats we wish to protect from devastation.

AN INACTION OF VIOLENCE

Such decisions – and passively allowing something to continue unabated is a decision we take – assume an added dimension if you consider that 'inaction', in the words of Faithless lyricist Rollo Armstrong, can be 'a weapon of mass destruction', and that sometimes doing nothing can be at least as violent as anything we could possibly imagine doing. If this idea of inaction being a form of violence is counterintuitive, consider how many humans and non-humans a year suffer or die through the lack of effective action on matters that are within our ability to do something meaningful about. This fits in with the Marxist conception of violence, 'in the sense that any harm caused by indifference and neglect is as much a part of human violence as the violent acts of revolutionaries',[44] and why wouldn't it be, if the results are exactly the same? As Engels wrote in *The Condition of the Working Class in England*, 'murder has also been committed if society places hundreds of workers in such a position that they inevitably come to premature and unnatural ends. Their death is as violent as if they had been stabbed or shot'.

In order to understand the violence of inaction, there is another critically important question to contemplate in all of this: whether the act of complicity is, to some degree, violent or not? Allow me to explore this for a moment with a thought experiment. A lone male assailant fatally shoots a woman for no apparent reason. In this case, it is generally accepted that the only person acting violently is the one who pulled the trigger in cold blood. However, it is not the person who shot her who is ultimately responsible for her death. No, ultimate responsibility lies with the bullet, as it was it and not the man that severed the main arteries of her heart. Whilst it is hardly controversial to say that this technicality does not mean the assailant is innocent of an extremely violent act, making the distinction has grossly underestimated repercussions for us. Why? Once we accept that violence can be enacted indirectly – in this case, the perpetrator was removed from the exact instance of physical force by one tiny degree – it forces us to be honest about our indisputable complicity in the horrific violence that invisibly plays itself out in our normal, everyday civilised lives.

Take another example to reinforce the point. A woman intentionally releases a ravenous tiger into a small room of schoolchildren, and it proceeds to tear one of them apart before eating him. Releasing the starving animal amongst kids would be classed as an extremely violent act by any reasonable person, yet she was removed from the exact instance of physical force that killed the child by one degree. Again, it demonstrates how we already recognise that a perpetrator of violence can be separated, by at least one degree, from the victim of their actions.

But why stop at one degree of separation when doling out responsibility for the violence of a particular act? In the earlier example, why not go back one degree further and state that the act of selling the killer the gun is all part of a long moment within which the pulling of the trigger was merely the penultimate motion? Why not traipse all the way back to the original sin and include the weapons manufacturer whose business is producing lethal shotguns in the first place? To paraphrase both Žižek and Brecht (see page 33), what is the violence of pulling the trigger compared to the production of millions of triggers?

Few of us, thankfully, are involved in either the manufacture or regular use of firearms. Unfortunately, there are more relevant and subtle examples. Take the caging of an animal for the entirety of its short life against its will, destined only to be slaughtered in conditions that Jewish Nobel Prize winning author, Isaac Bashevis Singer, once compared to those of the concentration camp in Treblinka. Many stages of this process of factory farming are undoubtedly violent, even through a conventional lens. Yet few, if anyone, would currently consider their act of buying plasticated meat from the supermarket an act of violence. They are simply buying veal or chicken.

While the consumer is separated from the consequences of their actions by a combination of clever marketing and long impersonal supply chains, in reality they are no less directly linked to the violent torture and death of the animal than the gunman is from the death of the woman. By handing over the cash in payment for goods, they are pulling a sophisticated trigger of sorts, releasing a bullet into the heart of the next animal. But because of the delusional sense of separation – in both time and space – designed into our culture, we remain blinkered to the violence of our civilised lives. In order for us to effectively respond to the challenges we are faced with, it is crucial that we no longer see acts as individual moments in time, but as an entire chain of events in which each of us plays a role. With this perspective, the metaphorical man who pulls the trigger has simply undertaken nothing more than the penultimate motion in one long, slow moment of violence.

The Wachowskis brilliantly depict this idea in the big screen adaptation of Alan Moore's classic comic, *V for Vendetta*. The scene in question takes place in the office of Inspector Eric Finch, head of the regime's police force known as 'the Nose', on the fourth of November. He and the other heads of the ruling Norsefire Party suspect that the film's protagonist – an anarchist freedom fighter in a Fawkesian mask called V – will attempt to ignite the fuse of revolution against their fascist government the following night by mindfully blowing up the Houses of Parliament in London.

With a metaphorical and grand display of thousands of dominoes falling one by one towards the final piece as a backdrop (symbolising the interconnectedness of every act), Finch begins speaking to his sidekick, Detective Sergeant Dominic Stone. He explains to Stone that the previous night, as he pondered V's case and the events leading to what his anagnorisis made him realise was utterly inevitable, he 'suddenly had this feeling that everything was connected. It's like I could see the whole thing, one long chain of events that stretched all the way back before Larkhill [the concentration camp that "produced" V]. I felt like I could see everything that happened, and everything that is going to happen. It was like a perfect pattern, laid out in front of me. And I realised we're all part of it, and all trapped by it'. As he speaks, images from past and future events pop up before the viewers' eyes, and by the end it becomes irrelevant what order the events occurred in.

Once we are honest about our own integral roles in the hyper-violence that plays itself out in our economic habits every day, the question presented to us no longer revolves around whether or not we should partake in violence. We superficially peaceful civilised folk already do, and we do so in the extreme.

No, the unfortunate but real question becomes an uncomfortable one: in these times, what are we to be violent towards? You might well ask if we need to be violent towards anything at all, a perspective not without its merits, yet hidden within it is the underlying assumption that choosing not to take effective action against an ecologically tyrannical regime is an act of nonviolence.

Should we continue to wage war against the Earth, the community of life we share it with, those already in poverty and, ultimately, ourselves? Or in the interests of creating a genuinely peaceful way of living, one that respects life, do we redirect our current levels of extreme and ongoing violence towards a politico-economic system – and its bureaucratic and physical infrastructures – that is forcing us to do things that our hearts and minds, in their rare moments of self-honesty, cannot bear?

In contrast to pacifist understanding, and by the definition of violence I am about to propose, it could rather ironically be argued that it is the final act in this domino-esque long moment of violence – the blowing up of the Houses of Parliament – that is the only truly nonviolent act in the entire domino display in *V for Vendetta*. Everything that the fascist government enacted before its fall was 'intended' to inflict more control and suffering on the population, whereas V's plan had the opposite intention: the liberation of the people from an oppressive government and an end to much of the systemic violence it was forcing its population into. In doing so the Wachowskis illustrate my point that the so-called 'necessary evil', in effectively bringing down a hyper-violent fascist regime, is by its necessity not evil at all. Instead, I propose that it would have been the 'act' of not dealing with the Norsefire Party effectively that would have been 'the *unnecessary* evil', and the most violent one.

This idea of intention is crucially important to our ability to distinguish between real violence and acts of genuine courage or love. For example, say my friend has a really sore tooth at the back of her jaw. She hates going to the dentist, and she cannot seem to get the knack of the traditional door-slamming trick. So she asks me to give her a swift punch on the side of the jaw. I give her a left jab, and the tooth comes out. Whilst punching someone in the face is usually considered to be a violent act, it is obvious that in this instance it is an act of love. To this effect at least, the dictionary is correct to include the notion of intention at the heart of how we understand the subject.

Related to this point, 'one of the first things to understand about violence in human affairs is that it is not the same thing as force',[45] and therefore it is important to distinguish between 'force' and 'violence', two words often used synonymously. If a dentist yanks a sore tooth from our jaws, it is indisputable that he has used force yet has in no way acted violently towards the patient. In fact, the opposite is true, as pulling the tooth was the most caring thing to do. However, if a torturer pulls a tooth out of the mouth of an unwilling person whom he wants information from, it is clear under any common sense understanding that he has used both force and violence. Along with the willingness (or lack thereof) of the recipient of the force, the intention behind the act is often key. If something is done with a loving intention – and Nelson Mandela or Che Guevara claim that such a spirit was behind their revolutionary and seemingly violent actions – there lies the possibility that what may seem to be an act of violence to the uncritical eye is, in reality, something altogether different; perhaps even an act of compassion or empathy. Of course, not always – but sometimes.

I've heard it said that violence could be regarded as the injurious, excessive and unjustifiable use of force, and to some extent there is merit in this. Killing for food in ways that involve zero or minimal cruelty would, under this understanding, not be considered violent, nor would using physical force to stop an assailant attacking an innocent bystander. But this is an understanding of violence that doesn't go nearly far enough for me, as it fails to adequately acknowledge systemic violence, the violence inherent in inaction at certain moments, nor the violence of complicity. Not to mention the fact that it leaves the difficult question of 'who decides what force is justifiable?' hanging in the air like someone else's fart.

As it stands, the state holds the monopoly on such answers, a scenario that one would have to question the wisdom of, considering the state's unrivalled aptitude for hyper-violence (both direct and systemic) and its ideological and financial partnership with a corporate world which pro-actively seeks to convert life into profit.

So is there a definition, or understanding, of violence that can take into account these perspectives, and the idea that inaction – the act of witnessing gross injustice and doing nothing within one's power to effectively combat it – is its own form of violence? Considering that philosophical heavyweights such as Sartre, Engels and Hegel have tried and failed to convince me, I do not hold out much hope of convincing you, the reader of a book, by a considerably more feeble-minded author than those. However, I will try. At worst, it may do no more than prompt you to question what the notion of violence means to you from this day forth. At best, we may agree and face the convergence of ecological, social and personal crises together with a more nuanced understanding of pacifism, nonviolence and violence, and the new opportunities for creating deep change that this may provide us with.

VIOLENCE TRANSFORMED

Perhaps the first thing to question is the premise that there is such a thing as violence. In *The Failure of Nonviolence*, Peter Gelderloos suggests that 'violence does not exist. It is not a *thing*'. In it he claims that 'violence is whatever the person speaking at the moment decides to describe as violent', and that 'if it is done to me, it is violent. If it is done by me or for my benefit, it is justified, acceptable or even invisible'.[46] Gelderloos believes that 'violence is a social construct that is applied to some forms of harm but not to others, often depending on whether such harm is considered normal within our society'.[47] On the basis of this he now prefers to use more accurate words such as 'illegal', 'combative', 'conflictive' and 'forceful' when referring to the 'body of methods or tactics that are usually excluded by nonviolence'.

In many ways Gelderloos is correct. This question of violence versus nonviolence is a distraction, a debate had by civilised folk who, through little or no fault of their own, have never had an opportunity to experience natural peace – that of The Wild, that strange place where life is dependent on death and where healthy biodiversity is dependent on fierceness and gentleness in equal measures. Pacifists who protest war while living in cities – which are without exception founded upon, and fuelled by, extreme hyper-violence – are no less deluded than Jains who live in cities because their religion commands them to harm no living thing, something which they understand is impossible when one is living directly with Nature. While admirable through an urban lens, both groups are simply sub-contracting what they deem to be violence to others.

That said, even Gelderloos admits that 'it would be silly to abolish it [violence] as a word.' Therefore if we decide to use this word to describe a certain action (or inaction), in a way that is consistent, not subjected to or limited by the norms of one species or social class, what broad definition of it would aid us in living holistically healthy and harmonious lives?

The closest I have come to a holistic understanding of this phenomenon is not from one of our celebrated philosophers, but from the largely unknown Kelly Booth. Booth defines violence as 'the imposing of a form, or a set of conditions, on another party without regards to the others' interests, or without sensitivity to their situation'.[48] This is an interesting understanding of it, as on analysis it works on many levels: physical, emotional, psychological and even spiritual.

Take the hunter-gatherer, or the lioness. Is the hunter-gatherer imposing a form on another being, for example, a deer? Yes. Is she doing it without regard to the other's interest or sensitivity to their situation? Most likely not. If you look at anthropological studies of the wide range of tribal peoples, and their understanding of their role in the intricate web of life, you would have to say that, in general terms, the taking of life for food is done out of necessity and with the utmost of sensitivity, both in the spirit and technique in which the animal is killed. This is especially true when you appreciate that they have a deep understanding that their role as predator is crucial to the health of the ecosystem as a whole. Therefore under this understanding, the hunter-gatherer's method of eating is, in my estimation, the antithesis of violence.

Compare that to us, as agriculturalists, who destructively turn the soil regularly with little or no consideration of its health and well-being or the life-forms that make it up, not to forget the plethora of other wildlife whose survival depends on the health of that soil. Within conventional terms and anthropocentric moral parameters, digging and turning over the land, in order to allow a limited range of human developed plants to extract nutrients, is not regarded as violent in the slightest; in fact organic gardening is even celebrated by environmentalists and most peace activists in my anecdotal experience. Yet under Booth's definition, conventional horticulture is intensely more violent than primitive hunting, in that the former is almost rarely done with any real regard or sensitivity towards the life in the soil, and in that at the very least it is extremely destructive to the habitat of the billions of life-forms that live, mostly invisibly, within every few square metres of it.

What I like about Booth's definition is that it can also be used to better understand more subtle forms of violence. Here, the imposition of a certain economic system that is in no way sensitive to a local economy that has evolved over millennia can be seen for what it really is: violent. It is not suggesting that there are not instances where there is a conflict of interests, as in the conflict between the indigenous person's need for food and the animal's visible desire to live (though from a more holistic perspective of the Earth as a whole organism, such as in Lovelock's *Gaia* hypothesis, even this is questionable). Instead, unlike other descriptions, it recognises the dance of life, this transformation of energy. In doing so, it suggests that when life is taken with sensitivity and consideration, and from a deep awareness of its role in the health of the whole, then a case can quite easily be made for it not being considered violent. Not entirely peaceful perhaps, but existing in that wild space between such rudimentary labels.

Still, despite Booth's definition being the closest thing to making sense that I have encountered under a more holistic perspective, and one that has the potential to widen the parameters of moral consideration to include all of the community of life that we share Earth with, it contains flaws and, more importantly, does not go far enough for me. Therefore, I propose the following definition for violence, to ensure that even though we may not agree on it, you at least understand the assumptions I am using when I speak of it:

> *Violence is the unjustified use of force in ways that are intentionally or culpably injurious to another entity, or insensitive to that entity's own needs or The Whole of which it is one part. It encompasses actions that, through wilful neglect, indirect conscious complicity,*

or the imposition of a set of conditions, contribute to the injury of
another entity.

The proof, as they say, is in the pudding. Take the example of gang-rape that I mentioned in the introduction (see page 16). According to the dictionary definition of the term, the person who takes up whatever weapon is at hand and uses it to either limit or prevent violence towards the obvious victim is still seen as committing a violent act, despite the fact that it may be one which most people may ludicrously refer to as a necessary evil. If a loving and courageous act is deemed necessary to effectively stop an act of aggression – such as Frodo's heroic journey to destroy Sauron in *Lord of the Rings* – why it is still called an evil act of any sort is beyond me. Is someone who heroically puts their body on the line for the sake of something outside of their own self, however futile it may end up being, someone we would seriously consider a violent person? Not at all, and in such cases we would agree in broad terms that it was an exemplary act, especially in contrast to the cowardly violence of inaction that would have been the case if no intervention had taken place.

Now take my definition. Under this, the act of stopping the gang-rape can be seen as nonviolent, in that it is justifiable in its defence of another from a physical attack. The acid test of whether an act of force is justifiable often lies in whether or not it is carried out in defence or attack. By viewing violence through a more holistic lens, it takes the violent stigma out of acts that are only committed in defence of Life, and puts it into acts that have for too long had a peaceful façade but which are, in felt experience, much more deserving of it.

By taking this stigma out of loving and courageous acts of life-defence, there lies the distinct possibility that an overawing amount of latent energy could be released amongst activists of all persuasions, and harnessed towards the pursuit of effectively co-creating a more authentically-peaceful, ecologically-sound and socially-just world. By redefining it, it helps us to start supporting each other in our efforts to wipe out systemic violence, potentially enabling us to get involved in things that we may have previously been stigmatised out of endorsing or participating in.

This new understanding of what violence is, and isn't, also holds true for food. As I mentioned earlier, eating is by all accounts regarded as violent under the dictionary definition. This is an obvious absurdity. Whereas under the definition I suggest, eating – a natural part of life – can only be considered violent if the processes involved are not sensitive to the needs of the animal or plant whose life you are taking, or the delicate web of life within which their kin plays an essential role. The way in which a hunter-gatherer is known to have killed for food usually displays such sensitivities, and so is rightly not deemed a violent act.

I ought to be clear that although I believe the act of inaction can oftentimes be more injurious than anything we could possibly do, not all inaction in the face of brutality is an act of violence either, as this would be equally nonsensical. The act of inaction is only violent when a person witnesses an injustice that they can do something about, to some degree, but makes the decision to 'do' nothing. If the violence witnessed is of a systemic nature, such as industrialism, then the appropriate time scale to tackle this is long term, and will probably involve the enacting of many tactics and strategies along the way. In this instance, sleeping is obviously not violent, nor is spending time with family and friends, as both these activities are absolutely necessary for the type of psychologically, physically, spiritually and emotionally healthy person required for such a long haul cause. However, if the act of violence is of a more immediate effect, such as an act of rape or assault, then going for a power nap for 30 minutes is not an appropriate time scale of response. There will, of course, be many examples which lie between these two extremes, but these are things that intuition and common sense are more than capable of figuring out.

Whilst the importance of putting our understanding of key concepts to the test is grossly underestimated, considering the release of frustrated energy that new meanings and understandings often release in our heads, hearts and hands, I do not want to labour the point. Depending on your own morals, cultural narratives and philosophical assumptions, you should put my definition through your own rigorous testing, and see if it stands up to the examination. If it does not, then expand your own parameters of moral consideration or change your definition of violence accordingly. Either way, the point is to question it, and not to mindlessly accept the versions of violence that the dominant culture we live within wants us to believe.

As Jensen sums up in his foreword to Ward Churchill's controversial book, *Pacifism as Pathology*, 'Churchill doesn't, of course, argue for blind, unthinking violence. He merely argues against blind, unthinking nonviolence.'[49] This is a sentiment expressed by the Blekingegade Group – a small group of revolutionary socialists who spent 20 years robbing banks (amongst much other legal activity) in Denmark as a way of providing material (and not merely moral) support for liberation movements in Third World regions – in their article *It is All About Politics*:

> *We have no romantic relationship to violence. We have seen the civil war in Lebanon with our own eyes. We have seen torched villages in Rhodesia. On television, we have seen bombs dropped from B-52s over Vietnamese cities, and we have seen children burned by napalm running from the jungle. However, we have no romantic relationship to nonviolence either.*[50]

In response to my definition, people will no doubt make all sorts of criticisms. The most common is the notion that 'you cannot fight violence with violence'. This idea is best encapsulated by the phrase 'an eye for an eye will only make the whole world blind', often misattributed to Mahatma Gandhi (though it was used by his biographer, Louis Fischer, to describe Gandhi's views in a way that The Gandhi Institute for Nonviolence agree with). This phrase can seem to make sense, in that it can be seen to explain the futility of endless cycles of violence. Yet on examination, it does not stand up for itself very well. From the viewpoint of those fighting for the future of life on Earth and social justice, blinding the powerful forces driving the problems surrounding us could limit or end their ability to blind anyone else in the future. A blinded man is, at the very least, more impotent in his endeavours to blind others who were previously weaker than him. Blinding him may even encourage others to metaphorically maim him, diminishing his power to inflict violence on innocent others even further, while letting him know those who were his victims will no longer have their sight taken from them whilst they are on their knees. Therefore, an eye-for-an-eye does not necessarily leave the whole world blind; on the contrary, taking out the right eye in the most effective manner may lead to a world of exploited people finally regaining their sight.

Likewise, when critiquing this definition or generally arguing the virtues and tactical prowess of nonviolence, many may point to its capacity to transform the hearts and minds of people, a perspective which not so much suggests that you cannot fight violence with violence per se (though it is usually implied), more that it is best to respond to violence with peace. Many nonviolence practitioners, when proposing the merits of this, will refer you to stories such as *The Buddha and The Terrorist*,[51] in which the latter, known as Angulimala, roams towns and villages, brutally killing the locals and adding their fingers to his gruesome necklace. As panic spreads throughout the village, the Terrorist stumbles upon the Buddha, and informs him of who he is and what he has done. On seeing that the Buddha is not bothered in the slightest by his murderous antics, he says to him, 'Do you not know that I could kill you without blinking an eye?' The Buddha duly responds by telling Angulimala, 'Do you not know that I can be killed without blinking an eye?'

In the story this bold and brave move by the Buddha stops the Terrorist in his tracks, and he begins a process of transformation, in which he is eventually reintegrated into society as a servant of the people. By all accounts, this is a wonderfully inspiring tale with many important lessons, but it has one little drawback: it is a ludicrous story when applied to the real world of politics and big business. If the corporate-state coalition (in this example, the lumber company and the police) told environmental activists blockading a road to a piece of ancient woodland, 'Do you not know that we will arrest you all and destroy this ancient woodland without blinking an eye?', and the protesters responded with, 'Do you not know that we could be arrested, and allow you to annihilate this forest, without blinking an eye?', do you really believe that the police, the lumber company and the government would suddenly call a halt to the whole operation, enter a period of personal and institutional transformation, and put an end to clear-cutting as state policy? I don't think so either. We need to make a clear distinction between our responses to individual people, and to institutions. In an economic system where the political and corporate realms are dominated by the ecologically illiterate and those who display psychopathic tendencies (see page 149), the more appropriate response from an enlightened movement might be to say, 'Do you not know that we will do whatever it takes to make sure you do not destroy this splendid forest and all of the life thriving within it?'

In further, less metaphorical terms, both historical and anecdotal evidence would suggest that you can successfully combat violence, particularly systemic violence, with violence. As we will see in chapter five, 'monkey-wrenchers' in the U.S. have regularly dismantled or destroyed machinery in such a way, and to such an extent, that corporate endeavours – such as the clear-cutting of a forest or the wanton slaughter of wild horses – were effectively prevented from happening. These activities, against private property, would of course be deemed violent under conventional terms. Yet viewed through a more holistic lens, these acts of valour would not only be seen as nonviolent, but actively peaceful. As Paul Watson, founder of Sea Shepherd Conservation Society once said, 'Pardon me for my old fashioned ways, but I believe that respect for life takes precedence over respect for property which takes life'.

As I alluded to at the beginning of this chapter, there are a number of reasons why, if we want to face the convergence of crises facing us effectively, it is crucial that we question our understanding of violence. Primarily, how we perceive force and violence will have a huge influence on the ways in which we tackle the ecological, social and personal problems facing us, potentially opening up avenues to us that are free from the unnatural constraints imposed on us by those who cling to business-as-usual. But not only that. If we are serious about creating genuinely peaceful ways of life, then we will all need to end our complicity in economic habits which we know inflict systemic violence on others, the symptoms and consequences of which would make a vicious beating in a pub seem relatively pleasant.

Whether you agree or disagree with my definition is almost irrelevant. What really matters is that we question our narratives concerning what violence is, and just as importantly, what it isn't. This is especially important in a culture that considers destroying a bottom-trawler as violent, and flying to a meditation retreat in Nepal as unquestionably nonviolent; a culture in which an attack on the infrastructure or top personnel of an international weapons manufacturer (or the banks which finance them) is inexcusably violent, while selling billions of dollars worth of laser-guided rockets to whichever warmonger will buy them is sound business practice.

By employing a more considered and holistic perspective than our dominant culture would like us to use, I want to show how our current politico-economic model is without doubt the most violent system money can buy.

CHAPTER TWO

THE MOST VIOLENT SYSTEM
MONEY CAN BUY

How is it conceivable that all our lauded technological progress – our very Civilisation – is like the axe in the hand of the pathological criminal?

Albert Einstein

We come upon a contention which is so astonishing that we must dwell upon it. This contention holds that what we call our civilisation is largely responsible for our misery, and that we should be much happier if we gave it up and returned to primitive conditions.

Sigmund Freud

I N *THE RATIONAL OPTIMIST*, MATT RIDLEY – an Etonian aristocrat, economist and the chairman of Northern Rock when it became the first U.K. bank in over a century to suffer a run on its finances – argues that life has never been better, and that because 'ideas are having sex with each other more promiscuously than ever', producing more complex technologies at increasingly cheaper prices, it will continue to get better at an accelerating pace. The question is: exactly who or what on Earth has life never been better for?

While possessing exorbitant wealth does not preclude one from having a sense of social justice, or solidify one's views into a certain mould from birth, it seems too obvious to suggest that The Viscount Ridley's objectivity on such matters was compromised, to some degree, the moment he was born into extreme privilege. In expressing such views, he certainly does not speak for the billions of humans for whom the consequences of our politico-economic system are already, or are becoming, palpably intolerable. What may be less apparent to the naked eye are the cultural narratives and silent ideologies that govern everything that not only an aristocrat, but those of us from all social classes, think and do not think, say and do not say, do and do not do – ideologies that legitimise what is, as we'll soon see, an all-out industrial-scale attack on Life under the misnomer of progress.

Underlying all our actions and ideas are assumptions about the world that were planted into the collective mind before the time of Aristotle and Plato, refining themselves and taking new turns for the worse during the so-called Age of Enlightenment, and manifesting themselves in the most commonplace everyday habits of e-Homo Sapiens. If you were to survey people in the street you would find that few have ever read any of the works of Socrates, Descartes, Bacon, Voltaire, Locke, Newton or Rousseau, yet every day we enact their outdated philosophies and scientific theories, unbeknown even to ourselves. While most of us labour under the illusion that we're a free-thinking people, John Maynard Keynes was closer to the mark when he wrote that we're all 'slaves to some defunct economist'.[52]

One of the most significant notions that we have culturally inherited is the almost omnipresent attitude of anthropocentrism. This term represents the viewpoint of people who believe that humans have a higher moral status or value than any non-human life-form on the planet, and describes the human-constructed lens which inculcates us into perceiving ourselves to be at the centre of the universe, and the apex of its creation. According to feminist philosopher Val Plumwood, anthropocentrism plays an analogous role in ecological theory to ethnocentrism in anti-racist theory and to androcentrism in feminist theory.[53] Most importantly, it's a worldview that has provided the invisible underlying conditions for the emergence and intensification of the Industrial Revolution, for without such a confused perspective there is no way we could – legally or morally – commit the daily atrocities of industrialism on a non-human world that, in reality, is just as worthy of the respect and consideration we extend to our fellow humans.

It's no coincidence that the Industrial Revolution emerged shortly after the Enlightenment, when the world's most prominent thinkers – Descartes et al. – were convincing the rest of humanity that somehow humanity was the only thing deserving of respect on Earth. The likes of Descartes (who argued that man was the only living thing to have a soul) were merely standing on the shoulders of religious giants – the Old Testament in particular – when they began spreading this myth, a fact that should be a source of some unease to secular humanists who, in general, share a surprisingly similar outlook in this respect. Strangely, verse 1:26 in the *Book of Genesis*, which states, 'And God said, Let us make man in our image, after our likeness: and let them have dominion over the fish of the sea, and over the fowl of the air, and over the cattle, and over all the earth, and over every creeping thing that creepeth upon the earth', still silently infiltrates much of humanist thinking today, which in turn perpetuates the anthropocentric fantasy that humanity can successfully dominate and control something incomprehensibly bigger than itself.

If you think that you do not share this ideology of human supremacism to some degree, you are probably fooling yourself. Ask yourself if you would have as much problem slapping a stranger who has mildly annoyed you as you would have buying plastic toys for your kid, poisoning a rat, ordering cheap factory-farmed fried chicken or cutting down some old-growth trees that block the views from your house; if you answered no to any of those, you're either seriously aggressive towards humans or unknowingly indoctrinated into an outdated anthropocentric philosophy. As Žižek points out in *The Pervert's Guide to Ideology*, it is exactly when we think we live outside ideology that we are fully immersed in it.

How exactly we came up with this notion of human supremacism is anyone's guess, especially when you consider that our belief in this story intensified during the time of the scientific revolution, when rationalism and logic were supposed to have been coming to the fore. Various reasons have been put forward at one time or another for this persistent form of discrimination, which Peter Singer has termed 'speciesism':[54] people point to our capacity for foresight and morality, higher IQ levels, our manual dexterity, or perhaps the rather unique desire to trade that Ridley is so fond of. Perhaps the most convincing argument, however, is that such a worldview has been adopted because it fits so perfectly into the dominant culture and therefore gives us the excuse we need in order to exploit the rest of life on Earth, whilst still feeling like good, peace-loving people throughout it all.

Whether or not this is the case is far from conclusive, but it is a theory that would seem to explain our irrationality on the matter. George Monbiot once argued that the acceptance of American ecologist Garrett Hardin's economic views, outlined in his essay *The Tragedy of the Commons*,[55] by the political status quo of its time is explainable by the same theory. The essay's influence was not based on the flawlessness of Hardin's ideas, as the essay contains much erroneous thinking. Instead, Monbiot claims that 'for authorities such as the World Bank and Western governments it provided a rational basis for the widespread privatization of land'[56] at the time. Just like our specious belief in human supremacy, it gave those in power a seemingly justifiable excuse to do what they already wanted to do.

Despite the best efforts of religion, industry and The Establishment towards implanting and reinforcing the scientifically baseless notion of anthropocentrism in the human mind, the reasons used to justify this value system cannot hold their own when put to the simplest of tests. A pig, to take one example, beats a child with a severe intellectual disability on many of the criteria put forward by believers in human supremacy as the basis for their discrimination, yet few today would dare suggest that we grant pigs similar entitlements and protections to those the disabled child can already avail themself of.

Not only that, but any ecologically literate human knows that when we are in our rightful place, living in rhythm with Nature, we fill no greater or lesser role than any other species in our landscape. Cheetahs can run faster than us. Salmon can find their way back to the place of their birth from thousands of miles away, without recourse to printed maps or signposts. Many birds can transverse great oceans without any need for mechanical engines or fossil fuels. Characteristics like these do not make them any better than us, or more worthy of living a dignified, meaningful life in accordance with their nature. It simply means they are different to us. And vice versa. The world of plants is no less deserving of respect and consideration.

This anthropocentrism, embedded deeply in the modern psyche and an illness of the modern human mind, stands in stark contrast to 'ecocentrism',[57] a term coined by Aldo Leopold which argues that all living things on earth, human and non-human, have intrinsic value, regardless of their usefulness to humans. Ecocentrism indicates a more nature-centred, as opposed to human-centred, approach to life and represents a set of values that encourages people to respect non-human life for its own sake, and to give its needs fair consideration. Surprisingly to most of us civilised folk today, many indigenous land-based human communities gave fair consideration to the entirety of their biotic communities – some of the few left still do.

Paula Underwood Spencer encapsulates this spirit in a story about the Oneida, a First Nations people that were one of the five founding nations of the Iroquois Confederacy in what is now known as Upstate New York. This story took many different forms amongst First Nations people in particular, but also amongst indigenous peoples throughout the world. In her book, *Who Speaks for Wolf*, she says:

> ... the ancestors of the Oneida once grew in population so much that some of them had to go look for a new place to live. They found a wonderful place, and the people moved there. After moving, they found that they had 'chosen the Center Place for a great community of Wolf.' But the people did not wish to leave. After a while, the

THE MOST VIOLENT SYSTEM MONEY CAN BUY 57

people decided that there was not room enough in this place for both them and Wolf. They held a council and decided that they could hunt all the wolves down so there would be no more. But when they thought of what kind of people they would then be, 'it did not seem to them that they wanted to become such a people.'

So the people devised a way of limiting their impact: In all of their decisions, they would ask, 'Who speaks for Wolf?' and the interests of the non-human world would be considered.[58]

Who speaks for Wolf amongst us now? Or the Dodo, the Tasmanian Tiger, the Po'ouli, the West African Black Rhinoceros or the Passenger Pigeon, all of whom were forced so far out of their habitat that the only place they had left to go was extinction, their timeless splendour replaced by electric toothbrushes, chocolate laxatives and human microchip implants. I ask again, who speaks for Wolf?

Not Matt Ridley, that's for sure. Or most of us for that matter.

Considering that the majority of us will go through our lives without ever encountering the term anthropocentrism, let alone displaying any awareness of how it plays out in our lives and its consequences for the world around us, why does it even matter if Ridley, The Irrational Anthropocentrist, is corrupted by delusions of human grandeur or not? It is precisely the fact that we do not recognise the destructive ways that ideologies such as anthropocentrism – which permeates every single movement of our hands, filters how every single phenomenon is perceived by our senses – play themselves out in our lives that makes them so dangerous, and therefore so crucial to draw attention to. Just as in the realm of addiction, until we become fully aware of the extent of the damage our individual and collective behaviour is causing, we hold no hope of changing it.

Questioning the anthropocentric delusion – amongst many other deeply-held but baseless assumptions about the world – is the critical first step we must take in expanding the moral parameters within which we not only make our own everyday decisions, but which shape the public policies that in turn control our lives. The expansion of our value systems to include the Great Web of Life is fundamental to any attempts we might make at creating authentically peaceful lives for ourselves and the biotic communities we live amongst. Until we recognise the inherent value of the rest of Life, we will never care for it, never respect it, never savour and appreciate it to anything remotely resembling the extent that many of our ancestors did.

Through our abuse of the Earth and its inhabitants – upon whose health we are all dependent – we will not only continue to inflict violence upon it but, ultimately, on ourselves. The father of 'deep ecology' (a school of thought contrasted to the 'shallow ecology' of eco-capitalism), Norwegian philosopher Arne Næss, identified anthropocentrism as a root cause of the ecological crisis, and the mass extinction of species, that we are embroiled in, a view shared by many of the more radical environmental groups who have, to varying degrees, decided to keep the full range of tactical options open to them in their defiant defence of both human and non-human life.

There is another reason for shedding light on human supremacy, however, of more significance to the focus of this book. Until we see anthropocentrism for what it is, and its fundamental role in the politico-economic systems of our time and the institutions borne out of it, we will continue to labour under the notion that we can be a nonviolent people while these institutions continue to exist. The torture and slaughter of 989 million animals (plus 40 million who get put out of their misery because of injury)[59] every year in the UK alone, for example, can only ever be imagined to be nonviolent if on some level we believe we have fulfilled Descartes' dream and become the 'lords and possessors of nature', whose worth depends primarily on how much value and utility we humans can derive from it. Likewise, the ecocidal, communicidal and suicidal acts of daily civilised life that I am about to touch on shortly are only possible under the same worldview.

Until we are honest with ourselves about these types of systemic violence, inherent not just in the culture and economic model we were born into (and which by our actions and inactions we reinforce) but in the entire scheme of ideologies and myths underlying it, our resistance to the attack on life by the corporate-state coalition will also continue to be limited to the use of nonviolent means that are entirely ineffective by themselves. Why? Because as we'll see in following chapters, history teaches us that if our resistance is to be effective, it must be full spectrum; and the only way that is going to happen is if the people involved in our pacified movements for change drop any pretensions they have of being nonviolent in the first place. We cannot pretend to be nonviolent, after all, once we realise that all the modern conveniences (like electricity, buses and blenders) that we cling so tightly to are borne out of the fruits of our War on Life.

As I alluded to in the introductory chapter, even industry's self-professed victories are predicated on a hyper-violence that would make Rambo look like Mother Theresa in comparison. Dialysis machines and ambulances – as symbols of the kinds of complex technologies that even intelligent, thoughtful environmentalists and peace activists desperately clutch at – are both violent technologies, and though they may appear to save some human lives in the short term (increasingly from diseases, conditions or injuries rooted in industrialism), the industrial processes they rely on will eventually make Earth uninhabitable for much of human and non-human life. For if you deconstruct one ambulance and examine the raw materials involved, all of a sudden you can see The Machine itself unfold before your eyes.

To make just one ambulance you need people working on oil rigs and in factories, quarries and mines. But these workplaces of death and ecological devastation would be infeasible if society was only demanding ambulances and a few other 'good' products; it only becomes financially feasible when we demand unimaginable tonnes of plastic and the billions of litres of oil that we do every day, which are then turned into all sorts of gadgetry, consumables and the tat that fills our attics. The factories that make this stuff need machines and tools which themselves need to be produced in ever more factories, quarries and oil rigs, all connected through a system of roads that bring foul air and relentless noise to every inch of our lands, intoxicating our lungs and gnawing at our souls. You then need armies, police forces, prisons and court rooms to enforce the contracts that are needed to facilitate such global trading; they need weapons, which in turn need additional factories to produce them at scale, and all the implications of that. This goes on ad infinitum, like an industrial *matryoshka* doll.

If you want one ambulance or dialysis machine you must accept a militarised world full of poisoned rivers, mediocre livelihoods, toxic oceans, dead soil and an atmosphere full of greenhouse gases and pollutants. It is a source of great irony that by trying to keep everyone alive we may inadvertently, through our ecological illiteracy, kill everyone and much else besides. This is a hard reality for anyone – such as myself – who has had a loved one 'saved' by industrial medicines or technologies to accept, but one that we must address if we're not going to inflict future generations with all the same physical and psychological diseases of our toxic culture.

While pondering hard-to-digest perspectives such as these, we ought to take a moment to ask ourselves why we have become so dependent on industrial medicines in the first place. It almost seems too obvious to suggest that a civilisation whose people survive on a diet of sugar, prescription drugs, caffeine, highly processed food laden with chemicals, anti-depressants, tobacco and alcohol – and who are thrown on top of each other in cities whose air and water are laced with a deadly concoction of toxins – will be a civilisation with a big demand for industrial medicines and vaccines. Less obvious to note are Ivan Illich's theories of 'social and cultural iatrogenesis'[60] and the medicalisation of life, which argue that pharmaceutical companies and medical professionals have a vested interest in two undesirable things: sponsoring illness by creating unrealistic health expectations around ailments that are simply part and parcel of life; and annihilating the ways by which people have traditionally coped with pain, illness and death down through the ages, so as to create an unwarranted dependency on industrial-scale healthcare.[61] This is especially insidious once you understand that industrial imperialists continue to consciously destroy or weaken indigenous cultures and, with it, their knowledge of how to naturally maintain and treat their own health. You would also have to be fairly naïve to rule out the possibility that, in an industry driven by an intense pressure on high-flying executives to make multi-billion dollar profits, pharmaceutical companies genetically engineer viruses which they are then able to produce the much-coveted vaccine for.

While the last remark is mere conjecture, the next one is a strangely celebrated fact: the sickness industry is big business. Call me a cynic, but a healthy population isn't healthy for corporate profits or GDP, which is why pharmaceutical companies' marketing budgets dwarf public spending on the promotion of good health maintenance. Global spending on prescription drugs alone is due to top the $1 trillion mark in 2015. For those of you who think that businesses should be able to make billion dollar profits if they are doing their job well, consider the millions who die every year due to a lack of affordable healthcare for industrial diseases, such as cancer, which their natureless culture has made them dependent upon. People are literally dying in the millions because of corporate greed, yet our culture considers this good business whilst simultaneously labelling those who target its bricks and mortar as violent.

Once we accept that violence pervades our own everyday lives, even our healthcare systems, labels such as 'pacifism' and 'nonviolence' become irrelevant for both ourselves and others, and we can approach change with a more nuanced appreciation for the complexity of the mess we've inherited. A nonviolence that allows us to feel good about ourselves, but which does not achieve what it needs to, should not be worn as a badge of honour; taking effective action to stop extreme systemic violence ought to be the only badge we wear, if we must wear anything at all. Otherwise we will continue to be fined and sent to prison – peacefully of course – for our nonviolent actions, as if there were so many fighting on the side of Life that each foot soldier could be easily spared.

This willingness to get incarcerated for bearing witness to state-sanctioned violence, on the understanding that our altruistic and selfless actions may melt the hearts of those in power, is a tactic that I believe to be misguided. I agree with Robert Paul Wolff who, in his essay *On Violence*, said:

> In a futile attempt to deny and affirm the authority of the state simultaneously, a number of conscientious dissenters have claimed the right to disobey what they believe to be immoral laws, so long as they are prepared to submit to the punishment of the state. A willingness to go to jail for one's beliefs is widely viewed in this country as evidence of moral sincerity ... Now tactically speaking, there is much to be said for legal martyrdom ... but leaving tactics aside, no one has any moral obligation whatsoever to resist an unjust government openly rather than clandestinely. Nor has anyone a duty to invite and then to suffer unjust punishment. The choice is simple: if the law is right, follow it. If the law is wrong, evade it.[62]

Unless we reassess our approach to social change, not only will we continue to suffer from the imposition of unjust laws, we will continue to allow ideologically corrupt governments to wage war on sovereign nations whilst doing little more than raising our banners in protest and expressing our right to 'freedom of speech', all the while self-policing our right to 'freedom of action'. We will continue to fool ourselves that those who really govern us – the City – care about our placard-raising, petitions and letters, or our conversations over cappuccinos in organic cafés, when the policies and behaviours we are campaigning against play integral roles in their business models. Our raging nonviolence has become so out of control that nowadays we even communicate to the police in advance that we are about to hold a demonstration, a sure sign to those in power (who have no problem using violence themselves) that our indoctrination into nonviolent civil disobedience (which is, when ineffective by itself, an obedience to those who inflict suffering on ordinary people for their own private gain) is now complete.

These pacified demonstrations have also become the scene where much of what masquerades as nonviolence can be seen for what it is: the cowardice of the political comfort zone. Gelderloos describes a classic scene from the modern-day protest, which nonviolent protesters seem to claim ownership of (shouting things like 'stop ruining *our* protest' to those who employ a diverse approach). During the 15M mass movement in Spain, nonviolent protesters 'lined up in front of banks to protect their windows from vandalism, and in front of cops to shield them from the insults of the crowd'. This would have, at least, demonstrated some conviction in their nonviolent principles had it not been for the fact that 'when the police started shooting rubber bullets at the crowd, these same activists ran away instead of putting their bodies on the line'.[63] It is easy to appear brave and moralistic, after all, when you're on the side of the rich and powerful – those with the guns.

This is all part of a culture that tells us that as long as you hug a police officer at a demonstration, or do not strike back at those who are destroying the basis of life on Earth, you are a nonviolent person, and by association in our culture, a good person. Yet paying an oil company to extract fossil fuels on your behalf so that you can drive to the protest march is as violent as anything you could possibly imagine doing once you arrive at it. When this veil of nonviolence is dropped and we accept the hyper-violence we are all enmeshed in, we can free ourselves from any pretence to muddled ideas such as pacifism for the time being, and instead embrace the entire spectrum of tactics and strategies that may actually bring about an authentic peace, one that is inclusive not only of humans but the entire biotic community in the long term.

We live in the most violent times, however much marketing executives try to blind us to it with their razzmatazz. By way of our scientifically outdated and inconsistent philosophies, we have created a politico-economic system that perpetuates this violence every moment of every day. At the heart of this system is the ideology of industrialism, a core idea that has played the role of protagonist in modern Capitalist, Socialist and Communist models alike. In this chapter I will look at the violence industrial civilisation inflicts on life in three different realms: violence towards the entire biotic community of which we are but a mosaic piece; the violence towards our own human communities that has led to their widespread breakdown; and the violence that the dominant ideologies of our time force us to commit towards ourselves and each other, not just physically but to the human spirit and soul, along with the injuries we endure every day to our sense of dignity, integrity, autonomy and freedom.

In doing so, I hope to shatter any lip-service to nonviolence or pure pacifism that anyone concerned with social justice or personal and ecological issues may cling to, so that we may unite towards creating genuinely peaceful ways of living that are inclusive of not just black and white people, not just women and men, not just working- and middle-class folk, but all of life. Otherwise, we will continue to subjugate Nature in the same way that we have, for the longest time, subjugated women and black people.

The first of these realms is what is now known as 'ecocide', the holistic equivalent of what we human supremacists call genocide, simply applied to the rest of life.

ECOCIDE

Genocide – a process that starts with one form of supremacist ideology or another before inevitably culminating with one form of brutality or another – has a deservedly bad reputation. Only sociopaths such as Hitler, or the British and European colonists, seem to be able to invent justifications for it. However, in defiance of all logic and reason, what has distinctly failed to achieve any similar level of instinctive revulsion in popular culture is ecocide, the application of the same ethics and rationale underlying genocide to the entirety of Life. Like the Nazis, Christopher Columbus and other harbingers of genocide, the dominant culture of anthropocentric, industrial civilisation eerily resembles the 'fictional character Hannibal Lector from *Silence of the Lambs*: refined, urbane, sophisticated and a cannibalistic psychopath'.[64]

While what constitutes genocide, and what differentiates it from homicide, is never a clearcut matter, Raphael Lemkin – a Polish lawyer of Jewish descent – coined the term around the end of the Second World War to roughly describe the deliberate and systematic destruction, in whole or in part, of an ethnic, racial, religious, or national group.[65] Events at the time give obvious context to its emergence and, by labelling it, Lemkin enabled humanity to recognise it for what it was and to deal with it more effectively.

While the term 'genocide' was unknown in common parlance prior to 1944, it quickly gained traction. Similarly, the idea of ecocide has gained momentum since it became apparent that the intensifying extermination of life on Earth was akin to the extermination of Jews in Nazi Germany. There is no anti-Semitism in my thoughts here, but I would go as far as to say that, looking at the situation through an ecocentric lens, the brutal violence Hitler and his cronies inflicted on one ethnic minority pales in significance to the total biotic cleansing of over a hundred thousand species every single year. That is not to downplay the Holocaust in the slightest, but simply to put the scale of ecocide today into proper perspective.

According to Polly Higgins, author of *Eradicating Ecocide* and a barrister who is known as the 'Earth Lawyer', ecocide is 'the extensive damage to, destruction of or loss of ecosystem(s) of a given territory, whether by human agency or by other causes, to such an extent that peaceful enjoyment by the inhabitants of that territory has been or will be severely diminished,'[66] arguing also that it is a 'crime against peace'.

Unlike genocide, however, ecocide is what Higgins calls 'the missing crime of our time'; at the time of writing it is still not an international crime, a fact that illustrates just how influential the dogma of anthropocentrism has been. The good news for the Gray Wolf, the Blue Whale, the Green-backed Kingfisher and the Shortnose Sturgeon (or any of the uncountable other endangered species teetering on the brink of annihilation), is that the day where ecocide is unlawful no longer seems quite so impossibly far away. Plans are afoot to table an amendment to the Rome Statute to include an international law on ecocide, after which 'all countries can then adopt this Ecocide Act into their national legislation'.[67] Higgins has already held a two-day mock trial in the U.K. Supreme Court, where under the proposed legislation top lawyers and judges found the CEOs of two fictional fossil fuel companies guilty as a result of their extraction of oil from tar sands in Canada, though found another not guilty for the damage caused by an oil spill in the Gulf of Mexico. Bolivia has gone one further, and in defence of what their indigenous people call *Pachamama*, they passed their *Ley de Derechos de la Madre Tierra*, The Law of the Rights of Mother Earth, into their constitution in 2010. Ecuador has taken a similar, if less radical step, and has enshrined the 'Rights of Nature' in its constitution.

If the law does change to reflect the deepening of our understanding of the world, and our place within it, what will the crime of ecocide look like? To start with, those who have had a grossly disproportionate part to play in this violence towards life would have to radically change the way they conduct their affairs. Under the 'principle of senior responsibility', everyone from heads of state to Chief Executive Officers would be personally accountable for acts of ecocide. The repercussions for elected Ministers of Parliament or their unelected corporate equivalents has the potential to exceed the effect that the Slavery Abolition Act 1833 had on those companies facilitating the slave-trade throughout the British Empire. It would be nothing less than the encapsulation in law of our move away from outdated ideologies of anthropocentrism and into the more ecocentric perspective which both science and our primal instincts know to be true.

Higgins' work is an example of reformism at its best, and in its rightful place. If this law against ecocide becomes the Fifth Geneva Convention or something similar, there lies the distinct possibility that at least some of what would have been annihilated will be preserved until a time when human desire or capacity to wantonly destroy has weakened. It is pragmatic and *could* be effective to a meaningful degree. I emphasise 'could', however, as the chances of enough governments voting it in seems slim, to say the very least. When you consider that the wealthiest nations and heaviest greenhouse gas emitters in the world cannot agree to do anything meaningful about climate change – something the overwhelming majority of scientists believe to be the biggest threat facing humanity today – enshrining something as radical as a law against ecocide into international law, and then enforcing it upon the same companies who fund the political campaigns of those in power, seems like a million miles away. Much less radical green legislation is struggling to get passed, and those green initiatives that do exist are always under threat from political elements. As time is running out if we are to avert the most damaging symptoms of climate chaos, I would not put all my eggs in the legal basket.

Even if ecocide somehow does get accepted as the fifth crime against peace, it only represents part of the solution. Within a globalised, industrialised capitalist economy, there is only so much a law can do to prevent widespread devastation, and only so deep that it can go. For example, Bolivia is still a major exporter and consumer of hydrocarbons, something its own economy has become dependent upon both in terms of fuel and for its balance of payments. This is despite the fact that such economic practices contravene both the spirit and the letter of *Ley de Derechos de la Madre Tierra*, which enumerates seven specific rights that *Madre Tierra* is entitled to, including the right to clean air, water and to live free from contamination.

But what can they do? The lives of those who live in La Paz are fully dependent on the fruits of ecocide. This means that, on the off-chance they actually wanted to, their government would only be able to prosecute the worst and most symbolic offenders of ecocide, in the same way that animal rights activists might target McDonald's (as the biggest purveyor of violence towards the animal kingdom) and not every small fast food outlet with factory-farmed chicken on its menu. It does not mean that other fast food companies are not guilty of (or at least accomplices in) committing acts of ecocide, but simply that the state recognises that such levels of violence are integral to the industrial economic system they have based their entire lives, values and institutions upon.

The problem of scale seems to be tricky here, and the big challenge with defining ecocide lies in deciding what scale of environmental destruction will constitute a 'crime against peace'. If insects and their habitat are to be included in this (and logic would suggest they should), then pesticide use will have to end in Bolivia immediately. We know that this will not happen as, like us all, they have created an agricultural system that has destroyed their biodiversity to such an extent that they believe they cannot now live without chemicals to grow their food.

I highlight this point not to criticise the courageous and bold actions of the Bolivian people and those who serve them, as it is a pioneering move in the most trying of circumstances and a significant step in the right direction. I illustrate it solely to show how difficult implementing laws such as this will be within the existing anthropocentric framework. We are all complicit in uncountable acts of ecocide every day, and though some are more responsible than others, we have designed entire ways of lives, food systems, factory production techniques, technologies, expectation levels, educational and prison systems, transport networks and methods of governance around everything that a law against ecocide would have to attempt to outlaw. No state or corporation in the world is going to pass and implement a law that effectively threatens the validity of their own institutions and their underlying assumptions about the world.

To compound the problem, due to the natural complexity of global ecosystems, it will be almost impossible to lay the blame for the biggest manifestations of ecocide on one company or CEO. Take climate change for example, which is likely to kill millions of people in the decades to come.[68] Who do we put in the stand on the charge of causing climate change? Or for the ecocide of bees? It would be more difficult to pin 'non-ascertainable' activities such as these on a particular legal entity than it would be to charge someone with causing breast cancer, as the ideology of human supremacy and its physical manifestations has forced us all to be complicit in them to varying degrees. The entity which really needs to be on trial is the one that never will be: our entire industrial culture.

This is why a diversity of tactics must be employed. The role of reformist action is to limit the destruction in whatever ways are most effective. The role of revolutionary action is to take the weapon out of the hand of the assailant to begin with.

Aside from the difficulties involved in outlawing ecocide, there would be potential long-term benefits if it were successful. As I will argue in chapter four, setting a law against ecocide could also act as a precursor to a law protecting what I call 'the right to holistic self-defence', where an inhabitant of a certain territory will be able to claim self-defence in a court of law if she was defending a threat to the life-systems of that territory which her own life is dependent upon. The consequences of this would be profound for those whose only experience of violence is that which is inflicted upon them from the top of the hierarchy downwards, the only direction violence is ever allowed to flow.

Whether or not the law courts of any nation – whose industrial economic model means ecocide will have been designed into their philosophical and practical foundations – ever recognise ecocide as a crime against peace, or not, does not change the fact that ecocide happens. If the Convention on the Prevention and Punishment of the Crime of Genocide had not been adopted by the UN General Assembly in 1951, it would not mean that genocide was any less wrong or that it did not exist; it would have simply meant that international legislation was not in place to protect the people of the Earth.

Unlike the mock trial in London, ecocidal acts are really happening every moment of every day. As E.F. Schumacher pointed out, we are in 'a battle against nature, a battle in which, if by chance we win it, we will find ourselves on the losing side'.[69] This is nowhere more visibly apparent than in our flat-packing of the world's forests.

The rate of deforestation – enacted for lumber, *The Daily Mail* and books such as this – would still be ecocide in real terms regardless of its legal status. As a 2005 report by the United Nations Food and Agriculture Organization states, we are deforesting the Earth at a rate of 13 million hectares per year (or 3,667 acres per hour). If we continue on our current course, we will have destroyed every square inch of rainforest within the next hundred years. This is especially tragic when you consider that over 70 per cent of all of Earth's land animals and plants live in forests of one variety or other, and that the majority of these will not survive the wholesale destruction of their habitat. Replacing natural woods or old-growth forests with young monocultural tree-farms is not a solution, contrary to what politicians and their spin doctors will claim, as the latter is not a suitable habitat for many species. If you insist on clinging to your anthropocentric outlook, and therefore do not see commercial deforestation as an equivalent level of violence as bulldozing a housing estate in a suburb of London while all its residents are still asleep, ask yourself if effectively cutting off the oxygen supply to nine billion humans is enough to convince you. Because by clear-cutting the world's forests, that is exactly what lumber and pulp companies – aided by our cash – are doing.

This brings me onto the oceans, that complex and majestic world which phytoplankton call home. Few of us wake up in the morning and have a care in the world for the oceans, let alone phytoplankton, yet our lives are more dependent on it than they are on our spouses or parents. One of the biggest threats to our oceans (which make up 99 per cent of all the living space of the planet)[70] is the practice of bottom-trawling. For anyone who clings to the romantic picture of the fisherman, standing on the shore as I did with my dad as a boy, casting in for the odd trout, then think again. Bottom-trawling involves dragging a trawl, a fishing net of sorts, usually along the sea floor or just above its benthic zone. Along with a host of other relatively minor contributing factors, this industrialised method has led to 90 per cent of the populations of commercially attractive fish, such as cod, swordfish and tuna, being wiped out since industrialism took control of our lives, and 'scientists predict that if current trends continue, world food fisheries could collapse entirely by 2050'.[71] These trawlers also catch gut-wrenching amounts of unwanted fish and other marine life in the process, with anywhere from '8 to 25 per cent of the total global catch discarded, cast overboard either dead or dying',[72] equating to over 20 million tonnes of flesh and bones (no less sacred than a human's) being killed for absolutely no reason every year.

Bottom-trawling's partner in crime, longline fishing (which can often involve lines that are up to 80 miles long) kills around 300,000 birds annually alone, not to mention its significant role in the emptying of the oceans. On that basis, ask the dolphin – who incidentally gets caught in the crossfire – if the pacifist extremist who eats fast food sushi is as non-violent as she thinks she is, and see if you encounter a different perspective to our culture's claims of moral superiority.

Again, if you insist on the outdated anthropocentric outlook, the levels of systemic violence are still astronomical. More than 3.5 billion people depend on the ocean for their primary source of food, some of whom also rely on it for their family's livelihood. Considering that the UN Environment Programme have stated that if we keep going like we are, 'we are in the situation where 40 years down the line we, effectively, are out of fish', the health and economic consequences for humans alone make any retaliatory destruction of trawlers look strangely like acts of peace and compassion.

The ocean is not only full of fish. Amongst many other wonders, it is also home to phytoplankton, who are responsible for every second breath that both human and non-human animals take, and are also 'responsible for a host of different, invisible and interlocked parts of the metabolism of the planet'.[73] While all the aforementioned practices are not helping, anthropogenic warming and acidification of the oceans due to the rapidly increasing concentration of carbon dioxide in the atmosphere (caused by industrialism) is one of the biggest threats to both marine and terrestrial life. According to a foundation of marine conservationists, Save Our Seas, the problem – as far as scientists can work out – is this: warmer surface water 'leads to stratification, where valuable nutrients become trapped in the deep ocean'. This in turn 'prevents phytoplankton, which live near the surface, from transforming those nutrients into energy and making that energy available to higher levels of the food web. When the base of the food web is disrupted in this way, all other species are affected, including those at the top: whales, sharks, seals, tuna, and people'.[74] As Alanna Mitchell poignantly notes, 'if plankton vanished tomorrow, the marine food chain would fall apart'.[75] If this is not violent through a more holistic-looking lens, nothing is. By way of the anthropocentric lens through which most humans view the world, it's just normality.

Next up is the animal kingdom. Those animals we do not like having around, we wipe out. We are doing this at unprecedented rates, leading to what is now being called the Holocene Extinction. Cautious studies suggest that we are losing at least 10,000 species every year, but if we combine 'species-area theory' with 'upper-bound estimating', the current rate of extinction 'may be up to 140,000 species per year'.[76] Lonesome George, the last Pinta Island Tortoise to experience life on Earth, passed away into oblivion in 2012. There will be no more Baiji Dolphin, no more Golden Toad, no more West African Black Rhinoceros, all of whom have already joined an incalculable and rapidly growing list of evolutionary dead-ends, their stories and patterns having made way for the myth of progress.

Many of those animals that we do claim to love – and by 'love' I mean 'derive utility from' – we cage and abuse, all for the growth imperative and profit necessity inherent in our politico-economic system. Factory farming – aside from the torture it inflicts upon sentient beings through 'rearing' and the cruel slaughterhouse practices that have become the norm – kills 150 billion animals every single year,[77] not including those imprisoned on life sentences, without parole, for products such as mass-produced eggs and dairy. None of this is done with sensitivity to the animal's needs, or the health of our ecosystems as a whole, the kind of consideration that many tribal people continue to display. It is beyond injurious, beyond destructive, but only when you stop seeing the world through a 16th century Cartesian lens.

These are just a minute sample of the headline figures, and could never do justice to the millions of individual tragedies that unfold every week. The list of ecocidal acts by The Machine is almost endless, and their combined effect is causing a series of feedback loops that are altering our atmosphere and changing our climates, and thus endangering much of the life still existing on Earth. However, I do not want to bombard you with any more facts about what we are doing to life on Earth. The point is this: we live and take part in a pathological culture, and until we are honest with ourselves and each other about this, any pretence to nonviolence will be just that – pretence – and we will not respond effectively to the extent that is appropriate to the circumstances.

There is so much to lose if we fail to respond effectively. As Aric McBay eloquently puts it:

> *What is at stake? Whippoorwills, the female so loyal to her young she won't leave her nest unless stepped on, the male piping his mate song of pure liturgy ... Mycorrhizal fungi, feeding their chosen plant companions and helping to create soil, with miles of filament in a teaspoon of earth. Bluefin tuna, warm-blooded and shimmering with speed. The eldritch beauty of amanita mushrooms. The mission blue butterfly, a fairy creature if there ever was one. A hundred miles of river turned silver with fish. A thousand autumn wings returning home. A million tiny radicles anchoring into earth, each with a dream of leaves, a lace of miracles, each thread both fierce and fragile, holding the others in place.*[78]

If we refuse to defiantly defend our own habitat with the courage of the female whippoorwill, what is at stake? All the above splendour and beauty that the bureaucrats at the UN refer to as ecosystem services, and much more besides. At what point, as we witness this ecocide unfold before our eyes, do we say enough is enough? Wendell Berry asks 'why not wait until our cause becomes vivid and urgent enough, and our side numerous enough, to vote our opponents out of office? Why not be patient?' He too gives his own answer, adding that:

> ... *while we are being patient, more mountains, forests, and streams, more people's homes and lives, will be destroyed in the Appalachian coalfields. Are 400,000 acres of devastated land, and 1,200 miles of obliterated streams not enough? This needs to be stopped. It does not need to be 'regulated'. As both federal and state governments have amply shown, you cannot regulate an abomination. You have got to stop it.*[79]

How long do we wait before we do whatever it takes to defend Life, that most sacred of things our industrial culture is desecrating and turning into cash? This is a question Derrick Jensen asks of us in *Endgame*. He says: 'Give me – and more importantly yourself – a specific threshold at which you will finally take a stand.' How many of our friends, lovers and families will we have to watch die from cancer, and the many other physical and mental illnesses that our toxic culture produces, before we say 'enough'? Will we wait until only 2% of our rainforests stand proud before we ourselves take a stand with them? How about 1%? Or 0.5%? Do we feel that the decimation of our oceans has already gone far too far, or will we reach our limits of tolerance when only 3% of the numbers of fish that lived pre-industrialisation roam the Atlantic and the Pacific? Do we have to wait until every minutiae of our lives is mechanised, monetised, tamed, surveyed, regulated and geared towards increasing corporate profit before we can no longer take it? What is our threshold going to be before we fight back? As Jensen adds, 'if you can't or won't give that threshold, why not?'[80]

As Thoreau found out, saying 'enough' may involve breaking the law, if the law itself is unjust. Does this idea that we must not only create new laws, but break current ones, scare you? It should. If we are serious about preserving a beautiful, thriving planet not only for ourselves and our children, but the unborn of the millions of species whom we have weaved the web of life with, we need to radically change the way we live, the politico-economic systems that we live within, and the cultural stories underpinning it all.

Change on such a scale is always scary, always unknown. Yet instead of seeing it as something to avoid, we could embrace it as the biggest adventure that those of us born into this Age could embark on, something that could unite us under a cause that will reintroduce meaning and purpose into lives that have up to now been dominated by bureaucracy, assembly lines and clock-in cards. Instead of thinking of it involving the loss of all the modern conveniences that our plundering of the Earth has given us a false sense of entitlement to, we could look at it as an opportunity to reclaim aspects of our primordial nature that, because industrialism has never allowed us to experience them, we do not even know we have lost. By straightening our backs and not shirking the challenge of our time, we may find our way back to living a dignified life, in which we restore our intimate connection with the Earth and, through doing so, become no longer afraid to defend it.

It is not just the rest of Nature that is violated by The Machine and its underlying assumptions. No, we're also violating ourselves, or more precisely, allowing ourselves to be violated.

COMMUNICIDE

I think it is morally justified to resort to whatever means are necessary in order to defend our land from destruction, from invasion.

Edward Abbey

A neighbour and I were having a cup of tea one lunchtime, after he had been helping me with a bit of work on the land. The conversation soon got on to the deteriorating state of rural Ireland, a topic that gets far too little attention considering the scale and profound consequences of the problem. I made an obvious point about the way in which high technologies such as the automobile, World Wide Web and television had thoughtlessly destroyed a way of life that had served the people of rural Ireland well for many a year. My neighbour – who had lived through a much different (albeit recent) period in Irish history than I had experienced, one where most Irish people did not have two shillings to rub together – had a more subtle perspective. He suggested that the technology that ripped apart every thread of the fabric of small villages and parishes was not, as expected, industrialism's poster boy products such as the television, car, or the internet. Instead it was an unlikely suspect: the humble flask.

Intrigued by this revelation, I asked him to explain. When he was growing up around the 1960s, himself and his family would often go to the bog to take in the turf, along with most of the other families of the parish, all of whom would spend the day helping each other out with their time, skills and tools. Cutting turf in this way is convivial but hard work, and inevitably there ends up being as much tea drunk as there is turf dug. Every day one family would make up a campfire upon which the kettle would be boiled and around which tea would be savoured.

But the campfire had a much more significant role than hydrating people, an important thing in itself. It was the focal point that brought the entire community together during important seasonal events such as this. During the day people would chat and have some banter as the tea brewed, and in the evenings food would be cooked on it. Without fail, by nightfall neighbours would start getting up to no good – a bit of music would be played, a couple of jigs danced, and some young lad would hide some other poor bugger's wheelbarrow, providing endless entertainment the next morning. Working in the bog together was about more than simply meeting the physical requirements of life. It allowed people the pleasure of applying the age-old crafts that had been passed onto them with a sense of common purpose. In doing so, the experience weaved individual people into a strong community of folk who looked after each other physically, psychologically, emotionally and even spiritually.

Then one day, out of the blue, the simple everyday flask appeared on the scene. Like every technology before it, when it was first invented and marketed to us we were only made aware of the benefits it would bring us. In this instance, the flask meant that we could have hot water at any time, in any place. It seemed to be a no-brainer. Yet what happened next perfectly illustrates, in practical reality, the law of unintended consequences.

Within a short period of time people began boiling up their water on the stove at home, and taking it with them to the bog, a much more convenient option than making a campfire. This meant there was no longer as much need to build a campfire, as it was now designed out of the whole process, made obsolete after millennia of good service. No campfire meant no focal point. No focal point meant no singing, no dancing, no making merry with the neighbours. In a matter of years it produced a much less resilient and more alienated community. The flask therefore played its own part in the move towards individualism that goes hand-in-hand with mass consumerism. It gave people the illusion of independence. Of course, people were no less dependent than they were before, in that they were still dependent on something keeping their water hot. The only difference now was that instead of being dependent on the natural materials and people around them, something which is vital to maintaining healthy human and biotic communities, they had become dependent on industrial factories and people on the other side of the planet, people whose eyes they will never meet, people whose work conditions they will never witness, people who will not see them through thick and thin. The flask was just another product of a 'civilization committed to the quest for continually improved means to carelessly examined ends'.[81]

This story is distilled into a basic point by Charles Eisenstein. He notes that 'We find in our culture a loneliness and hunger for authenticity that may well be unsurpassed in history. We try to "build community", not realising that mere intention is not enough when separation is built into the very social and physical infrastructure of our society. To the extent that this infrastructure is intact in our lives, we will never experience community'.[82] He adds that 'community is not some add-on to our other needs, not a separate ingredient for happiness along with food, shelter, music, touch, intellectual stimulation, and other forms of physical and spiritual nourishment. Community arises from the meeting of those needs. There is no community possible among a people who do not need each other'.[83]

To blame the total destruction of community on a flask would be akin to blaming the genocide of a people on a bullet. The real culprit is the entire industrialised, globalised and monetised culture we in the civilised world have created today. What a culture that mixes the ideologies of industrialism, monetary economics, globalisation and capitalism in a large social test tube does better than anything else is give us the false impression that we do not need each other, an illusion that has not only destroyed healthy human-scale habitats such as rural villages and hamlets, but has added to the alienation and misery of overcrowded and strangely anonymous cities. Our most intimate relationships with both the land and the people, who have become as integral to it as the trees and the wildlife, are eventually denigrated into monetary transactions in order to fulfil the incessant growth imperative inherent in capitalism. Through doing so we have created a society that brutalises us physically, psychologically, emotionally, and spiritually, and a politico-economic system that has waged more violence on human-scale, sustainable communities than any war ever has.

This may seem like a wild statement to make. Let me explain. The real 'tragedy of the commons' was that the potent and simultaneous combination of the ideas of private property and industrialism forced people, both economically and physically, off their lands and into the cities. This had a terrible effect on people on every level, and as Jared Diamond once said when speaking about agriculture, it was another 'catastrophe from which we have never recovered'.[84] They had to leave places where *belonging* was most valued, and move to a place where *belongings* were most valued. Family, friends and community were substituted for strangers with whom one had no loyalty towards or trust in, eventually leading to a level and type of crime that was unimaginable in non-industrialised villages. Instead of applying their age-old crafts to make the physical necessities of life for those they had a meaningful relationship with, people were forced onto the conveyor belt of industrialism, working boring, specialised jobs that wrench at the human soul and deprive it of meaning and intimate connection. People were torn from communities where they had an authentic connection to the land under their feet and the friends and family whom that land had shaped, and were forced, as Jacques Ellul says, to 'live in conditions that are less than human'. He adds that the effects of this are particularly gruesome when you

> ... *consider the concentration of our great cities, the slums, the lack of space, of air, of time, the gloomy streets and the sallow lights that confuse night and day. Think of our unsatisfied senses ... our estrangement from nature. Life in such an environment has no meaning. Consider our public transportation, in which man is less important than a parcel; our hospitals, in which he is only a number. Yet we call this progress ... And the noise, that monster boring into us at every hour of the night without respite.*[85]

Livelihoods that were once sustainable, where people fashioned local materials into the shape of their own imagination and soul, became repetitive factory jobs that imported resources from all over the world, resulting in the 'production of too many useful things' that Marx said 'results in too many useless people'.[86] Traditional, sustainable skills died in this process and were replaced by jobs in web development, call centres and the pharmaceutical industry, none of which will outlive this short era of cheap and dirty energy and the industries founded upon the mythical belief in their infinite abundance. Such modern skills will also not be of much use to people when the time comes that humanity is eventually forced by Nature to live in a harmonious, sustainable relationship with the Great Web of Life once again. This loss of knowledge of real economics – of soil and wood and bones – where one knows how to meet her needs from the local landscape, has the potential to wipe out massive urban populations once the unsustainable systems that support them (through the wholesale destruction of other areas) can no longer be fuelled at a price that our financial and ecological capital can afford.

Of course, young people today are no longer physically forced into cities. While economic factors play a strong role, as the institutionalised rituals of industry and commerce reinforce their hold over our minds, the influence of industrialism has become much more subtle. One of the revolutionary technologies that has popped out of the mechanical anus of industry – the television – has long since sold us aspirational lifestyles, aspirational sex and aspirational homes, none of which becomes the experiential reality for anyone other than the exorbitantly wealthy. These images take hold in our minds, however, and the effects are much the same as the enclosures: an intensifying decline of sustainable rural areas alongside a rapid increase in the size of unsustainable cities and large towns. The growth of dull, inanimate greyness of such unnatural habitat as these led to what became known as 'the Avatar effect', referring to the wave of depression and suicidal feelings that followed the release of the movie *Avatar*, as people longed for the ecologically bountiful and diverse moon of the fictional Pandora, a world where life was thriving and its inhabitants were, quite literally, connected to The Whole. I watched it myself, and I too felt a sense of grief for the loss of a way of being that I have never even experienced, but which my primal self still remembers and is still alive somewhere in my DNA.

Make no bones about it, our current politico-economic system is continuing to force itself upon the 5,000 indigenous cultures (whose homelands constitute 20 per cent of the land surfaces on earth)[87] we still have remaining, including regions where uncontacted tribal people have lived in harmony with their landscape since time immemorial. The Machine desperately needs the resources these people live amongst to keep its own military-based economies running, while Growth demands that the people themselves must be turned into consumers of industrialised products, whose relationships can be monetised and redistributed to the already financially wealthy through profits, salaries and taxes. This industrialisation of land-based peoples is *always* violent towards its direct victims, and by way of creating, growing and fuelling cities that themselves depend on the destruction of other far-flung places through resource extraction (and the wars required to procure those resources), it is indirectly violent to the entire biotic community.

This is not a system that will voluntarily reform itself, as it could not do so without self-destructing, and there are far too many vested interests for that. Therefore it is a system that we need to do whatever we can to bring to a long overdue end, using whatever means and strategies are necessary and most effective. Otherwise things are only going to get worse. Yes we have destroyed thousands of unique cultures and languages, and made extinct innumerable species, in the last few hundred years alone, and this is a terrible loss for the world, even if most of us don't realise it yet. But there is still so much to play for, still so much to lose. Unless we fight back, in defence of Life and in solidarity with those cultures that have thus far managed to resist the onslaught of The Machine, we will deserve the generic, monoglot cultures we will have created for ourselves.

THE TYRANNY OF THE MACHINE

Dante, when composing his visions of hell, might well have included the mindless, repetitive boredom of working on a factory assembly line. It destroys initiative and rots brains, yet millions of British workers are committed to it for most of their lives.

E.F. Schumacher

Myself and a few hundred like me emerge from a London tube one morning, all busily scurrying along towards some business meeting, appointment or workplace. Most people are plugged into one sort of device or other, with electronic music and not-so-social media sedating the concrete and steel dullness of our immediate surroundings. It is rush hour and the station is heaving. As I approach the escalator, I notice that a huge crowd is gathering at the bottom, staring upwards, in the same way that a child who does not know what to do will look up at a parent. People are steadily gathering behind them, all looking equally puzzled. At first I thought someone must have had an accident, but it soon became clear that it was nothing more serious than the fact that the escalator had just broken, and had therefore turned into what was known in my youth as a set of stairs. A fully functional set of stairs at that. Yet there they were – fully mature, adult human beings – staring at it completely baffled as to what they should do. It was not until someone (presumably still grounded in their own body) at the back of the crowd shouted 'just use your legs' that those at the front started to walk up the motionless escalator, after which those behind trundled along, some looking decidedly the worse for wear for having to spend roughly 40 seconds climbing up steps. Everything I had believed about our current human culture was laid bare in an instant: The Machine has taken us over, mind, body and soul.

Unfortunately, this phenomenon plays itself out in ways much less comical than this. Through the increasing influence of not only the practical functioning of The Machine, but also the application of its underlying philosophy (such as scientific precision, maximum efficiency) to people with emotions, feelings and longings for diverse creative expression, industrial civilisation is not just biting the ecological hand that feeds it, it is also biting its own hand.

We live and work within a machine economy. Not only is our economy increasingly run by machines, we ourselves have become its cogs in the process. In saying this, I am not speaking metaphorically; we have, quite literally, become the interchangeable parts of the Mumfordian mega-machine. If you labour under the impression that this is not the case, think again. If Franz Reuleaux's classic definition of a machine, described 'as a combination of resistant parts, each specialized in function, operating under human control, to utilize energy and to perform work',[88] is accurate, then the great labour machine that is the modern workforce bears an eerily close resemblance, and as Lewis Mumford points out is 'in every aspect a genuine machine; all the more because its components, though made of bone, nerve, and muscle, were reduced to their bare mechanical elements and rigidly standardized for the performance of their limited tasks'.[89] At a time when it is commonly said that machines, through technologies such as artificial intelligence, are becoming humanlike, what is noticeable by its absence in the public discourse is its inevitable parallel: humans are becoming machinelike.

The Machine, despite the plethora of gadgets it clutters our world up with – all shinier, faster and cheaper than ever before – does not serve us well. It gives you the impression that it does; after all, we buy the stuff it produces, therefore we must desire it on some level. Desiring something, however, is no sound indication that it serves you well. Heroin addicts desire heroin not because it improves their lives, but because it has become an addiction, having initially been consumed to fill a void, a gaping wound sliced open by the blades of progress. The Machine's technologies have the same effect. They work in the same way that the advertising industry does, in that they wilfully and skilfully mask some real need, such as the longing for deep connection, and sell us a toxic substitute to soothe the pain of the loss.

Advertising, that dark art that I myself was indoctrinated in during my undergraduate degree, actively works to destroy the self-esteem of its victim first, before going on to offer the products and services that, once purchased, may restore some of the self-confidence destroyed by their deceitful adverts moments earlier. It's like a chocolate laxative, which through its marketing jumps out at us and shouts 'Do you have consti-pation? Eat more of this chocolate!', exactly the type of food that can trigger chronic constipation in the first place.[90]

Psychologically and emotionally healthy people, content within their own skin, are not what an advertiser desires. They need people to feel the ultimate poverty, the type where, no matter how much you earn or how much you have, it is never enough.

The women's magazine industry is a prime example of this. First you see the image of an airbrushed woman looking unlike any real woman ever could. Below it there is an advert telling you that if you buy this or that tanning or diet product, you just might look like her. Of course looking like her is impossible, as even she does not look like her. If you think this is a cynical attitude and that advertising executives are not so full of ill-intent, consider the fact that culture-jamming magazine *Adbusters* once tried and failed to place adverts with three leading women's magazines, despite offering to pay the going rate. Instead of making women feel inadequate as standard adverts are intended to do, in their own Freudian way, the unpublished *Adbusters* adverts simply told the reader that they were beautiful just the way they are. There was no product for sale. Yet all three magazines refused to publish it, for the simple reason (though not the one they gave) that encouraging women to be happy with themselves as they are would be to the long-term detriment of their businesses. If this is not an injurious attack on the emotional, psychological and ultimately the physical health of a person, I do not know what is. If you believe that the advertising industry – which depends on us consuming its products and services at an ever-increasing rate – can be reformed into a sustainable economy, you are grossly mistaken.

The Machine, and the gadgetry that comes off its conveyor belts every second, works on the same principles. It has destroyed, and continues to destroy, our deep connection to kith and kin, and offers us a toxic mimic in its place. Of course this toxic mimic seems novel and appealing to begin with and, like the flask, we initially only see the benefits it brings us. The companies flogging us their wares never sell us the consequences of their products in their adverts, as these consequences are usually violent towards everything it is to be human, to be animal. Like other addictions, these toxic mimics offer us release from the inner pain caused by the gaping wound their predecessors created. Inevitably the effects of the numbness wear off, and we go chasing a bigger hit, tying ourselves in all sort of chains, such as debt, in the process. As Ran Prieur warned, 'every technology begins as a key and ends as a cage'.[91]

Believe it or not, it has not always been like this. There was a time when we did not merely consume products and services; instead, we actively participated in life. We foraged or produced and cooked our own food. We made our own music and stories, and performed them around fires for family, friends and our immediate communities. We carved out our spoons and bowls in the shape of our own soul. We made our booze together, and drank it together. But gradually the ghostly spirit of The Machine infiltrated our minds, and possessed them. Now instead of living lives that are rich with diversity and which allow us to express a thousand aspects of ourselves in a thousand different ways, we specialise in one particular job or another, doing more or less the same thing every hour of every day in an attempt to replicate the mantra of 'maximum efficiency' of The Machine, a quality which has an undeservedly good reputation. Efficiency is 'a word that has been elevated to almost holy status in the neoliberal lexicon, but in reality has become a shameful euphemism for the sacrifice of human dignity at the altar of share prices'.[92] As Mumford astutely observes, 'power, speed, motion, standardization, mass production, quantification, regimentation, precision, uniformity, astronomical regularity, control, above all control – these [have become] the passwords of modern society in the new Western style'.[93]

This obsession with efficiency has not only enabled us to efficiently destroy much of life on Earth, it has also led to the death of truly sustainable and meaningful livelihoods, work that was once carried out at a human-friendly scale. The skill and slower speed of the human hand of a craftsperson can never compete with the functional efficiency of The Machine, meaning human-scale livelihoods have been put on the Endangered Species list, and one suspects that before long they may go the way of the Dodo. While few of us no more consciously mourn this loss of meaningful work than we do the loss of the Passenger Pigeon, we do so in a more subtle way every Monday morning when we awake to an alarm clock already wishing it to be Friday evening. This imposition of industrialism inflicts a subtle, systemic violence on us every day of our lives, and it is an ideology that it is utterly unreformable. If you are to believe Darrell J. Fasching, Professor of Religious Studies at the University of South Florida, 'modern technology has become a total phenomenon for civilization, the defining force of a new social order in which efficiency is no longer an option but a necessity imposed on all human activity'.[94]

The Machine has not only had a seriously damaging effect on our livelihoods, and the emotional and spiritual aspects of ourselves that are wrapped up in daily work, it also has acutely negative consequences for us physically. It is creating industrial illnesses – such as cancers, heart diseases, auto-immune disorders – which it conveniently then makes us believe only industry can cure. In doing so, it has made us totally dependent on a entire global infrastructure that is unsustainable in the extreme, and overwhelmingly damaging towards the health of the entire planet (and thereby the health of humanity also).

It has robbed us of all the healing skills we once had, skills that allowed us, in general terms, to live the 'optimum lifespan' of a human, instead of the maximum lifespan we strive for today. Of course, it's quite a natural thing to want to live for as long as you can, especially in a culture so disconnected from the natural cycles of life as ours. But if you think that living as long as is artificially possible is the ultimate goal of a human, ask yourself what the consequences would be for both ourselves and the planet if we found industrial medicines that allowed us to live until we were 300 years old? Or 500 years? The planet could not support such numbers of humans consuming even a fraction of what we do today, as it cannot even cope with our current population levels. Therefore we must accept that the optimum lifespan is not the same as the maximum lifespan. The optimum lifespan is that which gives you a healthy, natural way of life that does not prevent the rest of the community of life experiencing the same.

When we think about it, it becomes obvious that longer is not necessarily better. If we lived an extra 200 years, we would be beset by all sorts of physical ailments to an even higher degree than we are today. Replacement hips would be the least of our worries. Quantity is no sign of quality, and once quantity exceeds its optimum level, quality is the price we pay. If I said to you that because women in Ireland live, on average, four years longer than men, their lives must be better than those of men based solely on this statistic, you would rightfully point out that it is not just the quantity of life that counts, but the quality of it, and that in a patriarchal and male-dominated society, this sense of quality has been a lot more difficult for women to achieve. Yet we apply this flawed thinking to civilised society, endlessly pointing to our longer life span to extol its virtues, as if this was the ultimate indicator that proved we were living more meaningful, happier lives. We're not. Ask yourself this: would you rather live 60 years in freedom and deep intimate connection to the world around you, or 80 years in a cage with invisible bars? What's more, implicit in this fervent desire for longer life is an abnormally intense fear of death – itself a strong indicator that we aren't living in a healthy relationship with the Great Web of Life.

One look at the real indicators of human happiness shows that, despite the fact that those of us in the global West have never been financially wealthier, we have never been unhappier. In the U.S., where the ideologies of The Machine play out like nowhere else on Earth, anti-depressant use is soaring. In 1998, the number of U.S. residents using these drugs totalled a whopping 11.2 million. By 2010 it had more than doubled, weighing in at 23.3 million.[95] What kind of societies have we created for ourselves when so many people are so unhappy they have to take industrial drugs, with all their side-effects, to sedate the pain of living in a world devoid of intimate connection, meaning and a sense of authentic community and belonging? How many more trudge through life with feelings of depression, loneliness, isolation and discontent?

Despite ever-increasing levels of brute force and violence by police officers, armed soldiers and the legal system, crime levels continue to increase (rape, robbery and assault rose by more than one third from 2010-12).[96] People who live in healthy, connected communities do not commit the kind of crimes that we commit against each other today, and certainly not at the rate in which we do. Yet the criminals who commit them are usually victims themselves, forced into carrying them out by the systemic crimes of the entire culture we have created, one which we have to destroy if we are to have any hope of creating genuinely peaceful lives.

Perhaps the greatest violence industrial civilisation inflicts upon us is one much more subtle. The Machine has cut us off from the Earth, destroying our intimate connection with it and our conscious state of interbeing with it. As Rollo May, in *The Cry for Myth*, says, 'technology is the knack of so arranging the world that we do not experience it'.[97] We no longer experience the richness of the world. We do not have time to enjoy a butterfly passing from wild flower to wild flower in a meadow. We no longer feel the soil under our bare feet. Unlike Tom Brown Jr., we cannot see the tracks of a human foot and from that alone understand what mood the person who made them was in.[98] We do not have time to be slow, to fully immerse ourselves in a moment, or to be free from the guilt of the past or worry about the future. Because of ideologies such as industrialism and its inherent need for efficiency, we can no longer look at a stream, a swallow or an earthworm, and deeply understand how our lives are all inseparably interconnected. From this primary violence, uncountable secondary acts of violence inevitably occur, and will continue to occur until we rid ourselves of this ghost that has possessed us.

It must become clear to us that our way of life – the anthropocentric culture of industrial civilisation – inflicts more violence upon life in a moment than we can even comprehend. Every ounce of our efforts towards a more just, ecocentric world ought to be given towards dismantling The Machine, nut by nut and bolt by bolt. As Thoreau proclaimed in *Civil Disobedience*, 'let your life be a counter-friction to stop the machine', adding later that 'if I repent of anything, it is likely to be my good behaviour'.[99]

Civil disobedience, as our rulers would have us believe, is not the threat facing us today, and never has been. For as Howard Zinn pointed out:

> *Our problem is civil obedience. Our problem is the numbers of*
> *people all over the world who have obeyed the dictates of the leaders*
> *of their government and have gone to war, and millions have been*
> *killed because of this obedience ... Our problem is that people are*
> *obedient all over the world, in the face of poverty and starvation*
> *and stupidity, and war and cruelty. Our problem is that people are*
> *obedient while the jails are full of petty thieves, and all the while*
> *the grand thieves are running the country. That's our problem. We*
> *recognize this for Nazi Germany. We know that the problem there*
> *was obedience, that the people obeyed Hitler. People obeyed; that*
> *was wrong. They should have challenged, and they should have*
> *resisted; and if we were only there, we would have showed them.*[100]

If we are wise we will not overly worry ourselves with culturally-indoctrinated notions of violence and nonviolence, but instead concern ourselves only with the taking of the most effective action in protecting all that is beautiful about our world from the fall-out of the arrogance of human supremacy. There was a time when white supremacists (who were also human supremacists) and their views were regarded as normal and acceptable, something we have started making a little headway on, however superficially, in the last half-century. It will be interesting to see if history will view human supremacists – all of us – in the same light at some point in the future.

In the meantime, our ability to protect the victims of human supremacy, and ultimately ourselves, will be strengthened if activists of all persuasions unite in solidarity. The mystic poet Rumi once told us that 'out beyond ideas of wrongdoing and rightdoing, there is a field'.[101] It is in this field that both nonviolent and full-spectrum resisters ought to meet, listen to each other's perspectives and learn to respect each other's calling. It is from this field that a dignified resistance to The Machine may begin in earnest.

CHAPTER THREE
REFORMISM IS FUTILE

You may either win your peace or buy it: win it, by resistance to evil; buy it, by compromise with evil.

John Ruskin

'LOWER YOUR SHIELDS AND SURRENDER your ships ... your culture will adapt to service us ... you will be assimilated ... Resistance is Futile.' This is a quote often attributed to the Borg of *Star Trek* fame, but there is a growing body of evidence to suggest that they plagiarised it from the Industrialists, a virus-like race from planet Earth whose ways came to prominence during the Age of Separation.

This misattribution is understandable. For those of you who, like myself, are not fanatical Trekkies and can't speak Klingon, the Borg are a collection of species that have become cybernetic organisms – part organic, part artificial. Feared by other species and races, they spend their days marauding the Universe, violently forcing other starships, societies and entire planets to assimilate into their culture, a process that involves the integration of sentient beings along with their cultures, techniques and technologies. On encountering an 'undiscovered' planet or starship, the Borg take them by force and turn the inhabitants – in both body and mind – into drones, so that the Borg collective can use them for its own ends. From the perspective of their one-time spokesperson, assimilated Captain Jean-Luc Picard, this is all done to 'raise the quality of life' of those they aim to assimilate.

Sound disturbingly familiar? If not, it should. The bad guys from *Star Trek* play a frighteningly analogous role to the Industrialists, a dominant culture whose captains maraud the Earth forcing smaller, less technologically 'advanced' communities to domesticate and assimilate into their way of life. One of the Industrialists' key objectives on their frequent raids is to force indigenous people to relinquish their lands, before taking the minerals and energy reserves from under their feet and turning them into plastic gadgetry for them to then buy. This, they claim, brings these poor barbaric people (who it is assumed are too ignorant and stubborn to know what's good for them) whom they conquer out of poverty, thus raising the quality of their life. The culmination of this cunning plan is the monetisation of even the most intimate relationships of those vanquished, leading to the erosion of their skill-base, their connection to the land and each other and, eventually, the obliteration of their entire culture.

This has gone to such an extreme that those freshly conquered quickly cease being participants in life, but become mere consumers of it, entirely dependent upon those who invaded their lands to begin with and totally inculcated into their deathly ways. The dominant culture has been so successful at this that Ward Churchill provocatively, but perhaps insightfully, remarked that in what is now known as the U.S., 'white domination is so complete that even American Indian children want to be cowboys. It's as if Jewish children wanted to play Nazis'.[102]

What is crucial to any invading entity, as Clausewitz alluded to in *On War*, is that one way or another the invader must make those they wish to dominate feel that 'resistance is futile', something that draws upon military strategist Sun Tzu's advice that 'supreme excellence consists in breaking the enemy's resistance without fighting'. Just as in a duel or in a fight between a pair of wrestlers, the goal of those engaged in a war is to 'annihilate the enemy's capacity to resist', while simultaneously 'preserving and enhancing one's own capacity in the face of the enemy's application of force'.[103]

This can be done physically, by destroying their means for survival; and psychologically, by successfully wiping out any hope the enemy has of being able to put up a successful resistance. The latter is often attempted nowadays by the type of 'shock and awe' strategy undertaken by the invading U.S. forces in Iraq (with limited success due to strong resistance and insurgency by Iraqis) during what was known as, by way of smart propaganda, Operation Iraqi Freedom. As a sweeping glance around the cultures dying on the periphery of civilisation would attest to, such overawing strategies undertaken by industrialists often succeed in doing so. The more races and species The Machine assimilates, the easier it becomes, as the more resources and cultures they steal, the more powerful they get. This is Capitalism 101.

Despite what The Establishment would like us to believe, resistance is never futile, whether the resistance be by violent or nonviolent methods, or a combination of both. First and foremost (as I will explore in chapter six), and regardless of the final outcome, resisting tyranny is fundamental to a genuine sense of self-respect, dignity and honour that is shamefully absent from those of us who see the wholesale devastation inflicted upon the entire biotic community, ourselves included, and do not react appropriately.

It can also act as a unifying force that brings people together, in opposition to a common aggressor. Peter Gelderloos gives the example of Jews that took part in the Warsaw ghetto uprising in 1943. Using 'stolen, smuggled and home-made weapons', the rebel Jews 'fought for weeks, to the death, tying up thousands of Nazi troops and other resources needed on the collapsing Eastern Front. They knew they would be killed whether they were peaceful or not. By rebelling violently, they lived the last few weeks of their lives in freedom and resistance, and slowed down the Nazi war machine.'[104]

On top of that, their efforts inspired other revolts in extermination camps and ghettos throughout German-occupied Eastern Europe, which saved many thousands of Jewish lives. Two death camps in particular, at Sobibór and Treblinka, were closed down after rebellions and never reopened, significantly reducing the Nazis' ability to inflict extreme violence on those they wished to exterminate.

This innate drive to resist those enslaving us, against the most seemingly hopeless odds, is not a phenomenon limited to the human realm. Other creatures, without hope of ever winning freedom for themselves, have been known to rebel against those who attempt to dominate them. Take one colony of ants from the genus *Temnothorax*, who are annually invaded by a rival colony of ants from the genus *Protomognathus americanus* (their name might signify their tendency to invade), and have their young brood stolen from them. These unhatched ants are taken away with the conquerors to new nests, where they grow up to become live-in slaves, whose job it is to look after the families of their masters. Again, sound familiar?

This is where it gets interesting. Biologists who studied them found something they weren't expecting, but which those who took part in the ghetto uprising in Warsaw would have instantly recognised. Initially scientists assumed that the captured ants would not revolt, on the basis that they had no chance of reproduction and were therefore coming to an 'evolutionary dead-end' regardless of what they did. What they found in actual practice astounded them.

These slave ants, born into that regime and knowing nothing

different, eventually stopped looking after their masters' young in their care, often resulting in the latter's death. But they didn't stop there. Groups of them would often incite all-out revolt and kill the young of the masters' colony. Having puzzled a team of biologists including Tobias Pamminger for a while, they eventually realised that such seemingly hopeless rebellions were not as evolutionarily unfathomable as they first seemed. The conclusion they came to was much the same as those in Warsaw: that 'while mutinous slaves may not be able to save themselves, by rebelling they can reduce the number of slave masters who prey on nearby relatives'. As Pamminger found out through observing the oppressed, resistance can only ever be considered futile if one is only thinking about their own skin-encapsulated ego, and absolutely nothing else – and even then it's never futile if, as we'll see later, it brings a sense of dignity back into the lives of those it has been stolen from.[105]

As ant colonies and Jews know from experience, resistance has historically only succeeded when those resisting chose to consider the full spectrum of means at their disposal, and not the truncated range that dogmatic practitioners of nonviolence limit themselves to. Not that they would accept this fact; after all, as we'll see in chapter five, they have claimed that peaceful means alone won their flagship victories – the Indian Independence Movement, the African-American Civil Rights Movement and so on – a deceitful and dangerous revision of history that is nothing short of pacifist and state propaganda.

The truth of the matter was much less nonviolently romantic, as we will examine in more detail in chapter five. Sometimes nonviolent means have been used with some degree of success as part of what, in reality, were full-spectrum campaigns, such as in the Indian struggle with the British, though in these examples success has often meant great compromises that only changed the colour of the flag or the uniforms of those in power, leaving the structures of exploitation intact.

At other times violent means predominated, as in the armed struggle of the Viet Cong that eventually forced the U.S. imperialists out of their lands (the U.S. peace movement made audacious claims that it was their placard-raising, and not the relentless armed resistance by the National Liberation Front along with other political factors, that finally stopped the war). Peaceful resistance also played a small role, including such pacifist acts as self-immolation. But advocates of a diversity of tactics would never deny this; it is only those who follow the doctrines of nonviolence and pacifism who claim that all successful resistance or revolutionary movements in the past have come through their means alone. Real victories have *always* come through taking a pluralistic approach to resistance, a fact that modern movements for change, which in the early 21st century have become dominated by advocates of non-violence, would do well to remember if change is actually what they want. As Ward Churchill reminds us:

> ... *there simply has never been a revolution, or even a substantial social reorganization, brought into being on the basis of the principles of pacifism. In every instance, violence has been an integral requirement of the process of transforming the state.*[106]

Aside from the dignity that people achieve by resisting a tyrant of one political creed or another, the situation is rarely, if ever, as hopeless as the tyrant would like you to believe. Many resisters (though they may not have been known by that term prior to the French Resistance of the Second World War) throughout history have fought powerful forces and emerged stronger than if they had not. Indeed, if it were not for a lethal cocktail of understandable fear, the hegemony of pacifist ideology and a lack of genuine international solidarity, there is a strong argument to be made that other oppressed people may have more successfully defended their cultures, communities and lands. As Terry Eagleton once quipped, 'if you do not resist the apparently inevitable, you will never know how inevitable the inevitable was.'[107]

The list of those who realised, by employing the full spectrum of tactics available to them, that the inevitable was not so inevitable is encouraging. As Subcomandante Marcos and the women and men of the Zapatistas (a land-based revolutionary group based in Chiapas, Mexico) would attest to, standing up to a tyrannical power is undoubtedly better than watching everything and everyone you love being pillaged and raped while you are down on your knees – something I explore in more depth in chapter six. Emma Goldman went as far as to say that 'resistance to tyranny is man's highest ideal.'[108] When you consider the tyranny of The Machine over Life, it becomes clear what we need to do if we are to live dignified lives: resist it by whatever means are appropriate.

What categorically must be resisted, if we are to preserve what fragments are left of our cultural and ecological biodiversity, is the march of The Machine towards the goal of converting the world's entire physical and social capital into cold hard cash. This march, as I am about to explain, will – at best – only be temporarily impeded by reformist actions or – at worst – will be aided by them, inasmuch as they make its unbearable effects bearable. It is this simple: if we are to preserve any of the remaining beauty in the world and our own hearts, we need to start revolting. Building a strong and diverse resistance movement is an important part of any revolution.

When I speak about revolution I am not referring to the New Age, 'inner revolution' that has become fashionable to extol within some circles of the counter-culture movement. No, I am speaking about a political revolution, where a population of people (a village, region or nation) take power out of the hands of a few and clear the path for some new form of social relations to take its place. Such political 'outer revolutions', which always involve a diversity of tactics, have a bad reputation amongst many of those in what is loosely called the New Age movement (a term I dislike), who usually argue that what we need is 'evolution, not revolution'. By doing so they forget that revolutions are little more than particularly intense periods existing within our evolutionary process, mini-spirals spinning amongst the great spiral of evolution.

For any new child to be born into the world naturally, a short moment of absolute intensity – an orgasm – is required. The same is true of new societies. Revolutions are the orgasms that bring new political life into the world, and are just as much a part of evolution as the reformist measures that people commonly associate evolution with. It is absurd to think of revolutions existing outside of the evolutionary process – nothing can.

If we are to create healthy cultures and communities, these revolutionary processes must not merely change the colour of the neckties of those who control our lives, which has been the general outcome of the largely nonviolent 'colour revolutions'[109] that have taken place around the world. Instead, those who resist and revolt would be wise to begin the long process of eradicating global industrial capitalism from their economic systems, and start working on ways of living that are unique and appropriate for their locale. What ultimately takes the place of The

Machine is anyone's guess, but while this lack of 'one big idea' is a source of criticism for many commentators, the absence of a formulaic solution is precisely what is worth fighting for. Trying to enforce a 'one size fits all' solution on all the peoples of the world (and their widely diverse cultures, values and landscapes), as if we were all the same, is a large part of what has gotten us into this bloody mess in the first place.

As Paul Kingsnorth made clear in *One No, Many Yeses*, these solutions cannot or should not be a homogenised, standard politico-economic theory applied to people the world over as has been the case throughout modern history. Human ecology ought to reflect the diversity of the natural ecology it is a part of. As the status quo collapses, or is overthrown in a process that can sometimes seem to be sudden and quite extreme (but which usually has been fomenting for generations and is merely coming to a head), a hundred thousand new solutions need to fill the void, all formed according to the needs of each particular people and the landscape they are a part of. As the empire of The Machine falls like every other empire before it (whether through the weight of its own complexity, the 'undermining'[110] of it by revolutionaries and resisters, or a combination of forces), these solutions will emerge and germinate organically out of a soil fertilised by the decomposing remains of what has died. And though the plant of industrial capitalism has already gone to seed, it will be the work of the next generations to weed it out whenever and wherever it is revealed.

This is why, in this book, I don't even attempt to impress you with the types of generic, prescriptive solutions, which are inevitably laced with arrogance, that most non-fiction publishers love their authors to offer up, except this – resist The Machine in whatever way is meaningful to you, tackling whatever aspect of it that you are most passionate about. Only you know what that means to you.

However, if one is looking for inspiration and practical ideas on how to initiate such a resistance to the inhumanity of industrialism, they could do worse than to draw upon the experiences of the people of Marinaleda, a rural community in the Spanish region of Andalusia that Albert Camus once described as 'the native land of the rebel'.[111] Now dubbed a 'communist utopia' amongst Spaniards and the international media, Marinaleda's resistance was born out of the abject poverty of 1970s post-Franco Andalusia, and became a four decade long (and counting) struggle inspired by its mayor, Juan Manuel Sánchez Gordillo, and a people who knew that another world was possible. Around the time Gordillo became mayor, Marinaleda had 60% unemployment, despite people desperately wanting to work. They came from a long line of peasant pueblos who shared the political ideal of anarchism and a history of resistance and struggle, and yet because the lands around where they lived were owned by a few rich and powerful people, they had no land to work with. They had such shortages of food that in 1980 a quarter of their population undertook a 'hunger strike against hunger' (the rest were just hungry), an act that got the attention of the world.

But instead of following the example of the rest of the world and just accepting the apparently inevitable, they said 'enough is enough', and fought back. They took on absentee, aristocratic landlords and expropriated their land, to be collectively owned and run by the people. They invoked their new way of living with the spirit of resistance and revolution: street names were changed from things like 'Plaza de Franco' to 'Plaza de Allende',[112] and their sports stadium was emblazoned with a mural of the iconic Che Guevara, whom their mayor is known to quote from, along with the likes of Emiliano Zapata. Their motto is *'La tierra es de quien la trabaja'*, meaning 'The land belongs to those who work it'. At a time when 40 families a day were being foreclosed on in the Andalusia region, they created a housing system where apartments are self-built and communally owned and which cost occupants only €15 per month (or under a third of a day's wage, which itself is twice the Spanish minimum wage).[113]

Instead of getting machines to do the work in a more efficient manner, the collective consciously chose to plant crops that required the most human labour, so that they could begin to wipe out the unemployment that was hurting its people on all levels. Gordillo himself went on a march across the south, urging fellow mayors not to repay their debts. He even expropriated food from supermarkets before redistributing it, Robin Hood style, to food banks for those in Andalusia who could no longer feed themselves. They've chosen not to have a police force, and as the inhabitants of Sir Thomas More's fictional island *Utopia* would relate to, theft is not a problem; after all, what is the point of stealing what you already have access to?

It comes down to this: they fought back against the seemingly inevitable, and so far they've made a lot of headway. However, since the collapse of their financial economy, Spain's elite cannot afford to have more than a little village of 2,700 people not playing entirely by the rules. Therefore, if this approach to change took off and spread across the Iberian peninsula, the Spanish government and military would inevitably move to quash it by whatever means are at their disposal, which history has taught us would be when people such as these Andalusians would have to adopt the full spectrum of tactics to protect the way of life they have worked so hard to achieve. Not only that, but if Gordillo and his comrades were to move from resistance to revolution, and attack the institutionalised power structures that forced his people, and millions of others, to beg for financial help from the state (which Marinaleda utilised as much as they could) in the first place – something somebody is going to have to do at some point – then the response from the state would without question look a lot different.

Therefore the lesson we learn from places like Marinaleda and (as we'll see later) Chiapas may be this: resist the invasion of The Machine into every nook and cranny of your culture in whatever way is appropriate for your community's own specific circumstances now, and through doing so remember to start laying the foundations for more revolutionary change to the politico-economic system that forced you to resist it in the first place. Otherwise you only live in a state of perpetual struggle.

None of this talk about the ecological and social necessity of a politico-economic revolution means to suggest that the inner revolution is not needed; of course it is, otherwise you only keep repeating the same mistakes over and over again. Without a simultaneous inner revolution, these physical symptoms will keep reappearing and the illness will be a recurring one. I am simply pointing out what ought to be obvious: that unless the inner revolution that many people are undergoing at some point becomes an outer revolution, the mass extinction of species will continue unabated, children will be born into a world in which they are likely to be a glorified slave for the entirety of their adult lives, and the global West will continue its cultural imperialism of the world, ravaging it in the process.

Unless we look at our futures through a more honest lens, we will have no hope of putting our best efforts towards the creation of something with depth and longevity. Instead we will continue to be conned into believing that techno-fixes and the like will stave off the Grim Reaper, somehow forgetting how our experiences have taught us that every new technology only serves to increase our dependency on an industrial infrastructure which will not – which *cannot* – stop until it plunders every square inch of Nature.

When you are engaged in a war – and The Machine economy that we all contribute towards is engaged in a full-blown War on Life – it is reformism, not resistance, which is utterly futile. Consider the futility and madness, for a moment, of trying to reform an invading army by appealing to their logic with statistics, data, PowerPoint presentations and well-reasoned arguments about why conquering your people would be unjust and against their own long-term interests, and why they should peacefully return to their own lands on that basis. Or the futility of any attempt to transform them, soul by soul, into a peace corps, whose *raison d'être* would become the welfare of those whom they were originally intending to either assimilate or annihilate. It's an absurdly naïve thought, right?

Yet we continue to delude ourselves into thinking that reformist measures such as these have any hope of stopping the juggernaut from tearing its way through the intricately woven fabric of Life. Industrial civilisation has the same imperialist goals as an invading army, and from the perspective of indigenous human and non-human life on Earth, it *is* an invading army. This is a view shared by former Earth Liberation Front (ELF) spokesperson Leslie James Pickering, who said:

> ... *the vast majority of efforts made in the name of environment-alism are done so through state-sanctioned means of social change. But when the system itself is precisely what is enabling and promoting oppression, how is it logical to expect that same system to provide avenues towards liberation?*[114]

If I want to illustrate the failure of reformist methods, I need give you no better example than my own life's works. While I am now on the path to becoming a reformed reformist, I have been sweeping the dirt under the rug for years. Before I began a three year period in which I completely gave up money, I embarked on 'a year without oil', an experiment in localised living that included banning petroleum-based products, such as plastic, from my life. This was an interesting experience for myself personally, and it gained some media attention that, from what people told me in emails and in person, provoked other people to reduce their use of fossil fuels and excess packaging. What is wrong with that, I hear you ask? On one level, absolutely nothing. Living a life without fossil fuels, and showing that it can be done within the context of how we live today, is by all means a potentially useful endeavour for many people, and helps lay the psychic groundwork for what may come after this Age of Industrialism.

The problem begins when people believe that actions such as mine will make any tangible difference to the violent destruction of life on Earth, unless it is part of an active, full-spectrum resistance movement against industrialism in its entirety. It simply won't. It simply can't.

Oil production corporations are hardly going to decide to leave the couple of gallons of oil you saved in the ground, out of respect for your decision. Under the current tyranny of The Machine, that oil will be drilled and sold like every other litre that lies below us, until there is not a drop of even the dirtiest, most difficult to obtain oil left to be sucked out. At the rate we burn petroleum-based products globally, I can't work out if my decision to give up oil shortened the Age of Industrialism by less than a millisecond, or actually extended it – either way, who cares, it's a millisecond.

Due to the supply and demand mechanisms that are fundamental to capitalism, even if thousands of us did give up oil, all that would happen, in reality, is that the price of oil would temporarily come down. This, in turn, would mean that those who are happy to keep burning it would use more of it, meaning your resource savings would become someone else's cheap oil. Not exactly your motivation I would imagine.

Even if we convinced a million people to stop using oil completely – something that seems desperately unlikely amongst environmentalists, let alone a less ecologically literate general populace – oil companies would still continue to produce it, and not stop until every gallon has been extracted from the Earth. And as the case of the tar sands in Canada proves, they will go to increasingly extreme lengths to make sure they get it all. The Establishment won't enact policies to force energy companies to keep it in the ground either, so you can give up on that deluded hope too – politicians have become too dependent on their political campaign funding, back-handers and tax revenue to allow that to happen.

Heavily influenced by Mahatma Gandhi's quote, 'Be the change you want to see in the world', I then went from this experiment in living without oil to one that was popularly portrayed as even more extreme: living without money. Considering that our species has lived without oil or money for the overwhelming majority of our time on Earth, and the often forgotten fact that every other Wild species still does, why living without either is seen as extreme is beyond me. Again, people have told me that this action I undertook made them question their own relationship with money and how they meet their own needs, to the point where a growing number of people have begun living without – or at least with less dependency on – money too.

But let's be frank here for a moment. Did it make any significant, perceptible difference at all to the onslaught of The Machine in its drive to convert the splendour and beauty of life into cash? Not at all. Throughout my years living without money, the relentless drive to increase GDP that is inherent in our politico-economic system continued at pace, with all the world's politicians, CEOs, marketing executives and modern-day robber barons (and their billion dollar budgets) joining hands in an informal ideological partnership, working around the clock to ensure that the show must go on unabated, and at any cost.

Of course, if everyone withdrew themselves from the monetary economy, the complex financial system we have created would fall like the house of cards that it is, disabling the Financial Empire's ability to inflict devastation on biotic and human-scale communities. This is a view shared by David Holmgren, co-originator of permaculture, who has argued that a move towards 'largely non-monetary household and local community economies'[115] is our only hope of salvaging much of our beautiful world, and the emergence of something more intimate, more meaningful, more deeply connected to kith and kin in its void. But there are a number of issues here.

First, unless the politico-economic system we are in is overthrown, and new sets of decentralised social relations established in its place, such a move would be impossible for all but a few. People have rent and mortgages to pay, and to do so they need to get a job on the conveyor belt of industrialism. In trying to fulfil the insatiable financial demands of modern life, who has enough spare time to fully educate themselves on issues of ecology and social justice (neither of which are taught in schools), less still devote themselves to political action of one sort or another?

Even if we could, is the likelihood of such an outlandish scenario some-thing that we want to pin all our hopes on in our attempts to successfully address the convergence of ecological, social and personal issues humanity now faces? Only a lunatic, or a hardened reformist, would think so.

The problem with 'being the change you want to see in the world' is that it feels hard to become it when the change you want to see is nothing less than the end of violent industrialism. How does one become 'an end to industrialism' on a personal level, if we are to accept that simply making individual choices will be futile unless carried out as part of a wider resistance movement, one that recognises it needs to tackle our problems on every level with a diverse approach?

In saying this I am in no way suggesting that 'being the change' is not a positive thing to do, or that the experience of doing so will not have a deeply profound effect on you, leading you to all sorts of other understandings and changes in life purpose that logic or reason could never predict. Nor am I saying that the change you embody will have no effect on the world around you, as it inevitably will to some degree; after all, none of us live in a vacuum.

What I am saying is that this individualistic approach to tackling political scale issues, itself a symptom of the doctrines of liberalism and individual choice (try choosing to live outside of capitalism and the state and see how much choice you really have) and something promoted largely by proponents and practitioners of capitalism, cannot ever be sufficient in and of itself. To believe otherwise is delusional, with no basis in political reality. Being the change must be part of a pluralistic approach to resistance and, if necessary, revolution, if we are to have any chance of creating ways of life that are in harmony with The Whole.

Of course there are more macro-active ways in which we can try to reform the system, and many people are committing their lives to these approaches. It is true that petitioning, to take one form of reformism, has had some minor, irregular successes in limiting or preventing some of the milder symptoms of the disease that afflicts us today. This is its role, and it is one of many tools we should continue to use as long as it serves us. The problem begins when we con ourselves into thinking that our clicktivism (or 'slacktivism' as it is sometimes pejoratively called) amounts to us 'doing our bit for society', and that through doing so we conveniently wash our hands clean of the blood spilled during the manufacture of the computer whose mouse we are clicking.

The danger with such forms of activism is that they can soon become a substitute for more effective actions that have the potential to stop our pathological culture in its violent tracks; if, that is, they were to be engaged in by anything close to the millions of people whose activism involves the clicking of a computer mouse. Although not its original intention, petitioning has become a way of making ourselves feel good, assuaging the guilt we hold around our complicity in the strip-mining of our communities and lands, while at the same time posing no serious threat to the politico-economic system we derive benefit from. You can see why clicktivism is popular – it allows us to feel like we are doing something about all the issues we sign petitions for, all the while continuing to enjoy the technologies that come from the system that creates all these issues in the first place.

Green consumerism, that inherently paradoxical term, is perhaps the most common way in which people actively try to reform the system without thinking of themselves as activists. It involves buying products that are 'more' environmentally-friendly than other alternatives on the market. Notice how environmentally-friendly something is always gets described in relative terms (such as 'more' or 'less') and not absolute terms. In the short term, buying greener products is less destructive than buying the worst that The Machine has to offer, which isn't much of a compliment. When considered over a longer time-frame, it is an obvious absurdity to anyone with any literacy in economics and ecology. Consumerism is an ideology that encourages people to buy products and services in ever-increasing quantities, which taken as a whole requires colossal amounts of resources and vast amounts of energy inputs, even if they are processed from recycled materials. Trying to buy our way to real sustainability is no less ludicrous than trying to shag our way to virginity. Environmentalists claiming that green consumerism will help us revitalise a decaying planet into a healthy, thriving one is akin to Marxists suggesting that capitalism is the most effective path towards communism.

Projects such as Transition Towns, a global movement of localised initiatives whose goal is to inspire and encourage communities around the world to reduce their dependency on fossil fuels and become more resilient to external shocks in the process, are another example of a reformist approach to change. The Transition Network is one of the few movements of recent times that has a genuine ability to harness the power of communities, across a wide age demographic, to face issues like ecocide and communicide in an empowering way, and for that it has to be applauded. However, unless it is undertaken within the context of a much wider resistance movement, which has as its goal a revolutionary changing of the political and economic guards, there is an argument to be made that its ability to make the intolerable a bit more tolerable, something admirable and desirable on many levels, could in fact render it counter-productive when viewed through a wider lens.

While staying out of politics, as far as one can, enables a movement to be inclusive of a wide spectrum of people in each local community, it inevitably means that a lot of people who are genuinely interested in deep and radical change have their limited time and energy taken up by endeavours that could well be deemed criminally inadequate by future generations. If the Transition movement becomes an informal part of a wider resistance movement, one which has a revolutionary overhaul of the politico-economic system as its long-term goal (and many within such movements understand that capitalism and industrialism are inherently unreformable), then it has strong potential to serve life on Earth to its fullest. Otherwise, it could just become a well-meaning distraction that sidetracks those who desperately want deep-rooted societal change.

Monetary reformists – many of whom labour under the idea that our problems reside within the global nature of money and the way it is created, and not the whole notion of money itself – look to alternative and local currencies to reform the system within which we live and work. For those who come from an ecological perspective, the problem with this approach to change is that a local currency can only be localised to the degree by which the physical economy it intends to facilitate economic exchange within is localised. Of course these currencies can encourage localisation in terms of simple things like fresh food, which people can produce almost anywhere, but they cannot help localise complex pro-duction processes where the components have an inherently global nature. Therefore, as long as we remain an industrial culture with industrial desires, using technologies that require components from every continent on Earth, the localisation of money to any meaningful degree will remain a fantasy, as the scale of our money has to be aligned with our degree of economic globalisation. A global economic system requires global exchange mechanisms, and the degree to which it does is the inverse of the degree to which we are genuinely sustainable and respectful to Life.

For those who come from a social justice perspective, there are other problems. It is important to remember that those who hold political and economic power maintain their privileged positions by collectively earning trillions of dollars every year from our corrupt monetary systems staying exactly as they are. Again, if I were a betting man I wouldn't put a fiver on them agreeing to radical monetary reform voluntarily; instead they will do as they have always done – that is, fight tooth and nail to make sure it stays as it is. This is a political reality monetary reformists cannot afford to sweep under the rug. Therefore energy would be better spent applying resistance to the cogs of The Machine – whose primary goal these days seems to be the production of the financial oil it needs to run itself – as local currencies, and alternative economic systems such as 'gift cultures',[116] will arise out of necessity once it grinds to a halt. Only when we admit to ourselves that it is our entire industrialised culture, and not simply fractional reserve banking, that is at the heart of our problems will we begin to stop spending our limited time and energy on reforming a financial system whose philosophical core is so rotten as to be beyond redemption. That said, the discussions monetary reformists have, and the trials they undertake, are potentially very useful endeavours for informing the kinds of economic structures we create after the inevitable fall of the Industrial Empire, as long as – and I cannot repeat this enough – they are undertaken within the context of a much wider resistance movement which aims to stop, amongst much else, the mechanisation, monetisation and, ultimately, the devastation of Life and all that makes it worth living.

Professional lobbying, and attempts to get new laws and regulations passed to protect the environment, runs into its own limits, as Bolivia is finding in relation to its new legislation, The Law of the Rights of Mother Earth (see page 65). No government in the world can or will outlaw the very practices on which the government itself is premised. No court in the world can or will outlaw the very practices on which the court itself is premised. Courts and parliaments are largely based in cities, which are entirely dependent on the (usually) lawful but violent importation of enormous levels of resources to keep their lights on, a process that leads to the wholesale destruction of the places from which these resources come. It is these lawful practices that must cease if we are to create genuinely peaceful and sustainable livelihoods, yet it is precisely these lawful practices that the current regime cannot, and will not, outlaw.

Another reformist activity, aboveground education, suffers from similar limitations. Because of the hegemony of nonviolence and industrialism in both mainstream and counter-culture arenas alike, radical and revolutionary views on the extent to which we need to change things rarely, if ever, get any serious exposure. The fact that this book was published is more of a testament to the courage and bold vision of the publishers than it is an indicator of a media that is as open to the diversity of opinions that it deceitfully likes to pride itself on. This is why the only references to sustainable living you will see in the corporate media are tips on how to be a little more environmentally friendly (lightbulb changing and plastic recycling), actions which make a minute difference but have a feel-good factor attached to them. It is an approach to change that is sometimes described as 're-arranging the deck-chairs on the Titanic'. The reason you will rarely see, hear or read ideas such as deep ecology in anything other than the most honest media comes down to the same problem that the courts encounter, in that it is difficult for an institution to endorse or promote ideas that are in opposition to its own philosophical and practical foundations, or promote courses of action that would eventually lead to its demise and replacement by truly Life-friendly endeavours.

Because of these underlying ideological premises, the corporate media is entirely unreformable to any perceptible degree (the Leveson Inquiry, in the U.K., proved that even minor operational reforms are dismissed by political leaders who don't want to upset the press), and through its vice-like ideological grip over the minds of the masses it is proving to be a serious and stubborn obstacle to meaningful social change. The media, after all, has long since snuggled itself up in bed with the big businesses whose adverts help fund it, the politicians its ambitious editors are pals with, and the military-industrial complex its business model is dependent upon.

But to say that the media is in bed with big business would be wrong – it *is* big business. The same people who own it are often major shareholders or stakeholders in many of the companies, institutions and practices it should be reporting objectively on. The likes of Rupert Murdoch are the obvious examples, but the problem is more widespread, and more insidious, than most people would imagine.

Take the big talking point here in Ireland, where I live, at the time of writing: the installation of water meters, used to charge Irish people for their water. They've been introduced largely because the bankers almost bankrupted the country six years earlier, a situation that meant the taxpayer had to go cap-in-hand to the IMF and others for a bailout. One of the IMF's conditions for giving the Irish government a loan was that they would have to start charging the people they are supposed to represent for their domestic water, a condition to which there is surely more than meets the eye.

The Irish people were up in arms. Well, not quite. Instead they took to the streets in huge numbers to have their voices heard. The newspapers, it seemed though, were as uninterested in listening as the politicians. I remember walking past a newsstand in Galway one day and seeing a headline, in the *Irish Independent*, which read like a press release straight from the offices of the Irish Government, who themselves were under heavy pressure from undemocratic institutions to push through this new water charges bill at the time. The front page article in Ireland's most popular daily newspaper told its readers all the introductory sweeteners they would receive if they agreed to sign their water supply over to a newly-formed utilities company called Irish Water, and all the fines they would incur if they didn't – the trusted carrot and stick approach.

A lot of articles these days are press releases copied-and-pasted by over-stretched hacks, but this one seemed particularly devoid of journalistic input, or any sort of critique of the issues. It bore a greater resemblance to a very expensive-looking advert. So I went home and did the kind of basic research you would hope your nation's top journalists would do, and found some interesting things not mentioned in the paper. As it turns out the biggest shareholder in the media conglomerate who owns the *Irish Independent* is Denis O'Brien, who just so happens to also own the biggest stake in the company who won the contract to install the venomously-despised water meters. You couldn't make this stuff up if you tried.

To add insult to injury for the Irish public, another of O'Brien's outfits, the oil company Topaz, also won a €20 million national contract to supply fuel for the large fleet of paddy-wagons used by the *Garda Síochána* (the Irish police force), some of whom were captured on video assaulting peaceful protesters at water charge demonstrations. Of course, in the media the next day the protests were decried as violent and unacceptable.

Apparently someone threw a water balloon – or water 'bomb' as it was reported in the press – at the *Tánaiste* (The Irish Deputy Prime Minister) Joan Burton, while others delayed her passage through Jobstown (a town with an ironically brutal level of unemployment) by two hours, time which they spent banging on her very expensive, chauffeur-driven car. As per usual, these grassroots, bottom-up actions were labelled as both 'terrorism' and 'violent' in the media the next day (the *Taoiseach* [The Irish Prime Minister], Enda Kenny, dramatically claimed the car incident was akin to 'kidnapping'), while no articles, oddly enough, were written about the Garda who was caught, on video camera, aggressively throwing a woman into a metal post in Dublin.[117] She was lucky not to have been badly injured.

In Ireland it seems the military-media-industrial complex is not so complex – it's basically one man.

These are just a selection of the reasons why it is impossible for reformist efforts to change the way we live to any meaningful extent by themselves alone. What is a distinctly more important point is that, not only are reformist measures futile, there is a strong case to be made that they may even be counterproductive, making our situation worse in the longer term than if we had done nothing at all. This may appear counter-intuitive. After all, how can efforts to create decent communities within an indecent world make our lives worse on any time scale? How can hugging a police officer at a demonstration be detrimental to anyone involved?

SUGAR-COATING HEMLOCK

The real danger of reformism, aside from the amount of human energy it ties up in our multifarious and futile pleas to power to rein in their violence, is that it makes what ought to be intolerable more tolerable. Our industrial societies, like our over-processed meals, have been produced with toxic ingredients, and by sprinkling them with sugar we have a tendency to forget that industrialism, like hemlock, is fatal to humans. This was a perspective Rosa Luxemburg discussed in her influential pamphlet, *Reform or Revolution*, which she wrote at the beginning of the 20th century. While writing in a different political context – that of the class struggle between the proletariat and the bourgeoisie – her thoughts on the subject remain as relevant as ever, and transferable to the dilemmas facing us today.

Reform or Revolution is largely an argument against the revisionist and reformist ideologies – in particular those of fellow SPD[118] member and revisionist Eduard Bernstein – that were beginning to emerge in Europe after the internal debates that raged amongst Marxists at the Second International. In it she argues that Bernstein (and perhaps even Trotsky, to a lesser extent, later with his 'transitional programme') was a fantasist and a utopian if he believed that capitalism could be reformed into socialism. She went as far as to compare him to a prominent utopian socialist called Charles Fourier. In it she said:

> *Fourier's scheme of changing, by means of a system of phalansteries, the water of all the seas into tasty lemonade was surely a fantastic idea. But Bernstein, proposing to change the sea of capitalist bitterness into a sea of socialist sweetness, by progressively pouring into it bottles of social reformist lemonade, presents an idea that is merely more insipid but no less fantastic.*[119]

Luxemburg was hardly alone in this idea that the reform of an unreformable political structure is self-evidently impossible. A school of thought, known as Impossibilism, argued that socialism should not concern itself with the types of social reform that its adherents believed were, at best, irrelevant and, at worst, counterproductive to the goal of achieving socialism. It suggested that socialists should work towards revolutionary changes in society, as opposed to merely advancing social reforms. Marx himself, when addressing the Central Committee to the Communist League in 1850, said:

> *... the democratic petty bourgeois want better wages and security for the workers, and hope to achieve this by an extension of state employment and by welfare measures; in short, they hope to bribe the workers with a more or less disguised form of alms and to break their revolutionary strength by temporarily rendering their situation tolerable.*

In referring to key socialist and communist thinkers I am in no way proposing either of those two models in their industrial-scale form as a solution to our current predicament. Both of these politico-economic systems were, and still are, anthropocentric to varying degrees and resolutely preoccupied with industrialism in a way not too dissimilar to capitalism's fascination with it today. Instead, I am merely drawing on a logic that is transferable to the set of challenges we have before us today. To paraphrase Luxemburg, applying this logic to the modern context and the struggle at hand here, industrialism is not overthrown, but is on the contrary strengthened by the development of environmental and social reforms.

By permitting a range of reforms (such as carbon offsetting) that do not pose even the mildest challenge to industrialism's hegemonic dominance, those in positions of power give the impression that achieving more meaningful reforms is possible (which it's not) and, by doing so, take any heat out of a pan that could otherwise boil over into a serious challenge to their empire. They also reinforce the popular myth that we live in a genuine democracy, whereby political decisions are made with the people's interest in mind and not those of their friends and ideological partners working a few doors over in the City – the people who just so happen to fund their political campaigns every four years, and take them out to dinner in posh restaurants.

There is a related point here. By giving us a glimpse of hope that we can achieve some small reforms within its ideological framework, industrial capitalism acts like the Doorkeeper from Kafka's parable, *Before the Law*, who refuses the Man from the Country entry to the law.[120] The enmity between these two characters, the Doorkeeper and the Man from the Country, who eventually find themselves in a classic Clausewitzian duel, is eventually 'defused by the Doorkeeper's reformist gesture of refusing admittance *now* but leaving open the possibility of an entry to the law *later*'.[121]

This is exactly what the dominant culture's doorkeepers are doing today, stopping us from taking an appropriately dramatic course of action in the vain hope that, if only we practice the virtue of patience a little bit longer, we may get enough of what we want through industrial capitalism's own mechanisms. Of course we never get anything more meaningful than that glimpse of an authentic change that is perpetually just beyond our reach. This is a tactic used by the corporate-state coalition that resembles what those who subscribe to anarchist values and ideas might refer to as 'recuperation'.

In their perpetual attempts to manage dissent from those they claim to serve, The Establishment uses a carrot and stick approach. If repression is the stick, recuperation is the carrot. Recuperation is the process 'by which those who attempt to break away from current power structures to rebel are induced to rejuvenate those power structures or create more effective ones'. Contrary to popular belief, Peter Gelderloos argues that 'struggles in democratic societies are defeated by recuperation more often than by repression'.[122]

The state, and its precarious claims to real democracy need to keep up the illusion of social peace and to make people believe that its use of physical force and violence is the exception, other than the rule that it is. In order to do so, it acts like Kafka's Doorkeeper, but along with offering us the possibility of tasty sweets later if we are good little girls and boys now (though never actually giving us the sweets), it offers us stale bread immediately, in the hope that this will satisfy our hunger and make us forget about the sweets. What we end up with are toxic substitutes for what we really yearn for.

Gelderloos notes how the 'liberation movements in India, South Africa, and many other countries were recuperated when they decided to seek common ground with their colonizers and fight for a new government that would carry out all the same economic projects of the old government', effectively 'becoming local managers for international finance'. He adds:

> We can't overcome the destruction of our communities, but we can have a hundred friends on facebook. We can't keep the forest we played in as children from getting cut down, but we can start a recycling program. Indigenous people cannot have their land back, but one or two of them might get elected to congress.[123]

The problems with such an approach to change does not stop there. Reformism can act like a drug, sedating us to the pain of the world by helping us fool ourselves into believing that hanging a little air-freshener inside a bulldozer (giving its human operator a more pleasant experience, albeit one which is a toxic substitute for fresh air) will stop it from flat-packing the forest. The bulldozer, as a symbol of the type of economy that makes its manufacture possible, is designed precisely to convert Nature into products. It cannot be reformed, and it will not die voluntarily. This regrettably leaves limited options.

Having been asked by a member of the audience 'how many environmentalists does it take to change a lightbulb?', Derrick Jensen, with the brutal but refreshing level of honesty he has made his trademark, replied after some contemplation:

> *Ten. One to write the lightbulb a letter requesting that it change. Four to circulate online petitions. One to file a lawsuit demanding it change. One to send the lightbulb lovingkindness™, knowing that this is the only way real change occurs. One to accept the lightbulb precisely the way it is, clear in the knowledge that to not accept another is to do great harm to oneself. One to write a book about how and why the lightbulb needs to change. And finally, one to smash the fucking lightbulb, because we all know it's never going to change.*[124]

If we are to react appropriately to the scale of the challenges we face today, we need to feel the pain of the Earth, and that of those cultures and species that are being pushed into extinction for the sake of the gadgetry and so-called convenience goods (the soul-destroying tasks we often have to perform to afford them aren't so convenient) that we somehow have become dependent on. We need to cease our futile attempts to put reformist band-aids on the gaping wounds of the land and its inhabitants, and allow ourselves to fully experience what we are doing to Life. Only when we see the scale of this violence for what it is, and deeply understand how such a level of violence is inherent in The Machine, will we resolve to get up off our knees and approach this dire situation with the entire range of tools at our disposal.

Often the best tool for the job will be a nonviolent one, and this is always the ideal, the first port of call. However, as Pickering argues, sometimes other tools are necessary to prevent an act of systemic violence:

> *Like the tools of a toolbox, each has a specific use and specific results. Depending on the job you have, you choose a tool (or a set of tools) from your toolbox. You don't choose only the tools that fit most comfortably in your hand or that are the prettiest; you choose the*

ones that'll get the job done. Sometimes these tools do fit comfortably in your hands, but most of the time they give you blisters. No matter what, though, at the end of the day, the objective is always to have the job completed. It's idiotic to shun the sledgehammer when you're working to knock down a wall.[125]

RESISTANCE IS FERTILE

Resistance is feasible even for those who are not heroes by nature, and it is an obligation, I believe, for those who fear the consequences and detest the reality of the attempt to impose American hegemony.

Noam Chomsky

The idea of resisting or revolting against ideologies as ubiquitous as industrialism and capitalism, both of which physically manifest themselves in every nook and cranny of our lives, is an overwhelming thought. The corporate-state coalition seemingly keeps on getting more powerful and corrupt, and it can sometimes feel as though, with every day that passes, our economies are becoming more monopolised, our cultures more homogenised, and our lives more surveilled through the CCTV on our streets and the World Wide Web in our own homes. On top of that we have got mortgages, bills and rent to pay, families to rear, and our own little dreams to pursue.

Despite this, people across the world, against all odds and powerful forces, are saying 'enough is enough'. For some, the gross and increasing disparity between the world's rich and poor has been a rallying cry for their causes, as we have seen in the occupations of the plaza in Madrid to Wall St. in New York. For others, it is the protection of their lands and waterways, where people such as those near Rossport in Ireland and Ogoniland in Nigeria (a campaign that resulted in the execution of nonviolent campaigner Ken Saro-Wiwa) have tried to resist the invasion of Royal Dutch Shell who, in partnership with the state, want to destroy their lands, cultures and livelihoods for their own private profit. The people of Balcombe and Barton Moss in the U.K. have been putting their liberty at risk by defending their own habitats from being fracked by corporations such as Cuadrilla.

Each of these cases is inspiring, and it sends out the message that people are not going to lie down whilst their local landbase gets converted into numbers by the corporate-state coalition. That said, what is hampering them all from being more effective in achieving their goals is their insistence on a type of dogmatic, puritanical nonviolence that is nothing short of delusional. As Gelderloos explains:

> ... people have gone into the streets for the first time thinking that nonviolence is the way, because contrary to the claims of many pacifists, our society teaches us that while violence may be acceptable for governments, people on the bottom who want to change things must always be nonviolent.[126]

What could be a more violent spectacle than watching your community and lands get ripped apart because of your movement's stubborn insistence on using an impotent tactic against an invading force? It is worth repeating Mandela's words in this respect when he said, 'For me, nonviolence was not a moral principle but a strategy; there is no moral goodness in using an ineffective weapon'.[127] This is a sentiment and perspective that agrees with Saul Alinsky when he suggests that we ought to ask 'of ends only whether they are achievable and worth the cost; of means, only whether they will work',[128] while taking care to examine the most nonviolent means as the first port of call when considering the options available.

And this is exactly what genuinely radical movements do. Despite their 'extremist' reputation in mainstream media, movements such as the ELF, which were born out of the failures of reformist environmentalism, went to lengths to take that kind of care. As Howie Wolke, a co-founder of Earth First! made clear, 'If nonviolence worked in stopping the destruction of a Forest Service wilderness area by road-building, then that was the bottom line. If it was ineffective in a given situation, Earth First!ers would have to reassess their tactics.'[129]

Ted Honderich, an English philosopher, once referred to his 'principle of humanity' to attempt to distinguish between a legitimate and illegitimate use of violence, and came to the conclusion that an occupied people have the right to resist and, if necessary, to use violence in doing so. The difficulty today is that we in the imperialist nations do not have an obvious, tangible invader to resist. The king's soldiers no longer ride in on horseback to pillage our lands and rape its women in the traditional sense; conquest has become a more subtle affair. Instead, they come as dishonourable knights, bearing gifts of jobs (however soul-destroying), electronic gadgetry (however community-destroying) and the endless promise of financial growth (however Life-destroying).

The King's soldiers today know that they must occupy our hearts and minds first, invading us through our televisions and newspapers, laptops and shopping centres, as a precursor for the occupation of our physical spaces; and such has been the extent of their success that instead of resisting them, we welcome them and their thinly-concealed swords with open arms. What we seem to have forgotten is that when the modern knight comes with his machines to extract the dirtiest drops of energy from below our habitats, they come as conquerors, and that those who live there – the invaded – have the inalienable right to resist by whatsoever means necessary.[130]

Would the people of County Mayo in Ireland have achieved real success in keeping Royal Dutch Shell's gas refinery and pipeline out of their coastal lands if they had treated them like a more traditional invader – in their case, the British Empire, whom their forbears resisted and revolted against using every means at their disposal, with great success, not even 100 years earlier? Would the protesters in Balcombe and Barton Moss have served their causes better if they had taken off their nonviolent badge of honour, stopped chanting 'this is a peaceful protest' and simply asked themselves 'what is needed to effectively stop this violence being inflicted on us?'

The question is not intended to sound unfair; after all, they were out there doing it every day while I was mostly writing this book, and as Edward Abbey rightly said, 'Sentiment without action is the ruin of the soul. One brave deed is worth a thousand books.'[131] Yet it is still an important question. The answer, of course, is that nobody will ever know. What we can do, however, is look to similar examples where resisters did use a diversity of tactics, inclusive of what are commonly (but mistakenly) understood to be violent and nonviolent methods.

One important case study is that of the resistance of the Mohawk people that was documented in the film, *Kanehsatake: 270 Years of Resistance*. In what became known as the Oka Crisis, tensions erupted in Quebec in 1990 when the town of Oka tried to expand an exclusive nine-hole golf course, the *Club de golf d'Oka*, to the full 18 holes. The problem:

they wanted to build the last nine over what the Mohawk people of Kanehsatake considered to be one of their ancient burial grounds, within which stood the sacred tombstones of their ancestors.

Like the people of Mayo and Barton Moss, the Mohawks decided to resist. On hearing the news from the Mayor of Oka that the development would go ahead and that the remainder of the pines were to be cleared, they erected a barricade that obstructed access to the area. In a move that was much more about making a statement than it was about giving the white population of the town an extended few hours out playing golf, Quebec's emergency police force moved in and attacked their barricades with tear gas and stun grenades.

Unlike the people of Mayo and Barton Moss, however, the Mohawks were not going to allow the state to have a monopoly on violence. In accordance with the Constitution of the Iroquois Confederacy, they asked the women (considered the caretakers of the land) of their community if they should make use of the stockpile of arms they had. The women collectively agreed that they should use their weapons, but only in the case of self-defence. When tear gas entered the fray, they retaliated and opened fire on the police, and after a short gunfight, the police (one of whom was killed) retreated along with their fleet of cruisers and bulldozers. Heartened by a rare occasion of courageous resistance, First Nations people from both the U.S. and Canada joined them in solidarity, and together blocked off several roads (this time nonviolently), an action which caused serious traffic issues for the surrounding area. Despite millions of dollars being thrown at the crisis, and thousands of troops sent in, it ended after 78 days when the Mayor announced that the plans for the golf course were to be cancelled, and that the pineland and burial site could remain as they were.

It is almost impossible to say whether or not the resistance of the Mohawks was violent or nonviolent. It was neither and both, as they used different tactics at different times. Is shooting at police officers more violent than allowing the forest (and the life that inhabits it), their way of life and their dignity to be destroyed? As I will ask in the next chapter, is defending one's lands and culture an act of self-defence? These are difficult questions, but our responses to them require more subtlety than the civilised, pacified mind would care to admit.

One thing that is certain is this: their resistance was effective, and their sacred lands are still sacred lands.

CHAPTER FOUR

SELF-DEFENCE IN THE AGE OF REUNION

Humankind has not woven the web of life. We are but one thread within it. Whatever we do to the web, we do to ourselves. All things are bound together. All things connect.

Chief Seattle

When one tugs at a single thing in nature, he finds it attached to the rest of the world.

John Muir

A FEW HUNDRED CONFUSED-LOOKING faces stare back at me, all wondering (a) if the question I had just asked was designed to fool them or (b) why the devil was I even asking it. So I put it to the audience once again.

'Hands up everyone who believes that their leg is a part of themselves?'

With the exception of one man who was cheerfully waving his prosthetic limb at me, shouting 'mine's not!', most hands went up, the others presumably thinking they were too smart for such an esoteric trick. Though the relevance of the question at this point seemed quite unclear, it was one I would regularly ask at the start of talks I gave about my life without money, and the reasons behind why I chose that path. To the disappointment of those who kept their hands down, I reassured the crowd that with the exception of our one-legged friend, their legs were, for all intents and purposes, part of themselves. The process of breaking down the modern conception of self, however, was only beginning.

I decided to take it one degree deeper. 'So what about the bacteria in your gut, life-forms that are entities in and of themselves but which are also a crucial component of your digestive system – are *they* part of *you*, or not?' Chins were scratched, and brows furrowed. Hmm. This time only half the hands went up, and even those were a little less bold than the first time.

'Not so clear-cut, right?'

'Okay, what about the water in a stream that you stand beside and from which you're contemplating drinking – do you see this as part of you, or not?' The hands raised were now becoming increasingly marginal.

'No? What about that moment where you have cupped the water in your hands and it's at the point where it's just touching your lips and about to enter your mouth? Anyone?' Some go up and some go down, but I can now count the people who think so.

'What about the moment the water from the stream enters your body and is absorbed by it? Is it now part of you?' Suddenly lots of hands start waving enthusiastically again.

'If not it ought to be, considering the fact that a large percentage of your physical being – *you* – is made up of, and replenished by, this water.' Having established that almost everyone considered the water from the stream to be part of their egocentric selves at this point, I continued on the journey towards establishing a more scientifically sound, holistic sense of self.

'Why, then, did you not consider it to be a part of you in that split second before it passed your lips and entered into what Alan Watts called "the skin-encapsulated ego", that skin-bag of blood and bones that we normally think of as our selves? How is it that the stream suddenly becomes *you* when it passes the invisible boundary of your open mouth, even though you may have often drunk from that same stream innumerable times before?'

My point was this: the boundaries of our sense of self are delusional and a product of an age-old but incremental journey away from a deep sense of oneness with the rest of life, and towards a sense of individualistic separation from it all. We think of ourselves as a discrete 'object', bounded by our skin, but it's a perspective that is both scientifically and experientially hard to justify when even the skin itself is constantly exchanging atoms and energy with the universe it is a part of. Instead of the fleshy egos floating around in a Cartesian universe that Charles Darwin, Adam Smith and others have taught us is inherently hostile towards us (a worldview seemingly immune to the fact that the same universe freely supplies us with everything we need to live healthy lives), the reality is that we are part of a flow of life – energy, food, water, minerals, radiation and so on – constantly passing in, out and through us, much of which has no respect for the boundary of the skin at all. John Dewey, an American philosopher of the early 20th century, once said:

> *The epidermis is only in the most superficial way an indication of where an organism ends and its environment begins. There are things inside the body that are foreign to it, and there are things outside of it that belong to it de jure if not de facto; that must, that is, be taken possession of if life is to continue. The need that is*

manifest in the urgent impulsions that demand completion through what the environment – and it alone – can supply, is a dynamic acknowledgment of this dependence of the self for wholeness upon its surroundings.[132]

We are no more a bounded 'object' than a wave on the ocean is. Like a wave, we are a form through which many objects are passing. As Alan Watts lucidly notes, 'you and I are all as much continuous with the physical universe as a wave is continuous with the ocean'.[133] We are not, as contemporary culture would fool us into believing, glorious beings separate from the savagery of Nature, but instead glorious beings inherently part of glorious Nature. We are as much Nature as the grand oak or the humble chickweed is. Therefore the yet-to-be-drunk spring water is as much a part of the 'I' as the flesh, blood and bones that you more obviously consist of at any exact moment.

At a fundamental, particle level we are all one and the same: different assortments of the same basic elements (oxygen, carbon and nitrogen and so on). On the basis of this, should our sense of self, at the very least, not stretch to the landscapes – the streams, springs, trees, wildlife, plants and atmosphere – on which our lives inextricably depend? It is a sentiment Albert Einstein once alluded to when he said that:

... a human being is part of the whole called by us universe, a part limited in time and space. We experience ourselves, our thoughts and feelings as something separate from the rest. A kind of optical delusion of consciousness. This delusion is a kind of prison for us, restricting us to our personal desires and to affection for a few persons nearest to us. Our task must be to free ourselves from the prison by widening our circle of compassion to embrace all living creatures and the whole of nature in its beauty.[134]

The vast majority of the people in the crowd, though looking quite intrigued, had no idea why I had begun speaking about this in a talk that was meant to be about living without money, gift culture and economics. As I explained, however, our notion of self plays an entirely underestimated, though central, role in the types of economic systems we create. Our current monetary economic system – at odds with the culture of gift economics which humanity has used in various forms to meet its needs for the overwhelming majority of our time on Earth – was born out of our delusional sense of self. For if we dropped the illusory veil of separation, and accepted that we are part of a world constantly exchanging energy with itself, a world with no respect for boundaries such as the skin (which is as arbitrary as the border between France and Germany), then 'my self' charging 'you' for the gifts I manifest in the world (gifts, remember, that we have all been given freely) is no less absurd than me charging a tree for the nitrogen in my urine when I pee under it, and it then invoicing me for the oxygen it produces and generously supplies to my lungs. As Daniel Suelo, a man who has lived without money for over a decade in the U.S. once suggested, it would be no less ludicrous than for my hand to charge my face for scratching it.

As I have explained more thoroughly in *The Moneyless Manifesto*, money is both chicken and egg in relation to this incomplete sense of self. Whilst money originated as a mere symptom of the illusion of separation between ourselves and all other life, along with concepts such as debt and credit (which do not exist outside of the human mind) that stem from that, it has in turn perpetuated and greatly intensified the extent to which we feel disconnected from the rest of life. It does this primarily by increasing the degrees of separation between us and what we consume. Without a technology such as money, we would have to live within a localised economy, where we meet our needs through a direct and intimate relationship with the land under our feet and the people in our communities. Money enables us to trade with far-away people whose eyes we'll never meet, often by using supply chains which – due to the lack of visibility involved – rely on gruesome and violent practices that we would be hard pushed to witness if we were directly exposed to them and their consequences.

These new impersonal relationships, devoid of the sense of trust and friendship that local economies draw upon, rely on contracts and the armies, police forces and court rooms required to enforce them. Therefore, to the psychological and emotional discomfort of pacifists who love using the World Wide Web and who do not want to give it up, the reality is that they cannot have high technologies such as servers and fibre-optic cables without the very things they rail against: armies, prisons, and police forces, not to mention the global factory system that is injurious not only to the human soul, but to the entire biosphere. As much of a shock as this might come to us in the powerful, overdeveloped nations, people like the Ogoni do not want their lands destroyed so that we can feed our insatiable desire for tat, no matter how much money we offer them. Unfortunately for them and countless others who have been unlucky enough to live over 'valuable' resources, if The Machine can't buy you with its gold it will destroy you with its weapons. Nowhere is left in peace. For as Derrick Jensen poignantly noted in *A Language Older Than Words*, 'Throw a dart at a map of the world, and no matter the territory it strikes, you will find the story of cruelty and genocide perpetrated by our culture'.[135]

This institutionalised separation only serves to create an even stronger delusion, and that is where our problems really intensify. This constricted sense of self – manufactured in stages over millennia by the incursions of language, numerical systems, agriculture, money, indus-trialisation and global-scale technologies into our lives – has critical implications for the way we treat the Earth and its inhabitants. For if we do not see ourselves as connected to, or dependent on, our human and non-human communities, why would we bother respecting them? If we do not see ourselves as connected to, or dependent on Nature – or more precisely, *as Nature* – why would we defend it (ourselves) from the forces of The Machine which, though born out of Nature also, is an entity more analogous to a cancer which has taken over an organism whose vitality has been dangerously compromised?

Industrial civilisation has developed and encouraged a sense of self which implicitly denies these integral connections and dependencies – implicitly denies oneness – and the results of this have never been clearer: homogenisation of once diverse cultures; the Holocene mass extinction of species and languages; air, soil and water toxification; the rapid growth of cancer, asthma, diabetes, heart disease and obesity rates; rapidly increasing incidence of mental illness, suicide and depression; cults of celebrity, obsessions with physical beauty, and a fear of death. All of this makes up an epoch which Charles Eisenstein refers to as the 'Age of Separation'.[136]

The consequences of this limited sense of self do not stop there, either. The notion of a separate self has long since become a scientifically baseless premise for our legal systems, and therefore the ways in which we can defend our biosphere, and both the landscapes and human and non-human communities that comprise it. Let me explain. The concept

of the right to self-defence – the use of physical force as a countermeasure
to a threat of violence towards oneself (the skin-encapsulated soul), one's
'own property' or the safety of another human – is a legal justification
available in the vast majority of jurisdictions around the world, though its
interpretation and application vary from place to place. As Edward Abbey,
alluding to something deeper that I will flesh out shortly, explains:

> ... *if a stranger batters your door down with an axe, threatens your
> family and yourself with deadly weapons, and proceeds to loot your
> home of whatever he wants, he is committing what is universally
> recognized – by law and morality – as a crime. In such a situation the
> householder has both the right and the obligation to defend himself,
> his family, and his property by whatever means are necessary. This
> right and obligation is universally recognized, justified and even
> praised by all civilised human communities. Self-defence against
> attack is one of the basic laws not only of human society but of life
> itself, not only of human life but of all life.*[137]

It's a law so natural that it is difficult to even find a nonviolence practi-
tioner who doesn't accept it. Derrick Jensen recounts an experience with
an old friend of his, who had become a staunch pacifist since the last
time they had met. The subject of conversation got onto resistance, and
Jensen asked his friend what he would do if someone wanted what he
had and was prepared to do anything to get it. In his mind, when he asked
the question, were the words of the Oglala man Red Cloud, who said of
the colonisers:

> *They made us many promises, more than I care to remember. But
> they kept only one. They promised to take our land and they took it.*

His pacifist friend replied by asking 'But what is worth fighting for? Can't
we just leave?' Jensen, it turns out, could think of a good few things he
felt were worth fighting for: 'bodily integrity (my own and that of those I
love), my landbase, the lives and dignity of those I love', before reminding
his mate that the planet is finite, and that if The Machine is allowed to
industrialise acre after acre of the Earth whilst the pacifists flee lands not
worth fighting for, there will come the day where there will be nowhere

else to run away to. After some contemplation, even his friend admitted that under some circumstances, and at some point, 'you've got to fight back'.[138]

This idea of self-defence is an outlook that is deeply rooted in the natural world, one which allows us to defend our lives and our livelihoods using whatever means are appropriate for the threat at hand. What industrialism has done so successfully is to have somehow convinced us that our lives depend on The Machine, and not the land. But as Aldo Leopold succinctly expressed, 'we fancy that industry supports us, forgetting what supports industry'.[139]

Beans now come from a tin can, not the soil. Water comes from a tap, complete with chloride or fluoride, and not the spring or the stream. Our furniture comes from a supermarket, and not the woods around us. We no longer navigate our way around our habitat by way of the stars, but by gadgets with SatNav. We meet our needs by understanding how to use a piece of software instead of the age-old knowledge of plants, and their qualities, which were once abundant around us. Medicine comes neatly packaged in plastic containers from the pharmaceutical industry, and not direct from the world of plants like it still does for some indigenous peoples.

We have become the prison inmate who has been inside so long that he, on regaining his freedom, re-offends immediately, simply because he is dependent on the prison service – his chains have become normal. We are the slave who has become loyal to his 'owner', the hostage suffering from Stockholm syndrome, the battered wife who continues to stick up for her abusive husband, the cow who refuses to – or no longer remembers how to – run when the iron gates of her small concrete barn are opened. We have sworn our allegiance to The Machine instead of the Earth and its inhabitants, and this reveals itself in a myriad of ways, not least when pacifists decide to protect corporate windows from the likes of the Black Bloc, whom they don't seem so enthusiastic about protecting from the brutality of the police.

Jensen argues that, 'If your experience is that your food comes from the grocery store and your water comes from the tap, then you are going to defend to the death the system that brings those to you because your life depends on them. If your experience, however, is that your food comes from a landbase and that your water comes from a stream, well, then you will defend to the death that landbase and that stream.'[140] Until a time where we understand that our own well-being is dependent on the health of The Whole, we will not adequately resist a culture that seems hell-bent on pillaging every square inch of the planet, polluting our air, soil and waterways along the way. Unfortunately, nothing stops us from understanding our interdependency with our land better than the troika of industrialism, capitalism and monetary economics. It is yet another chicken-and-egg mess we seem to have gotten ourselves into.

To those of us who are deluded to such an extent that we act as if our lives are dependent on supermarkets, some of this may seem a touch abstract or theoretical. To those – such as the Pirahã, an indigenous hunter-gatherer people of the Brazilian Amazon – whose cultures have thus far resisted The Machine and who have retained a deep understanding of their connection to the Great Web of Life, the idea that human well-being is dependent on the health of the land, the air and the waterways is basic common sense, even if they have no need to intellectualise it.

To toxify their rivers would be to, quite literally, poison themselves. To annihilate the flora and fauna on which their own lives are intricately reliant, would be to annihilate themselves. To pollute their air would be to pollute their lungs, to erode their topsoil would be to directly diminish the vitamins and minerals that make up their own flesh and bones. Native, land-based peoples usually understand (or more commonly now, *understood*) this to a much deeper degree than those whose lives have been mechanised by industrial civilisation. This is why they are less afraid to defend their lands with everything they've got when they come under attack from the incursions of The Machine. They certainly do not bother to constrain themselves with civilised ethics that don't hold up to even the most gentle investigation.

The primal truth of interconnectedness can reveal a fragment of itself, rather ironically, when we attempt to conquer uncivilised people, or 'undeveloped markets', for our own short-sighted benefits. The European colonisers knew that the lives of First Nations peoples were heavily dependent on their land, in particular the buffalo, which is why they slaughtered the entire herds that once roamed their habitat, leaving them to rot on the plains that were their home for millennia. Part of the reason why we export heavily subsidised food to foreign markets is to further damage their self-reliance in food, making them heavily dependent on their economic conquerors. Wealth is thus parasitically sucked out of their nations and into the bulging coffers of the invading entrepreneurial industrialists. We promote the joined-at-the-hip ideologies of multiculturalism and globalisation so that communities – whose lives previously consisted of largely non-monetised relationships based on tightly knit bonds of community and shared values – are broken up and their peoples scattered all over the world, leaving them dependent on monetised goods and services (which The Machine conveniently just so happens to sell and tax). It's that age old tactic of divide and rule playing itself out once again, only now through the vehicle of sanitised warfare that is modern economics.

Despite the obvious truth that if we destroy or toxify that on which our lives depend then we will die with it, we (supposedly) intellectually superior civilised people persist in restricting the inalienable right to an appropriate defence of the things we think *we own*, and not the things *we are*, and which are us. If we are to have any chance of survival we need to take this natural right out of the Age of Separation and plant it firmly in the Age of Reunion, a new epoch in which we no longer delude ourselves with such clear distinctions of 'I' and 'other' and within which we can recreate our systems of economics, medicine, education, science and technology through a lens that 'seeks not the control or transcendence of nature, but our fuller participation in nature'.[141]

We need to defend the Earth with the same ferocity we would evoke if it were our home, because it is. We need to defend its inhabitants with the same passion as if they were our family members, because they are. We need to defend our lands, communities and cultures as if our lives depended on it, because they do.

While this more holistic sense of self is something that is becoming more widely acknowledged in both scientific and philosophical circles, my own route to this perspective was an experiential one. Through my adventures living without money, as futile as it was from a political perspective, I learned many lessons. I learnt that if I did not return nutrients to the soil, by means that were not detrimental to far-off places, I would eventually not be able to eat. I realised that if I chucked pollutants – such as petroleum, sewage or agricultural fertilisers – in the river that I lived by, I would soon not be able to drink. I gained the understanding that if I cut down all the trees in my habitat to fuel my woodburner at all hours of the day, I would no longer have anything left to use, and the birds who woke me up every morning with their indefatigable, exquisite song would no longer have a place to call home. For the first time in my life I became aware that the fate of myself, the ash tree, the robin, the spring, the stream, the bees, the owl, the badger, the trout and the stag were all one and the same – if they were wiped out or destroyed, myself and my kind would not be long after them. What was true for my little realm, is also true for the planet at large. This understanding of the world may appear profound or 'deep' within the shallow context of contemporary society, but it is only what many of our ancestors, and those still living in relative harmony with the landscape today, recognised as the basic facts of life.

I am the land, I am the salmon, I am the holly tree, I am the swallow, I am the earthworm, I am the pigeon, I am the hen, I am the fox, I am the ramson, I am the bluebell. When the robin eats the worm and shits onto the soil from which I eat, it is not violence, but Life giving life onto itself. Likewise, when I die I want to go out with humility (whose linguistic roots are in 'humus', the Earth). I want to be devoured by buzzards or, if they hadn't been exterminated from my landscape, a pack of wolves. It seems only fair.

If I see myself as the land, and all that it comprises, is it not an act of primordial self-defence to do whatever it takes to defend it against the forces who wish to convert it into cold, hard numbers for their own ends, ends born in the Age of Separation but which are obsolete in an Age of Reunion? Contrary to what we have been led to believe today, acting to defend 'the other' still fits perfectly into the scheme of logic that Ayn Rand, and those such as Adam Smith before her, describe as acting in our 'rational self-interest'. The only difference is that this sense of self has been tweaked to take into account this more accurate and consistent conception of it.

If we understand ourselves to be made up of the land, and its atmosphere and waterways, if we know that our flesh and bones are made of its wildlife, how can we sit passively by and let ourselves be attacked and robbed by those who are wielding their pathological axe and who, at the same time, are hypocritically telling us that it is immoral, unjust, illegal and futile to defend ourselves from their bludgeoning? The urgency of applying our right to self-defence to our holistic selves has intensified in tandem with the War on Nature. Mike Ryan suggests that the time to start taking decisive action is long past, and that enough is finally enough. He says:

> *If, as [Rosalie] Bertell suggests, we are sitting upon a dying earth, and consequently dying as a species solely as a result of the nature of our society, if the technology we have developed is indeed depleting the earth, destroying the air and water, wiping out entire species daily, and steadily weakening us to the point of extinction, if phenomena such as Chernobyl are not aberrations, but are (as I insist they are) mere reflections of our daily reality projected at a level where we can at last recognise its true meaning, then is it not the time — long past time — when we should do anything, indeed everything, necessary to put an end to such madness? Is it not in fact an act of unadulterated self-defence to do so?*[142]

At a time when the extent of ecological destruction has become so widespread that we are beginning to experience the sorts of extreme weather patterns that will soon become the norm, we need to wake up and admit that the longest petition in the world, or the most creative street theatre, will not persuade the likes of ExxonMobil to keep fossil fuels below the surface of the Earth – where they belong – and not consumed above it.

When we take 'self' defence out of the Age of Separation, and apply it in the Age of Reunion, the spectrum of responses available to us starts to look a lot more potent. We can stop burdening ourselves with misguided and inconsistent moral notions that tell us that defending our holistic self – the home of all life – with an appropriate level of force or violence is unjustifiable or morally and ethically wrong. Instead we can start defending our Great Home in the same way we would if someone entered our dwellings without permission and attacked us with a knife.

As the bulldozers invade our natural landscapes, willing and able to extract whatever it is they can sell, we can start to unjoin our circle of hands and put them to more productive use. We may take a break from singing 'give peace a chance' and start taking effective actions that more realistically 'give life a chance'. We can stop chanting 'this is a peaceful protest' to the police, and instead let them know through our actions that 'this is an effective protest'.

Otherwise we will be allowing a violence to be inflicted on the Earth – and all it comprises – that we would not think twice about stopping, by whatever means appropriate, were it being inflicted on our cars, houses, or our own flesh and bones.

If someone broke into your house at night with the intention of stripping it of everything it contained, would you round up your family and 'lock on'[143] to each other and the front door, whilst waiting for the police to come and arrest not the burglar but instead you, your partner and your children, so that the burglar could continue to do his job in peace without the threat of violence? It is, of course, a ludicrous thought, but it is exactly what we are doing in relation to attacks against our Great Home and our Great Family and, ultimately, to ourselves. It is important to note that, through their defence of the corporate-state coalition's self-created right to pillage our Great Home, the police are literally arresting us so that the burglar can continue to rob us in peace.

If we could reform legislation around the world to take account of this more expansive, holistic sense of self in a way that would allow it to be applied to the legal right to appropriate self-defence, the implications would be genuinely world-changing. Destroying The Machine's apparatus, and telling its human operators in no uncertain terms 'here, and no further', would no longer be seen as the act of terrorism it is cunningly being labelled today, but instead an act of self-defence that is no less justifiable than the defence of your ego-self.

No longer would indigenous people be forced to impotently watch imperialists invade their territories and destroy their cultures and ways of life, but instead have the same tool-kit available to them that an English home-owner has if someone breaks into their house. No longer would local residents – if they could prove how fracking is threatening their health and lives in a multitude of ways – have to allow the likes of Cuadrilla to drill in their communities, but instead they would be able to put up a full-spectrum resistance without having to worry about spending years in prison for doing so. No longer would the residents of places such as Rossport (see page 112) have to suffer the humiliation and despair of seeing their homelands invaded, and their traditional livelihoods made extinct, for no more logical reason than the sorry fact that our legal systems have not yet caught up with the emerging philosophical and scientific notions of self.

However, that is quite an 'if'. Unlike Polly Higgins in her campaign to outlaw ecocide, I do not hold much hope of the law of self-defence being applied in a holistic manner in the courtrooms of our states, no more than I see our politico-economic systems outlawing the very eco-cidal practices on which they are founded. However, this need not matter. Our own sense of justice has always had more sway on how we act than the laws that supposedly govern us, and rightly so. By and large we do not refrain from killing people because we are afraid of being caught and going to prison – we don't kill other people because we value human life and know the pain and sadness such actions would cause, and so on. We do not, in general terms, cease from stealing other people's things because we might get a fine or a custodial sentence, we do so because we do not want to do unto others that which we would not like done unto ourselves. Similarly, when a law is perceived to be unjust, people will break it, and the more this is done en masse, the more people feel confident enough to do it. Looting during riots is an example of this phenomenon, though the gnawing sense of social injustice the poor have towards rich corporations is revealed even in these acts.

Of course, changing the legal interpretation of 'self' would be a game-changing victory for a resistance movement to win, as it would mean a number of things: many more people would be prepared to resist; those who are already willing and able to fight back would be kept where they are needed and not behind bars; and actions would not have to be undertaken so clandestinely. It would be fascinating to have the 'right to holistic self-defence' argued in a court of law – perhaps as a mock trial in the same way that the law against ecocide was tested in the U.K.'s Supreme Court. But if we are unable to rid this constricted sense of self from our legal systems, a premise I feel needs to be presumed for now, then the least we can do is rid it from our minds, which are a lot more controlled by propaganda than they are by the threat of prison. Otherwise we will tie ourselves up in the chains that morally bankrupt ideas such as pacifism and nonviolence have created for our minds, a prison of sorts within which any chance we have of creating a world worth sustaining is arrested before it even begins. For as the poet Robert Frost once penned:

The strongest and most effective force in guaranteeing the long-term maintenance of power is not violence in all the forms deployed by the dominant to control the dominated, but consent in all the forms in which the dominated acquiesce in their own domination.

This is a sentiment summed up by Stephen Biko, a prominent anti-apartheid activist who was tortured to death by state police in the 1970s, when he said that 'the most potent weapon in the hands of the oppressor is the mind of the oppressed'.[144]

Let us stop listening solely to our heads, which have been compromised by a relentless process of cultural indoctrination since the moment we were born, and start acting from our hearts. We need to understand that we are the biosphere (and it is us) once again if we and much of life are to survive the death throes of industrialism. Most importantly, we need to start acting on this understanding, one which our hearts know to be true.

Though it may be our home, the Earth is not only that. It is us. We ought to defend it and its inhabitants with the same passion and ferocity as we would protect our own dwellings, their inhabitants, and our own flesh and bones. In doing so, we need not allow Power to dictate to us the ways in which we can defend ourselves and Life from its attacks.

CHAPTER FIVE

NONVIOLENCE:
POWER'S CHOICE OF PROTEST

Despotic governments can stand 'moral force' till the cows come home; what they fear is physical force.

George Orwell

WHEN LEE MINIKUS, A WHITE police officer who patrolled a predominantly black neighbourhood of Los Angeles, pulled over local resident Marquette Fry one autumn evening on suspicion of drink driving, he could have hardly anticipated that he was about to write himself into the history books. What began as a run-of-the-mill incident of police harassment and institutionalised racism would end up lasting six days, culminating in what became known as the Watts Rebellion, the most explosive event of the African-American Civil Rights Movement.

Despite U.S. President Lydon B. Johnson having signed the Voting Rights Act of 1965 into law only five days earlier (effectively prohibiting racial discrimination in voting), the incident lit the fuse of a rebellion that had been many lifetimes in the making, and one which quickly spread over 120 square kilometres of Los Angeles in the days that followed. Martial law was declared as 14,000 National Guard troops attempted to contain around 35,000 residents (with twice that in support), and by the time normality was restored 34 people had lost their lives, many more had been arrested, and almost a thousand buildings had been looted, damaged or destroyed. The saucepan had boiled over, and the chefs were cursing the water.

Probably the least notable, but perhaps most insightful, episode of the riots occurred when President Johnson 'urged Negroes to realize that nothing of value can be won through violent means'.[145] Regardless of whether or not the ex-President was correct – he wasn't – his statement smacked of the routine hypocrisy that governments profess in relation to their attitude towards violence, as this particular sound bite came at a time when President Johnson was fully engaged in the escalation of the Vietnam War. While we are all guilty of labelling actions as 'violent' only when they are inflicted *upon* us (but not *by* us), and of claiming to 'deplore violence when at the same time perpetrating it',[146] politicians have been condemning acts of upward violence while simultaneously imposing it downwards for as long as we've been foolish enough to listen to their words instead of observing their actions.

Such hypocrisy is what led Malcolm X to state that 'if they [U.S. Government] want peace, they should start by being peaceful'. Mandela echoed these sentiments when the self-confessed white supremacist (and one-time Prime Minister of South Africa) P.W. Botha offered him freedom if he would renounce violence, and the Nobel Peace Prize winner replied, 'Let him renounce violence'.[147]

President Johnson's comments during the Watts Rebellion raise lots of questions, the first being this: if violence really doesn't work, as our political leaders tell us is the case, why do they use the sword so often and wield it so brutally themselves? The answer is simple: it does work, something many indigenous people who have had their lands stolen at gunpoint, and subsequently industrialised, would attest to. As we will see shortly, The Establishment are not as alone as they would like to be in this realisation – those who defiantly defend their cultures and lands by whatever means are effective are also finding out that violence can achieve results in both directions.

My second question: why would those who want to radically change the dominant politico-economic system of our time accept advice on strategy and tactics from those who desire the exact opposite? In footballing terms, such logic is akin to the manager of one team (let's say Real Madrid) advising the manager of the other team (say Bristol Rovers) on the tactics he must employ if he wants to win the cup final, and this coach then doing precisely as he says, thankful for the advice. It is an absurd thought, and you don't have to be Gary Lineker to know who would be lifting the cup at the end.

My third question: why does The Establishment tell us that non-violence is the only moral and just way of effecting change, all the while inflicting a steady, quiet hyper-violence on us? Again, the answer is not mind-boggling: those in power do not want its subjects to have effective avenues for deep change open to them, especially when those avenues lead directly to their boardrooms and headquarters.

Dogmatic nonviolence, on its own, will never adequately challenge a military-industrial complex that has no intention of voluntarily dissolving itself. Do its advocates really believe that corporations such as BAE

Systems – who sell weapons of mass destruction to any nation that can afford to buy them, and often to those that can't – will one day suddenly be won over by the strength of moral persuasion, as if they had simply not realised that their products kill and maim masses of people every year? Those in power, whose institutionalised goal is economic growth and political control at any cost to human and non-human life, do not want the type of radical change that we need if we want to create authentically peaceful, genuinely sustainable livelihoods and cultures. Therefore why in the world would they espouse tactics for nuts-and-bolts change that have any realistic chance of succeeding? Instead they recommend courses of action that keep us running down alleyways that lead only to political dead-ends. When those in positions of power and privilege offer tactical advice to those who want radical grassroots change, a sceptical attitude towards it is the absolute minimum required.

I once had a friend tell me that an acquaintance of his, who was widely considered to be a successful and prominent campaigner for his role in a number of inspiring reformist movements, believed that his life, contrary to popular opinion, had thus far not been a success at all. Why? 'Because I've never had a death-threat.' Similarly, Dave Foreman, co-founder of Earth First! and a man who has had his fair share of death-threats, claimed that he was 'proud to be facing harassment by the FBI'[148] because of his actions.

Having some of the most powerful people in the world threaten your life, liberty and well-being is not most people's benchmark for success, but within this remark lay a strange but important point: that the litmus test of the efficacy of our actions in resisting the violence of the corporate-state coalition may, rather unfortunately, be the extremity of their response to it.

Those in power do not waste time or resources counteracting campaigns that they do not see as a threat; in fact, not only do they tolerate such harmless endeavours, they often implicitly support them. Reformists and The Establishment make peculiar bedfellows. Reformists (in general terms) tend to bemoan the hundred thousand illnesses that arise from industrialism in a hundred thousand different ways, yet still cling onto all the perceived modern conveniences that only industrialism can deliver. Likewise, The Establishment needs reformists as part of a strategic, long-term perspective. So-called democratic governments must appear to be open to being challenged, otherwise they lose an element of their manufactured credibility from which they derive much of their claimed legitimacy; that, or face the threat of all-out revolt. Therefore they make irrelevant concessions that take the heat out of the pan and stop it from boiling over.

Reformists provide this service for the state by asking for minor, acceptable tweaks to a fundamentally corrupt system. In doing so they help legitimise it, and inadvertently co-create the illusion of a liberal democracy which pretends to have the best interests of the people at heart. Reformism also diverts masses of potentially subversive energy, an inevitable phenomenon in unjust social models, down more harmless routes. Harmless, that is, to The Establishment's own interests, but not to those of the Great Web of Life.

The Machine will only ever grant reforms that, despite its extravagant protestations, secretly strengthen it overall. Granting traditionally oppressed people such as women, black people or the LGBT community a slow trickle of rights threatens its stranglehold on life in no way whatsoever (if anything, it strengthens it), as long as it means those people work more, pay their taxes and mortgages, consume its endless streams of tat and do not question its basic underlying premises. The moment a particular situation looks like it might get feisty, they'll whip out a baby carrot and recuperate those getting angry with some token gesture, whose ultimate function turns out to be nothing but a pacifier for them to suck on. This is not to downplay the inroads oppressed people have made over the years, which have been hugely beneficial to those who have fought for them, but to simply put it into overall context, and to remember that to the entirety of the non-human world, we humans – men and women, heterosexual and homosexual, black and white – are all supremacists, something we don't seem keen on admitting to.

Professional women and men, of all colours and sexual orientations, are better for the economy than mothers and fathers who live in direct relationship to the land, after all. If the dominant 1% thought that granting non-humans a few superficial rights would make them more money, they would no doubt do that too. However, it is difficult for a foie gras duck to join the union and strike over conditions, or for a forest to revolt against the extirpation of its wolf, and therefore their lamentable situations only seem to get worse.

The corporate-state coalition will never permit tactics that pose a genuine threat to its structure. From their perspective, why would they? Ward Churchill has said that 'demonstrations of "resistance" to state politics will be allowed so long as they do nothing to materially interfere with the implementation of those policies.'[149] Emma Goldman took this a step further, claiming that 'if voting changed anything, they'd make it illegal.'[150]

The problems with industrial-scale democracy are a subject for a different book, but needless to say that voting – in the pseudo-democratic systems we have today – changes nothing but the colour of the necktie of those whose job it is to convert Life into money. The nature of the media-military-industrial complex ensures that whoever wins, they will march to the beat of industrial capitalism's drums. Every four or five years we allow ourselves to be fooled into believing that this time it will be different. It could even be argued that by having the ability to vote for three or four different shades of hyper-violence, we are conned into thinking that we live in a free and fair democratic society, and are thus recuperated by The Machine.

As Gelderloos argues, such a type of democratic government 'exists on the same [political] continuum' as dictatorship. Academics, journalists and political commentators will argue that there is a distinction in that 'democratic elections are "fair and free" whereas the elections that confer office on dictators are manipulated', yet it is common knowledge that those three or four people we can choose to vote for are carefully cherry-picked by both the corporate media (with each newspaper backing its preferred option with positive spin) and those in the City who pay for the cyclical charade. He adds that:

> ... *Democratic governments have all the capacity for violence, repression, mass murder, torture and imprisonment as their dictatorial counterparts. However, democratic governments tend to tolerate non-violent movements, to keep them around, because such movements can be most useful to those in power.*[151]

Not only does The Machine not permit tactics that pose a genuine threat to it, its fear of them is exposed by the ferocity with which it chases and attacks those who choose to fight back using the entire toolbox. It is when movements engage in a diversity of tactics, with each employed in its right place, at its right time, that genuine challenges to business-as-usual occur.

THE GREEN SCARE

Around the time that the Stop Huntingdon Animal Cruelty (SHAC) campaign was gathering a head of steam, Will Potter – author of *Green is the New Red* – was working on the metro desk of the *Chicago Tribune*, where he would spend his days covering stories of rape, murder and other equally uplifting news.

In a self-confessed attempt to inject a bit of meaning and purpose into his life, he decided to volunteer with a local animal advocacy group whose aim it was to prevent animal abuse. Focused solely on getting results, himself and others took off to north Chicago on his first day, where they began distributing leaflets throughout the neighbourhood of a corporate executive of one of the world's largest insurance companies, Marsh Inc. At first glance, animal rights campaigners targeting an insurance company makes no apparent sense. However, this was the company who provided cover for Huntingdon Life Sciences (HLS), a U.K. based animal testing laboratory which, because of the routine cruelty involved in its practices, was incurring the wrath of a worldwide movement of people outraged by it. The leaflets, which contained a short history of the lab and its abuses towards animals, were given to this executive's neighbours, urging them to ask him 'to cease doing business with Huntingdon'. As Potter describes, 'the fliers made no suggestion of violence or property destruction, and they made no threats'.[152]

Approaching someone's neighbours may seem like an unfair type of action against what many would consider a fairly innocent businessman, to whom HLS was just another client. Such a perspective changes, however, when you put it into historical context, as this was exactly the type of potent strategy – a grassroots-led variety of economic sanctions – that was used to fight apartheid in South Africa. Such tools play an important role in dealing with those whose moral parameters exclude certain groups based on the colour or the furriness of their skin, and who therefore need to be persuaded to make less harmful decisions by appealing to other aspects of their value system: in this instance, their money and reputation. This time, instead of fighting for the rights of black people (whose oppression was culturally acceptable amongst many in South Africa at the time), activists were fighting to stop the systemic abuse of animals (whose cruel treatment is still culturally acceptable worldwide) using what they felt were the most effective means at their disposal.

Judging by the reaction they got from the corporate-state coalition that day, they were right. Not long after they began, police were called to the scene by security guards, and the leafleters were detained, handcuffed and brought to a police station without any explanation from the officers about the charges they were brought in on (Potter himself was followed by the FBI shortly afterwards, and received all sorts of threats – not a usual consequence of leafleting). Of course the reason the police officers couldn't present them with their charges was due to the fact that they had not broken any law. Leafleting that contains factual information, and which only encourages people to take nonviolent action, is not a crime after all. But that was, of course, hardly the point; its purpose was to obstruct their action, get their details and, more importantly, to scare them from repeating similar feats in the future.

The legal situation in the U.S., however, was about to change with the introduction of draconian legislation such as the Animal Enterprise Terrorism Act in 2006, a move which was one part of what became known in activist movements as the Green Scare.

The Green Scare is a wordplay on the Red Scares (or 'McCarthyism' as they are popularly known) that took place shortly after the Bolshevik Russian Revolution of 1917 and, more notoriously, in the aftermath of World War II. It was a term used to describe the propaganda used to escalate fear amongst the U.S. people towards socialist and communist ideas and revolutions. Similarly, the Green Scare refers to the witch-hunt being undertaken by the corporate-state coalition in the U.S. against the radical environmental and animal rights movements, involving a series of arrests, convictions, new legislation, grand jury indictments and, just as importantly, extra-legal measures such as intimidation.[153]

This crackdown was epitomised by Operation Backfire, in which the FBI and other agencies targeted members of the ELF and Animal Liberation Front (ALF) primarily, whose arson attacks had cost a couple of ecocidal enterprises around $80 million alone. Whereas communists were once the primary focus of the U.S. security agencies, attention, environmental and animal rights activists quickly became the target of 'green-baiting', another play on anti-communist rhetoric that sums up the persecution of groups or individuals fighting campaigns against the annihilation of non-human life (and, by dependency, human life) that has long been under way.

While Potter's leafleting efforts that day can only be described as entirely nonviolent, they comprised just one element of a diverse campaign that was gathering so much momentum that it ruffled the FBI's feathers enough for it to swing at whatever moved. This was largely triggered by the 'night work' of organisations such as the ELF, the ALF, Earth First! and SHAC, whose toolbox contained a handy implement known as ecological sabotage or 'ecotage', whose use was inspired by the adventures of fictional characters like George W. Hayduke and Bonnie Abbzug from Edward Abbey's classic, *The Monkey Wrench Gang*.

In their book *Ecotage!*, Sam Love and David Obst define ecotage as 'sabotage committed in an effort to defend ecosystems', and the term generally describes activities aimed at disrupting or stopping big business and state bodies in their relentless drive to liquidise the Earth's 'assets'. It includes everything that 'monkey-wrenchers' and other types of ecoteurs do in defence of the Great Web of Life: spiking trees (which can damage expensive blades in sawmills or, ideally, deter a lumber company from a specific timber sale), gluing locks, arson, pulling up survey stakes in wilderness areas to keep them road-free (necessary for maintaining corridors that threatened wildlife can move safely within), and the pouring of sand into the fuel or oil tank of bulldozers destined to destroy another huge swath of Nature.

As ecotage gained in popularity as a method of self-defence (in the holistic sense), the more refined and sophisticated it became. Before long it developed into a collaborative approach amongst a network of unconnected individuals and small, guerrilla-style groups working alone. Based on tips sent in from anonymous ecoteurs everywhere, Earth First!'s Dave Foreman co-edited a book called *Ecodefense: A Field Guide to Monkeywrenching*, an in-depth collection of practical ideas to stop The Machine bulldozing the Earth, providing some of the devilish details for Aric McBay's 'taxonomy of action'[154] outlined in *Deep Green Resistance*. Earth First! themselves published their own *Direct Action Manual*, giving guidance on everything from blockades, security and climbing to dealing with the police and the media. The ELF, true to their more hardline approach (and their belief that 'in some cases, burning a target is the most effective way of decommissioning it'), released a handbook titled *Setting Fires with Electrical Timers*. For those prepared to take resistance to an entirely more serious level, Joseph P. Martino's *Resistance to Tyranny* may be a better primer, with chapters focusing on the arts of booby-trapping, assassination, ambushing and encryption amongst much else; though as a retired Air Force Colonel, one can safely assume his aim was not to provide information and tools to those ready to defend Life against the military-industrial complex, through which he made a financially rewarding career.

While Foreman makes it clear that monkey-wrenching is a 'nonviolent resistance to the destruction of natural diversity and wilderness [that is] never directed against human beings or other forms of life [but instead] aimed at inanimate machines and tools that are destroying life',[155] not everyone shares his view that ecotage is nonviolent. This is partially because many people view property as an extension of their personhood, especially if their livelihood is dependent on the use of it. As ecotage generally involves 'damage [to] something', it also falls within the conventional dictionary definition of violence and the common – though utterly inconsistent – understanding of it. This is symbolic of the sad state of affairs we find the entirety of the world's jurisdictions in, whose laws regard an attack against a machine (whose purpose is to take animate life) as a crime, while at the same time treating the bulldozing of huge swathes of old-growth forests as not only legal, but good for the economy – precisely why it is legal.

The corporate-state coalition is not alone either; in an attempt to keep a seat at the negotiating table with those in power, many of the large mainstream environmental organisations disavow such tactics by underground movements such as Earth First! and the ELF, despite the fact they not only achieve the kind of results that aboveground organisations want, they do so without the hundred million dollar budgets that aboveground career environmentalists enjoy.

Ecotage, like sabotage, has an undeservedly bad reputation. The word sabotage was brought into common parlance by the actions of Dutch workers in the 15th century. Justifiably fearing that The Machine would replace them and destroy their livelihoods, these workers boldly threw their wooden shoes, called *sabots*, into the cogs of textile looms in order to break them, an act that inspired the Luddites[156] and infiltrated the daydreams of craftspeople for centuries afterwards.

Like most tactics, sabotage ought to have its rightful place. Whilst sabotage is almost always illegal (except in war, which is state-sanctioned violence) and condemned by public opinion that is itself sculpted by the corporate media, it is by no means necessarily immoral.

Deep ecologist Bill Devall, in an interview with Christopher Manes, argues that sabotage – like every tactic – has a role in the responsible citizen's toolbox. To affirm his point, he rightfully notes that he does not believe 'anyone would have any qualms about committing sabotage against concentration camps, and yet everything done at Auschwitz was legal under Nazi law', adding that 'ecotage responds to principles higher than secular law in defence of place'.[157] Sabotage usually comes into its rightful place when the law does not defend the most vulnerable from the abuses of the most powerful, and when the rights of both human and non-human life are being ridden roughshod by The Machine. Nelson Mandela, a man lauded by political leaders the world over (who themselves condemn sabotage) for his courage and tenacity in fighting apartheid, shares a similar outlook. In his later years he said that:

> I do not deny that I planned sabotage. I did not plan it in a spirit of
> recklessness nor because I have any love of violence. I planned it as
> a result of a calm and sober assessment of the political situation that
> had arisen after many years of tyranny, exploitation and oppression
> of my people by the whites.[158]

In doing so, Mandela recognised that sometimes, as Marx noted in *Capital*, 'force is the midwife of every old society which is pregnant with a new one'.[159]

While Foreman, Manes and other deep ecologists see ecotage as 'a means of self-defence',[160] others disagree and seem to believe that an inanimate bulldozer is more sacred than an entire biome. To this majority, ecotage is always an offence, and the law is always the law regardless of how unjust it is. In fact, ecotage and anti-apartheid-esque tactics (hacktivist group Anonymous's tactic of DDoS[161] attacks is a variation on this) pose such a threat to business-as-usual that the FBI and the Department of Homeland Security (DHS) have begun describing those who engage in it as nothing less than domestic terrorists. John Lewis, a top FBI official, went as far as to declare that 'the No.1 domestic terrorism threat is the eco-terrorism, animal-rights movement'.[162]

This is strange, but hardly surprising. On one level, it is understandable, as terrorism is often publicly associated with acts whose aim is to intimidate or coerce either the government or the civilian population into ceasing certain activities (such as the clear-cutting of old-growth forests). Under two of the FBI's three criteria that an activity must meet in order to be classified as domestic terrorism in the U.S.,[163] ecotage and other forms of ecodefence may, in some circumstances, tick the terrorist boxes. Activists themselves would certainly dispute the definitions involved, but as Potter astutely points out, 'terrorism is not violence for political purposes, it is violence for political purposes that "we" oppose' and can 'never be defined independent of the group doing the defining'. He adds that one of the 'unspoken tenet[s] of terrorism is that it does not apply to the systemic violence of people in positions of power against the powerless. It only applies when the flow of violence is redirected upstream, against government'.

To argue this point he notes that 'a bomb detonated by a guerrilla, killing dozens of civilians, is an act of terrorism. A bomb dropped by a military airplane, killing tens of thousands, is foreign policy.'[164] This is a sentiment summed up by the old adage 'one man's terrorist is another man's freedom fighter'. From the perspective of the directors of Louisiana-Pacific, HLS or BAE Systems, ecoteurs will always be terrorists. From the perspective of Gaia,[165] ecoteurs will always be freedom fighters. Whom you side with will depend largely on who you decide to swear your allegiance to: Power, or Life.

Regardless of the nicknames ecoteurs have received in the press, for any act to be officially classified as domestic terrorism in the U.S. Code it must be 'dangerous to human life [in a manner] that violate[s] federal or state law'.[166] Because terrorism has a potent stigma attached to it, labelling certain types of activism as terrorism frames how it is perceived by the public, and acts as a useful precursor to any governmental crackdown on it. Governments never need public opinion on their side in such matters, but it always helps.

There are a number of interesting points related to the phrasing of this condition. First, the fact that it is only terrorism if it 'violate[s] federal or state law' covers the government's own back against claims of state-sanctioned terrorism against people and planet; the state will hardly legislate against its own violence, after all. Second, many deep ecologists would argue that it is the corporations who seek to liquidise the planet, and convert Life into shareholder dividends, that are 'dangerous to human life', and therefore it's the industrialists who are the terrorists, and not those who attempt to prevent their legalised crimes.

Philosophical arguments aside, this is where the FBI's accusations fall apart. As the U.S. security agencies were claiming that the attacks by radical activists were endangering human life, Potter decided to investigate with a fine-tooth comb to see if there was any truth in the matter. The best place to start, he thought, was to go to the people most responsible for labelling activists as 'eco-terrorists' – the Foundation for Biomedical Research – who claim to be the 'only group in the world that tracks the crimes of eco-terrorists', and who had published a 'Top 20 List of Illegal Actions by Animal and Eco-Terrorists 1996-2006'. His logic being that, 'just as activists have an incentive to ignore or downplay violence, these groups have an incentive to display it'.[167]

What, then, did he find from trawling through the list? That 'the list of top eco-terrorism crimes from one of the top adversaries of these movements does not include a single injury or death'. One incident that is often mistakenly cited (due to propaganda manufactured by the corporate media in collaboration with the state) as an injury caused by the work of ecoteurs, is that of a sawmill worker at Louisiana-Pacific's mill in Cloverdale, California in 1987. As Manes reports, the *San Francisco Chronicle*, apparently primed for the event, printed a front-page headline saying 'Tree Sabotage Claims Its First Victim'. Another paper's front page read 'Earth First! Blamed for Worker's Injuries', while 'at a highly publicized press conference a Louisiana-Pacific spokesman [sic] faulted radical environmental groups "like Earth First!" in relation to the incident'.[168]

As it turns out, all of these accusations were nothing more than a tactic as part of the Green Scare, and a bid to turn public opinion (and especially that of mainstream environmentalists) against those who take a more radical and diverse strategy. Such tactics as these are nothing less than the age-old tradition of *divide et impera* – divide and rule – that the British imperialists used in the likes of India and Ireland when their people were rebelling. As Potter's investigations showed, 'years later, FBI files revealed that the Sheriff Department's primary suspect was not an activist but a disgruntled local who had admitted spiking in order to keep timber companies off his land'.[169] As is par for the course in politics, why let the truth get in the way of an agenda?

Using the FBI's own definition, this clear lack of injury or fatalities means that the vast majority of ecotage incidents may be a lot of things, but should not fall under the trumped-up charge of 'domestic terrorism'. In response to this inconsistency, the FBI had to create a separate, distinct term called 'eco-terrorism' in order to be able to describe ecoteurs in the media as terrorists, a sound bite with considerable clout. Language like this also helps instil fear into a public who, once sufficiently scared, become a lot more amenable to the inevitable draconian crackdown. The FBI now defines eco-terrorism as 'the use or threatened use of violence of a criminal nature against people or property by an environmentally oriented, subnational group for environmental-political reasons, or aimed at an audience beyond the target, often of a symbolic nature'.[170] Under similar terms, the sabotage of the Nazi war apparatus or concentration camps would have also have been described as terrorism.

This is not a view shared by Edward Abbey, who makes a clear distinction between ecotage and terrorism. From his perspective, 'sabotage is violence against inanimate objects: machinery and property', adding that 'terrorism is violence against human beings. I am definitely opposed to terrorism, whether practised by military and state – as it usually is – or by what we might call unlicensed individuals.'[171]

While the idea of becoming involved in activities not sanctioned by the corporate-state coalition is a scary prospect for those who, quite understandably, value their personal freedom, the grossly disproportionate level of the backlash against multi-tactical movements nonetheless provides a perverse insight into where opportunity may lie for those who have had enough of normality. Despite the fact that, to date, only a fraction of those who consider themselves ecologically and socially aware engage in non-reformist actions, this minority's successes provide us with valuable glimpses of the possibilities that exist if a greater percentage of movements questioned the doctrines of nonviolence and pure pacifism and instead embraced more diverse tactics, acting in solidarity with other like-minded movements.

The DHS admitted to this potential themselves, when in a bulletin to other law enforcement agencies they warned that 'attacks against corporations by animal rights extremists and eco-terrorists are costly to the targeted company and, over time, can undermine confidence in the economy'.[172] Not only that, but because many of the companies targeted make their money from tight profit margins gleaned from lots of large-scale projects, increasing the overall costs of any individual project (from increased insurance, damages, security etc.) often means that they become financially unviable.

As Pickering succinctly points out, 'these corporations exist to make money. All of a sudden they are losing money. So they have to reassess their activities.'[173] Foreman reinforces this point:

> *If enough trees are spiked in roadless areas, eventually the corporate thugs in the timber company boardrooms, along with their corrupt lackeys who wear the uniform of the Forest Service, will realize that timber sales in our few remaining wild areas are going to be prohibitively expensive. And since profits are the name of the game, they will begin to think twice before violating the wilderness.*[174]

Data on how much corporate profit is wiped out every year by such means is highly unreliable as, according to Manes, incidents go unreported as 'resource firms are anxious not to give their insurance companies another reason to raise rents in an industry already beset by safety issues'. Ben Hull, a special agent commissioned by the Forest Service to ascertain how much ecotage was being carried out, came out and said he would prefer it if his findings were not publicly released, as he did not want ecoteurs to know 'just how much havoc they're causing'.[175]

Despite these data constraints, Bondaroff conservatively estimates that between 1996 and 2004, a study of 600 actions by ecoteurs were estimated to have resulted in around $100m of damages and zero fatalities.[176] The reality could be many times that. This is bad news for the industries involved, but good news for Life. Taking profit away from the captains of industry is akin to taking the sword out of the hand of a psychopathic maniac. If such diversity of approach was applied by even a reasonable percentage of those who prefer solely reformist measures such as clicktivism, it could be enough to help bring such psychopaths to their knees.

If you think that the term psychopath is much too harsh to be applied to these fine captains of industry, who are usually well-regarded by society, a study published by the journal *Psychology, Crime and Law* would suggest otherwise. In 2005, psychologists Katarina Fritzon and Belinda Board gave personality tests to senior managers and executives from some of the U.K.'s leading companies. They then compared their psychometric profiles with criminal psychiatric patients locked up in Broadmoor, a high-security hospital that homes some of Britain's most notorious murderers. What they found was that some 'personality disorders were actually more common in managers than in the disturbed criminals',[177] leading the researchers to describe the bosses as 'successful psychopaths' and the criminals as 'unsuccessful psychopaths'.[178]

This disturbing fact is backed up by research conducted by Robert Hare and Paul Babiak who, in their book *Snakes in Suits*,[179] argue that because of the structure of modern bureaucratic organisations (such as the FBI) and corporations (such as banks), where team players have become less valuable than aggressive risk-takers, those with strong psychopathic tendencies are more likely to be selected, rewarded, and promoted. This led George Monbiot to quip that 'if you have psychopathic tendencies and are born to a poor family you're likely to go to prison. If you have psychopathic tendencies and are born to a rich family you're likely to go to business school'.[180] As Russell Brand said, 'we've built a society that rewards psychopaths'.[181] But not only are we rewarding them and allowing them to pillage the Earth for their own personal gain, we've also foolishly agreed to let them create both the laws and cultural norms that limit the ways by which we can hold them to account, without being imprisoned or excommunicated from society.

It's ironic then that it is these bureaucratic organisations that are labelling some activists – those who are putting their own liberty on the line for the sake of things other than themselves – as terrorists. This may be down to the fact that full-spectrum activists are taking on psychopath-led institutions in a manner which they find threatens the status quo, which they reap huge financial rewards from. Potter encapsulates the corporate-state coalition's concerns by quoting a 2008 DHS report titled *Eco-terrorism: Environmental and Animal Rights Militants in the United States*, which admits that 'animal rights and environmental movements directly challenge civilisation, modernity and capitalism', as their success would not only 'fundamentally alter the nature of social norms regarding the planet's habitat and its living organisms, but ultimately would lead to a new system of governance and social relationships that is anarchist and anti-systemic in nature'.[182]

If radical movements for change ever wanted an endorsement for their website or leaflets, they could do much worse than to quote from Homeland Security's own words.

There is good reason for the DHS to hold those views. That said, when discussing the successes of campaigns that employ, as part of their strategies, what could be popularly deemed as violent (or even terrorist) acts, there are a number of things that we should keep in mind.

First, those who argue that we should use the entire toolbox do not claim for a moment that violence is the first port of call. In fact, the opposite is true, as one must remember that these are usually people who are driven to put their liberties on the line out of a deep regard for Life, which is why not one life has been taken, or one injury caused, by their late night activities. The same, unfortunately, cannot be said of the actions of those institutions they target, which is precisely the reason they are targeted. Full-spectrum activists simply argue that sometimes, depending on the problem at hand, nonviolent methods are inappropriate due to their obvious ineffectiveness.

Unlike pacifists, radicals do not claim that every radical environmental action has been a success, or that those that have been were due to 'violent' means alone. Every time that the nature of social relations has changed in the past it has been down to activists employing a multiplicity of means, with the various actors following their own path of most resistance. As the corporations targeted never publicise the attacks on their property for fear that the idea behind it will spread, it is impossible to say exactly how many have been successful, or even how many have occurred.

STRENGTH IN DIVERSITY

There are some things we do know, however. We know, for example, that despite the revision of the history books conducted by pacifists and those in power, both of nonviolence's poster boy campaigns – the Indian Independence and the African-American Civil Rights Movements –

are, rather ironically, examples of the potency of movements which utilise the full range of tactics at their disposal.

The Indian Independence movement was much more diverse than the widely-held historical narrative would have us believe. You know the version, it goes something like this: the people of India, under the guidance of Mahatma Gandhi, won independence from the British through an almost totally nonviolent campaign (though suffering many atrocities themselves, Amritsar being one example)[183] involving peaceful 'protest, non-cooperation, economic boycotts, and exemplary hunger strikes and acts of disobedience',[184] which combined to make British rule unworkable. Through self-sacrifice, compassion, an indomitable will and an admirable ability to turn the other cheek, they won not only a victory for India, but for love, life and pacifism. But as Peter Gelderloos spells out in no uncertain terms in *How Nonviolence Protects the State*, the reality of the situation was a lot more complex.

For a start, pacifists and advocates of nonviolence seem to refuse to acknowledge that war, inadvertently, played a major role. Indian independence was granted at a time when the British armed forces were severely depleted from both the Second World War and the conflicts of Arabs and Jews in Palestine. The British feared that if some of the revolutionary elements springing up in India took charge, there would be no way their remaining armies could control over three hundred million people.[185]

But it wasn't only external military factors that were at play. In fact, the vision of a nation united under the nonviolence of Gandhi could not be further from the truth. 'Resistance to British colonialism included enough militancy that the Gandhian method can be viewed most accurately as one of several competing forms of popular resistance.'[186] When Gandhi called off the non-cooperation movement in 1922, after some civilians killed policemen in retaliation for them killing three local villagers in the Chauri Chaura incident, many people became disillusioned with nonviolence (and the doctrine of *ahimsa* as practiced by Gandhi) as an effective way of reclaiming sovereignty. Revolutionary groups such as the *Anushilan Samiti* (and its offshoot movement, the *Jugantar*), the Ghadar Party and the Hindustan Socialist Republican Association either sprung up or were radicalised, including noteworthy people such as Shaheed Bhagat Singh, Chandra Sekhar Azad and Subhas Chandra Bose.

Singh – whose life was a bit like a revolution: short, explosive and the stimulus for great change – was a very influential figure in particular, and by the time he was hung at 24 for his role in assassinations and bombings, he rivalled Gandhi in the popularity stakes. Like many in the Irish Republican movement around the same time, he didn't just aim for independence from foreign imperialists, but instead 'the overthrow of both foreign and Indian capitalism'.[187] Remember this was before the worst consequences of capitalism could even have been imagined. His execution by the British in 1931, after a 116-day hunger strike in jail, prompted a dramatic politicisation of young people in India, who were inspired to rise up to fight for Indian independence once again. Even India's first Prime Minister, Jawaharlal Nehru, said he was 'like a spark that became a flame in a short time [that] spread from one end of the country to the other dispelling the prevailing darkness everywhere', and that through what he symbolised – the honour of Lala Lajpat Rai, the man whose death he avenged – the 'popularity he achieved was something amazing'. However, because he didn't just want Indian capitalists to replace their British counterparts, he was seen as a much greater threat to the totality of British interests in the region than Gandhi.

The accepted historical narrative, as Gelderloos points out, also 'cannot make any sense of the fact that Subhas Chandra Bose, the militant candidate, was twice elected president of the Indian National Congress' in 1938 and 1939, and was only ousted because of the manoeuvrings of the Gandhi-led clique in the Congress Working Committee,[188] who didn't like the fact that Bose wasn't afraid to use force against the British if the situation demanded it. You have to ask yourself this: if India was so united under the banner of nonviolence, how did a revolutionary like Bose come to lead its biggest political party at the time? The answer: it wasn't. The movement was diverse, something any Indian will attest to.

None of this is a criticism of Gandhi, a man who had more conviction and courage in his nonviolence than I may ever have in anything. He walked his talk, in spite of what it cost him. I disagree with the abuse he gets from armchair revolutionaries as much as I disagree with the blind praise he gets from proponents of nonviolence. He was a great man who stood for truth above all else, and the truth is that the Indian Independence movement needed everyone struggling in accordance with their own nature. If anyone is to be criticised, then perhaps it ought to be addressed to those who do not have the same commitment to truth as their idol admirably had.

It was this collection of underground organisations and individuals, along with the nonviolent activities orchestrated by the likes of Gandhi, that formed a mosaic whose collective aim was to resist, and revolt against, the East India Company and the rule of the British Raj. The revolutionary parties and individuals played significant roles in the outcome, both by way of their own effect and, just as importantly, because they made Mahatma Gandhi look like a much more moderate option to negotiate with in comparison. This dynamic is analogous to the way that radical environmental organisations such as Earth First! made more mainstream environmental groups, such as the Sierra Club, seem like the voice of reason when it came to the important business of negotiating exactly how much wilderness was to be protected.

Despite the fact that the Indian struggle is not even the example of successful nonviolence that its proponents claim it to be, there is also an argument to be made that, in hindsight, it was only a success in very narrow terms. In a similar fashion to what happened with the Colour Revolutions that took place throughout various parts of the former Soviet Union and the Balkans during the early 2000s (largely by way of the nonviolent methods of regime change described by Gene Sharp in his book, *From Dictatorship to Democracy*), not much changed in the Indian parliament other than the skin colour of those who wielded power. Sri Aurobindo, an influential Indian nationalist and philosopher, even went as far as to argue, with some merit, that Gandhi's *satyagraha* movement was largely responsible for the partition of India in the end, as it blocked the more forceful actions that the Indian people were engaged in a few decades earlier, causing a delay in independence and allowing those who wanted a divided India to gain influence on the political landscape. Not only that, but industrial capitalism is as rife in India today as it is anywhere in the Western world, so much so that it is now considered one of the emerging markets of the 21st century.

This is a long way from the vision of *Swadeshi* – the idea that real sovereignty would only come through political independence and economic self-reliance – that Gandhi extolled. Though often attributed to him, the idea of *Swadeshi* in fact originated with a group including Bal Gangadhar Tilak, a man who spent six years in prison on a charge of sedition, for merely defending the actions of violent revolutionaries and calling for immediate *Swaraj* (self-rule). Because India accepted a deal which was significantly less than Gandhi and others had hoped for (a source of considerable pain to Gandhi), their struggle did little more than change the nationality and colour of the industrialists who control their lives and destroy their landbases. Indians are still controlled by foreign powers – the imperialists merely swapped their seats in Indian government for seats in Indian boardrooms.

Practitioners and advocates of nonviolence will quote Dr. Martin Luther King Jr. *ad nauseam* when preaching the virtues and effectiveness of the types of nonviolent action that he is famous for, but almost none of them will give a fair and honest account of the crucial role that people like Stokely Carmichael, Malcolm X and the Black Panther Party (which FBI Director J. Edgar Hoover called 'the greatest threat to the internal security of the country')[189] – all of whom advocated a diversity of tactics that many African-Americans resonated with more at the time – played in the success of their combined struggle. That said, it is also important to note that they were not the proponents of violence they are often painted as. They were all engaged in a struggle to fight a systemic hyper-violent American regime not out of a love for violence but as a pragmatic approach to their political reality. Malcolm X summed up his stance when he said 'we are nonviolent with people who are nonviolent with us.'[190]

Not only that, there was a lot more solidarity between groups represented by the likes of Malcolm X and Martin Luther King than either proponents of nonviolence or the state would like us to believe. As activist Mike Ryan points out, 'both Malcolm X and Martin Luther King shared a single long term goal', and that 'they could each be found at the same mass actions'.[191] In a lecture entitled *Conscience and the Vietnam War*, Dr. Martin Luther King Jr. said, 'Every man [sic] of humane convictions must decide on the protest that best suits [his] convictions but we must all protest. But across the spectrum of attitudes towards violence that can be found among radicals is there a unifying thread? Whether they read Gandhi or Frantz Fanon, all radicals understand the need for action – direct, self-transforming and structure-transforming action.'

Malcolm X, contrary to his popular portrayal, shared a similar feeling of solidarity and tactical diversity when, in a 1964 speech, he said, 'Now, I'm not criticizing those here who are nonviolent. I think everyone should do it the way they feel it is best, and I congratulate anyone who can remain nonviolent in the face of all [that confronts us].' While the quote 'I am only effective as long as there is a shadow on white America of the black man standing behind me with a Molotov cocktail' is commonly but wrongly attributed to Dr. King (scholars of his work have found no evidence of him saying this) by those pushing their own propaganda for violent revolution, an honest account of history shows that even in the deceit, there is a grain of truth. Dr. King and Malcolm X both knew they needed each other, and both played a valuable part in their common struggle.

Just as in the case of India, some commentators would also argue that the African-American Civil Rights Movement was only a success in very narrow terms. While the passing of the Voting Rights Act of 1965 was seen as a great success (correctly) for black people and (incorrectly) for proponents of nonviolence, little of real substance has changed. They still have both white and black bosses controlling their every move, still have life-long mortgages to pay back to primarily white bankers, and still have their planet ravaged by industrialists of all colours.

Again, none of this is intended to unjustly criticise or downplay Dr. King's efforts in restoring dignity to the people he represented. He was a man who committed his life to making the world a better place in the only way that he could, which may be more than the rest of us can say. It is intended only to give a more accurate description of how change actually came about in this famous campaign and the depth (or lack thereof) to which it succeeded, in the hope that it may inform how we move forward in an age where we must urgently do whatever we can to protect the Great Web of Life, and not just black humans.

The historical revisionism used to portray this civil rights movement as nonviolent is no mere mistake by those who write the history books and control the narrative. It is also often no mistake by advocates of nonviolence, who Ward Churchill accused of selective amnesia when he claimed that movements in the U.S. 'are currently beset by "nonviolent revolutionary leaders" who habitually revise the historical fact as a means of offsetting their doctrine's glaring practical deficiencies',[192] something he believes has 'done much to foreclose on whatever revolutionary potential may be said to exist in modern America'.[193]

Another problem that we encounter when discussing the successes of the types of diverse responses that I argue for is that, up to now, very few movements have been courageous enough to tackle the corporate-state coalition on its own terms. Despite this, those few who have dared to put their liberties on the line have often achieved more in one night than large reformist organisations achieve in years.

Some of these actions are depicted in *If a Tree Falls*, an Academy Award-nominated documentary that follows Daniel McGowan, Jake Ferguson, Suzanne Savoie and the likes as they recount their days of activism with the ELF. The film looks in detail at one incident in particular, where members of the ELF commit an arson attack on Cavel West, a slaughterhouse in Oregon where wild horses from government land were rounded up and culled en masse. The scale of the cull was so bad that on a number of occasions the amount of horse blood coming out of the plant was so large that it overwhelmed the town's water treatment facilities to the extent that they had to be closed down. For 10 years local residents tried everything to close the slaughterhouse, but to no avail. Everything, that was, except arson. The film, which portrays the ELF's activities in a balanced manner, describes the effectiveness of the action:

> ... on July 21ˢᵗ 1997, Jake Ferguson and three others slipped into the facility in the middle of the night and burnt it to the ground. The company was never able to rebuild and the arson became a model for the group. In one night they had accomplished what years of letter writing and picketing had never been able to do.[194]

A similarly effective incident occurred in Hawaii, where a wood chipper worth $250,000 was firebombed by ecoteurs in order to prevent a rare tropical rainforest from being reduced to fuel for a sugar mill. According to Manes, 'the company that owned the chipper was operating without a permit and subsequently went out of business'.[195] Many may remark on how attacks such as these cost ordinary workers their livelihoods. But within this logic the extremity of the anthropocentric mindset is revealed again; otherwise, how does one equate the short-term jobs of a few people over the safety and security of an entire town's water supply and the health of entire biomes. Not only that, it could also be argued that inflicting these costs on industry is simply a way of helping them internalise many of the detrimental costs they were hoping to externalise onto Life and the taxpayer, something they don't have the integrity, or the necessity, to do by themselves.

People have successfully fought the invasion of The Machine in a whole myriad of ways, and under a wide variety of banners, down through the years. Many have protected their culture and lands from its blades and weapons in ways that would not have been possible had they restricted themselves to purely nonviolent tactics. Gelderloos, speaking in generalised terms, explains that:

> ... *the indigenous nations that resisted colonization peacefully or tried to accommodate European settlers were exterminated, whereas the indigenous nations that resisted forcefully, using a variety of tactics, are still around today, and they also tend to be the nations with the strongest liberation movements. The Mapuche, Six Nations (Iroquois), Lakota and Coast Salish all went to war against colonization, many still consider themselves to be at war, and they represent some of the strongest indigenous struggles on the planet.*[196]

The people of Ireland have had a similar experience. Like all political change on their shores over the last few hundred years, things improved when the people took a wilder approach to the dealing with their oppression. It was the use of militant methods by *Conradh na Talún* (The Irish National Land League) during the bitter struggles of the Land War, together with the many nonviolent methods of others, that finally persuaded the British to allow Irish tenant farmers to buy back 'the land of Ireland for the people of Ireland'. This was land that they worked and had previously paid crippling rents to what were, quite often, absentee British landlords whose forbears had stolen the land through conquest to begin with.[197]

Resisters and revolutionaries have not only protected their own livelihoods, cultures and kin by taking effective action, they've helped protect non-humans too. Through property destruction and 'theft', those fighting against animal abuse have given innumerable hens, cats, dogs and guinea pigs (to name a handful of species) a second chance at life. Ecoteurs have saved huge swaths of wilderness – in countries where it still exists – from being pillaged for the 'resources' that lay peacefully within it, and have shut down enterprises who have knowingly put profit above the Earth. Many others have used the whole toolbox to send a message back to The Machine that if it continues to inflict its systemic violence on them, there will be consequences for doing so which won't be limited by the confines of a legal system rigged in favour of those who created it.

These successes have amounted to little more than damage limitation thus far. The reasons for this are manifold, but the almost total pacification of the public has played no small role in our impotent response in these matters of life and death. Whatever the reasons may be, hidden within these scattered victories for Life lie insights that ought to inform how we resist the invasion of The Machine into our homes, our communities, our lands, our relationships with the world around us, and even our minds.

The message they give is clear: if small groups of isolated people, and individuals working alone, can defend life from the incursions of The Machine, there is no limit to what we could achieve if we discarded the delusional cloak of nonviolence en masse and took up an approach that is more appropriate for the scale of the challenges before us.

Climate chaos, soulless jobs that can barely pay the rent, violent ecological devastation at untenable rates, disconnection from the natural world, the death of authentic community, gross disparity of financial and physical wealth, extreme energy extraction and use, industrial diseases of both the mind and body – none of these things are facts of life. We know what we don't want any more of, and we know that another world is possible. The questions presented before us, therefore, are these: are we prepared to leave our comfort zones in order to make this world a reality, and if so, how do we get there?

In the following chapters of this book I look at what a dignified, potent response may look like, exploring both the destructive and creative aspects of this, which in ecological terms are nothing less than two sides of the same coin. Sometimes in order for new ideas to germinate, the old ones need to die. If humanity wants to change tack and start moving away from the suicidal path it seems hell-bent on pursuing, and instead create a system of social relations that serves life on Earth in a much healthier way, then we are simply going to have to put a spanner in the works of The Machine. Otherwise we may no longer have a biosphere that can sustain life, or a way of life worth sustaining.

Nothing less than this will be enough, and hard choices will have to be made. We can no longer delude ourselves that we can have our Earth and eat it too. The task seems overwhelming, if not impossible. But to paraphrase David Fleming, who was speaking about the imperativeness of localisation: resistance and revolution stand, at best, at the limits of practical possibility, but they have the decisive argument in their favour that there will be no alternative.

CHAPTER SIX

A DIGNIFIED LIFE

The rebel is doomed to a violent death. The rest of us can look forward to sedated expiration in a coma inside an oxygen tent, with tubes inserted in every bodily orifice.

Edward Abbey

WHEN I WAS A BOY, growing up on the west coast of Ireland, I attended one of the De La Salle colleges, an all-boys school that in my father's time was run by an often vicious bunch called the Christian Brothers. Although the teachers had improved a lot in the space of that one generation – physical beatings for being a few minutes late for class were no longer considered appropriate – the increasingly industrialised nature of the curriculum paralleled that of society in general. Whereas children in pre-industrial times (and even more so in pre-agricultural times) learned how to forage, track animals, cook, carve tools and utensils, make their own dwelling, find water and heal themselves and their communities, our generation learned geography from a book, mathematical theories that seemed to have no relevance to our lives, a brand of economics that didn't acknowledge the greatest part of human existence, and foreign languages that grew out of lands we knew nothing about, less still cared for. So while the teachers themselves were honest people who wanted only the best for us as pupils, the lessons they had to teach were designed to breed workers for an industrial economy which, in turn, would help perpetuate a level of systemic violence against life that, when viewed through an honest lens, would make the Christian Brothers look like saints.

Although nothing like the bullying of the 21st century, where kids not only get physically attacked in the real world but emotionally and psychologically harassed through social media, our school had its bullies like every other post-industrial school. In a situation that mirrored civilisation at large, the couple of boys from each class who dished out the beatings always seemed to be from the central town, where I myself was from, while their victims almost always came from rural areas.

In the year above me there were a couple of notorious bullies, whom I will call James and Gareth, brutes who seemed devoid of empathy for anyone they perceived to be below them. The object of their attention most of the time was a younger boy – let's call him Paddy – from my year, who they believed to be a few rungs down the social ladder from them. Paddy had all the ingredients to be picked on: a slight speech impediment, a small stature, a lack of confidence and a simple, rural nature about him.

Paddy was tormented by these two and their lackeys on a regular basis. Most weeks I'd witness more or less the same event: they'd chase him around a nearby field, catch him, drag him back to the basketball court, before giving him what was generously known as 'the pole', where they'd grab his arms, spread his legs and proceed to repeatedly ram him into one of the poles that held up the basketball ring, hammering his genitals against it each time. He'd protest throughout, which only seemed to make it even more fun for the others.

Once bored, they'd drop him to the ground and pull his pants down to his ankles (much to the mockery of those in the madding crowd), and leave him there writhing in physical pain and severe psychological and emotional humiliation. I watched this happen every week for about two years, but I hadn't even the courage to tell the teachers about it (for fear of becoming the next target myself), let alone step in and defend my classmate. I felt ashamed by both the sense of impotence I felt in the whole ordeal and my cowardly lack of action, so I can only imagine how he felt.

As I sat by the court one evening after school, watching Paddy peel himself up off the ground and pull his freshly ripped trousers back up, I got the sense that, for the first time since I knew him, something had shifted within him. There was a look in his eye that somehow seemed to speak the word 'enough'. I went over to ask him if he was okay, but he said nothing; his eyes were fixated on the backs of James and Gareth as they strolled off laughing. I thought nothing of it, and went off to do my homework.

The next week, as Paddy put his bag on his back to catch his bus home, the inevitable happened again. Out came the bullies, running towards Paddy with a grin on their faces. To their surprise, and for the first time in his two years there, Paddy didn't budge. He dropped his bag, and at the moment they went to grab his arms he let fly with a sucker-punch that I had never imagined he could even be capable of, let alone carry out. With James down, nose bleeding, he made for Gareth with a head-butt under the chin before kneeing him in the face during a scuffle. As both

James and Gareth made to get up, shell-shocked but preparing to dole out some payback, a few onlookers decided that this was their moment to put their own shame to rest by jumping in to Paddy's defence, laying blow after blow until they both lay hunched up on the ground, wondering what the hell just happened. Paddy arose, covered in muck, bruised and much more cut up than usual, but this time there was one crucial difference: his trousers were up.

He stood there, as small in stature as ever, but now with a sense of pride in his eyes, and despite his dishevelled look, he appeared distinctly dignified. Not only was he never bothered again, those who got their comeuppance kept a low profile from that day onwards. His physical cuts did not take long to heal, and the last I heard he was working with inner city kids in Dublin.

We all have our own stories like this: battered women saying 'no more' to their abusive husbands; native people fighting back against colonial oppressors who want to destroy their culture and take their lands; activists taking on the corporate-state coalition; people everywhere resisting the dominant culture by refusing to partake in specific aspects of its violence, despite the constant social pressure to conform to its norms.

We also know another story, the one where we watch injustice after injustice unfold before our eyes – like I did with Paddy – and for reasons that are becoming less and less excusable, do not work up the courage to stand up to it.

A crucial difference between these stories is the element of dignity.

Dignity is one of those qualities that everyone recognises when they see it personified, but that is difficult to describe through the blunt tool of language. In ordinary terms it is most often used to describe conduct or speech that is indicative, in some way, of self-respect or a respect for some other that is deserving of it. Though it is a term often used in political, philosophical, moral and legal discussions to signify that a being has an innate right to receive ethical treatment and to be valued, its more commonplace usage attempts to convey a sort of Kantian notion of free will, where there is a causal link between our ability to retain agency in choosing our own actions and our sense of dignity.

In the face of such domination or loss of autonomy, dignity can take a million different forms for a million different people. To Gandhi, this may have been the taking of a baton across the head without flinching, a stance that, regardless of its ineffectiveness by itself alone, can none-theless be imbued with a rich sense of dignity. To Malcolm X, it would look entirely different. In his influential speech, *The Ballot or the Bullet*, he tells his audience that if they do not take more of an 'uncompromising stand ... [their] little children will grow up and look at [them] and think "shame"'.[198] Through his lens dignity depends not on one's ability to take a blow (that may damage you physically but not psychologically) and be able to rise above it, but on one's insistence on defending their psychological and bodily integrity by whatever means necessary.

For others, such as Count Claus von Stauffenberg – a man killed by Nazis for his part in the resistance and who said that he could have 'never look[ed] the wives and children of the fallen in the eye if [he] did not do something to stop [the] endless slaughter' – dignity means standing up for others and sharing the burden of responsibility in times of invasion or attack. To many of the spirited First Nations people of what is now called North America, accounts suggest that dignity was often only retained by meeting the violence of the colonial imperialists with everything they could muster.

As many slave narratives would attest to, the greatest loss of dignity can come not through personal sufferings, but through witnessing the abuse of a loved one while having little choice but to look on helplessly. As James C. Scott, an eminent political scientist, points out, the 'inability to defend oneself or members of one's family (that is, to act as mother, father, husband or wife) against the abuses of domination is simultaneously an assault on one's physical body and one's personhood or dignity.'[199] If the loss of dignity comes from the feeling of impotence and disempowerment in such dire situations, then regaining dignity must surely come from no longer looking on helplessly.

Whatever dignity is, we know it when we see it or experience it ourselves, and there are no end of opportunities to do so in a world where the levels of systemic oppression and violence are only eclipsed by the arts' desire and capacity to depict and communicate them. Our moral indignation towards all forms of violence in the real world (an indig-nation, remember, that is cultivated by those who dish it out the most) is betrayed by our reactions to the Fanonian counterviolence and resistance we experience in movies.

Take James Cameron's *Avatar*, a film about deep ecology and resistance cunningly disguised as a Hollywood blockbuster. Having severely depleted the Earth of its natural resources, the euphemistically-named Resource Development Administration (RDA) space-shuttle their way to Pandora – a moon in a faraway star system that is rich with life – on a mission to obtain unobtanium, a valuable mineral the indigenous *Na'vi* people of Pandora have in abundance.

One of the *Na'vi* clans, the *Omaticaya*, are a people deeply connected to each other and their land, and who communicate to their mother goddess, *Eyma*, via a neural connection to the sacred Tree of Souls, the pulsing heart of their culture. In a scenario indigenous people on real life Earth know all too well, the RDA decide to destroy the Tree of Souls, a move intended solely to demoralise the *Na'vi* through the calculated destruction of their culture. At this point the film's protagonist, Jake Sculley, decides that enough is enough and unites all the clans of Pandora into a resistance movement who, after an epic battle – and with no little help from Wild Nature – overcome the human imperialists. In doing so, the *Na'vi* successfully protect their land, and the unique culture which grew out of it, from being mined to death.

Of course, whilst this movie is fictional, the experiences it depicts are frighteningly factual. The 'civilised' have done this to The Wild and indigenous people (a label that would have been applied to us all until recently) for the longest time, and though the film is set in the future, it could easily be an historical interpretation. What is fascinating is how, when watching such movies, we find ourselves fist-pumping the resistance movement of Pandora to victory over the resource-greedy invading forces, Luke Skywalker as he destroys the Death Star, Simba as he takes on evil Uncle Scar, or most underdog, standing-up-for-honest-values stories for that matter. Yet when it comes to real life, we chastise, stigmatise and criminalise those who 'violently' fight back against the onslaught of The Machine, as if somehow their lives and cultures were less worthy of defence than those fictionalised on the big screen.

Resistance by people who value their dignity above all else is, thankfully, not limited to the realm of fantasy. Every day people across the world courageously stand up to those more powerful than them using a diversity of approaches. Nowhere is this more apparent than in Chiapas, a region of Mexico whose large indigenous population have fought back against those who want to destroy their way of life and pillage their lands.

THE ZAPATISTAS

As the rest of the world was resolving to stop smoking or start whatever fad diet was around at the time, resolutions of a much more political significance were being solidified in South America, and Mexico in particular, on New Year's Day 1994. On one side of the ideological divide you had the neoliberals celebrating the coming into effect of the North American Free Trade Agreement (NAFTA), a trilateral agreement between the corporate-state coalitions of Canada, the U.S. and Mexico, one that would significantly bolster the ideologies of industrialism and capitalism (central tenets of both Democrats and Republicans in the U.S.) in a part of the world not as traditionally susceptible to them as the West. On the same day, and on the opposite side of the ideological fence, the indigenous Mayan people of Chiapas declared war on the Mexican government through their newly-formed armed revolutionary wing, the Zapatista National Liberation Front (EZLN).

The Zapatistas and the indigenous people of the region took grave exception to NAFTA, and with good reason. Because of a decision made by the rich urban bureaucrats sitting in their offices far away in Mexico City (or, more precisely, Washington), NAFTA would effectively mean that – at best – the campesinos (peasant farmers) of Mexico would have their livelihoods and, eventually, their culture wiped out by the artificially fertilised, highly subsidised, genetically modified, mechanically harvested crops that would flood their country from the north, a system of food production which the peasants of Chiapas – who farmed traditionally and with respect for their lands – would never be able to compete with. More sinisterly, the Mexican government also agreed to the cancellation of the previously historic Article 27 of their constitution (an article that was a key element of Emiliano Zapata's revolution in the early 20th century), which had up to then protected the lands of the campesinos and the indigenous people from sale or privatisation, something their powerful counterparts in the U.S. and Canada felt was a 'barrier to investment' and were therefore unsurprisingly enthusiastic to change. EZLN Commander Major Mario described the effect that NAFTA had on their collective psyche and response:

Emiliano Zapata and his soldiers imposed that law [Article 27]
with their lives and their blood, and in a few hours, without

consulting the peasants, Salinas de Gortari wiped them out. When we
knew that our land could be sold or taken from us, when we heard
that there would be no more land for us, that nearly finished us.
At that moment my brothers wanted to rise up.[200]

Subcomandante Insurgente Marcos, the main spokesperson of the Zapatistas, declared NAFTA a 'death sentence'[201] to Indian communities across the nation, and whilst it was the trigger for a resistance movement that would inform and inspire revolutionaries and protesters against neoliberalism for the decades that followed (such as those in the anti-globalisation protests in Seattle in 1999), the Zapatista response had been no less than 500 years in the making. That the NAFTA agreement was merely the final straw in a centuries-old system of oppression was a sentiment articulated by Subcomandante Marcos in their first communiqué to the Mexican people the following day (titled 'First Declaration of the Lacandon Jungle'), when in capital letters they announced a phrase that would reverberate throughout their own writings, and those of resistance movements worldwide, from that historic moment onwards: 'Enough is Enough'.[202]

Despite – or, perhaps, because of – the 500 year warm-up, once they got organised the Zapatistas didn't waste time. Within hours of finalising their declaration of war, around 3,000 armed Zapatista insurgents seized towns and cities throughout Chiapas and set fire to several police buildings and military barracks in the area. The EZLN went to great lengths to state that they did not want their lives to be engaged in armed struggle, but that they felt they no longer had any choice due to the lack of results achieved through more peaceful means, an experience echoed by oppressed people both past and present.

Their gains came at a cost: while the Mexican government claims that only 159 insurgents lost their lives in the uprising, the Zapatistas say the figure is closer to a thousand. Since then the Zapatistas have become one of the most important examples of how a people can resist The Machine in its myriad forms. Though their successes thus far have been far from complete – they've not yet been able to establish political autonomy for the province – they have succeeded not only in creating a culture that is resilient and resolute in the face of a military-industrial complex intent on grabbing the land they were born out of, but also in retaining a strong sense of identity against homogenising forces.

Despite the grief of losing so many loved ones during the January uprising, you cannot find even a modicum of regret when you read through their communiqués and the fictional and factual stories they write. From what I can tell, as far as they were concerned, they were already the walking dead, a people without a face, a people without a voice. Fighting back reversed this: it gave them back their voice, gave them back their face, and they started to become fully human again.

Raul Hernandez, a 17-year-old Zapatista prisoner of the Mexican state, encapsulated the feelings of his comrades when he said, 'I watched my father die because there was no money in our village to buy him medicine for his stomach. That's why I went with the Zapatista ... I decided to fight because if we're all going to die it might as well be for something'.[203]

In a communiqué titled 'Dying In Order to Live', Subcomandante Marcos described this sentiment in more detail:

> *During these past ten years more than 150,000 indigenous have died of curable diseases. The federal, state and municipal governments and their economic and social programs do not take into account any real solution to our problems; they limit themselves to giving us charity every time the elections roll around. Charity resolves nothing but for the moment, and again death visits our homes. That is why we think no, no more; enough dying this useless death; it is better to fight for change. If we die now, it will not be with shame but with dignity, like our ancestors. We are ready to die, 150,000 more if necessary, so that our people awaken from this dream of deceit that holds us hostage.*[204]

One of the words that stands out in that piece – dignity – is a recurring theme throughout the entirety of their communiqués and stories. In fact, it is difficult to find a letter or tale which doesn't emphasise it. To them, dignity is a quality worth fighting for in and of itself, regardless of how sweet the fruits of their labour turn out to be. They believe that if your way of life, your lands and your people (or someone else's for that matter) are being annihilated, it is always better to die standing tall than on your knees begging for meaningless reforms that serve only to prolong the agony.

Taking the example of gang-rape that I described in the introduction, there is no scenario I can think of where walking away and pretending nothing is happening is a more dignified, honourable response than intervening and stopping the rapists by whatever means necessary. It doesn't matter how many men you are faced with, or how dangerous the situation, there is never any dignity in looking the other way. I knew this in my heart when I would watch my old schoolmate Paddy get beaten. The same goes for the systemic violence inflicted upon the Earth and its inhabitants – there is no dignity in pretending that recycling will stop the wholesale destruction of our cultures and land, nor honour in fooling ourselves that driving a hybrid car will somehow magically change the world.

When we face the enormous scale of the ecological, social and personal problems that stand before us today – climate chaos and ecological meltdown; extreme wealth inequality; soaring rates of serious crime, depression, industrial diseases and other indicators of an unhappy, unhealthy populace; the annihilation of our cultures and identities; the increasingly specialised nature of our jobs and the associated repetitious boredom; industrialised education, industrialised entertainment, industrialised food – when we face this multifaceted onslaught, fighting back can feel understandably hopeless, and therefore we are often paralysed by the sheer sense of scale of the challenge. Who are we to take on The Machine, and how could we possibly ever stop it?

To an extent, these feelings may be correct: maybe the scale of the problem has got too big, maybe industrialism and the forces driving it have become too powerful, maybe the modern human experiment is such a catastrophic failure that it is all a bit too late. What the Zapatistas and others are saying, however, is that regardless of the final analysis, we ought to be able to look at ourselves in the mirror and not feel ashamed about the person looking back. This sense of dignity can never be achieved by putting up a doomed-to-failure, pseudo-resistance to The Machine. It can only come through a careful, thoughtful analysis of the root causes, followed by a full-spectrum resistance utilising every available tool and method available to us. Only when we explore every avenue, use every tool, will we know if The Machine in its myriad forms was as powerful as we thought it was. Only then will we know how resilient the forces of destruction really were. Only then will we be able to look at each other in the eye and know that we have done everything we could.

Dave Foreman, when answering his critics about whether or not his radical efforts to protect wilderness areas in the U.S. would ever be enough, summed up such sentiments when he said:

> ... *perhaps it is a hopeless quest. But one who loves Earth can do no less. Maybe a species will be saved or a forest will go uncut or a dam will be torn down. Maybe not. A monkeywrench thrown into the gears of the machine may not stop it. But it may delay it, make it cost more. And it feels good to put it there.*[205]

For those who want to take positive action in defence of Life, what could feel more positive than unscrewing the cogs of The Machine's institutions that are intent on ripping communities and lands apart in the pursuit of never-ending profit? Foreman's friend Howie Wolke shared similar thoughts that were honest, realistic and pragmatic:

> *I doubt anything, including thoughtful radicalism, will bridge the gap between saving some wilderness today and creating a society that lives within its ecological means ... It's my guess, though, that thoughtful radicalism will save some biotic diversity in the short-term, and allow more to be saved and restored for the long-run. Then when [industrial society] finally, mercifully chokes on its own dung pile, there'll at least be some wilderness remaining as a seedbed for planet-wide recovery.*[206]

Truth be told, I have not got the slightest idea if anything other than the weight of its own complexity will bring down The Machine at this hour of the night. Like every empire before it, it will fall, though neither I nor anyone knows when. What I do know is that the very least we can do is help it to its knees. In doing so we may preserve enough links in the Great Web of Life to allow The Wild to take root and flourish once industrialism eventually does come to its inevitable end. This rewilding of the Earth – and ourselves and our types of activism in the process – is something I will come back to in the final chapter.

Another thing I know is that by resolving to resist the tyrant with every little inch of our lives, standing up to it and refusing to back down, we may regain some of the dignity that we have so evidently lost. Doing everything in our power to resist or stop the abhorrent levels of systemic violence we are embroiled in today ought to be a goal in itself. Everything after that is in the hands of Fate, but as experience teaches us, whenever we give our all to The Whole, She tends to give us everything we need in return.

When Paddy faced up to those bullying him there wasn't a shred of evidence to suggest than anyone else would jump in to help him out. Yet he did it anyway. When decent, dignified people see one small, insignificant person rise up against the mighty in a seemingly hopeless but righteous cause, strange things can happen. Never underestimate the ability of one determined fearless person to inspire an entire movement of people to do what they already knew needed to be done – Rosa Park's refusal to get up off her seat for a white passenger being one of many examples of this.

Dignity, it seems, inspires dignity.

If we need inspiration for the fight, we need look no further than Nature. Jensen recalls how, when contemplating the lameness of our response to what is effectively a threat to our lives, his mind wanders to

> ... the mother bear who charged me not one week ago, because she thought I was threatening her baby. I thought of the mother horses, cows, dogs, cats, hawks, eagles, chickens, geese, mice who have in my life attacked me because they thought I might harm their little ones. If a mother mouse is willing to take on someone eight thousand times her size, what the hell is wrong with us?[207]

Similarly, I often admire how my little dog Benji will ferociously defend his patch by chasing every car that drives past, despite the fact that he has been hit by them on a couple of occasions. I sometimes look at him thinking, 'I really wish you would stop doing that, you're going to get killed!' But most of the time I say to myself, 'I wish I was as fearless as you, little man.' That car could end his life by changing course or speeding up at any moment, yet he shows his teeth to every single one that drives past. If that is not a source of inspiration for everyone who feels too small to take part in the battle between Life and The Machine, I do not know what is.

As McBay has said, 'We must fight back not only to win, but to show that we are both alive and worthy of that life.'[208] Fighting back is not about violence. It may include acts that are deemed violent (under current delusional notions of it) when force is the only adequate and effective course of action, but fighting back is a hundred thousand different things, the majority of which will be decidedly peaceful. A resistance movement needs people who know how to grow food and reclaim their own food sovereignty. It needs foragers, craftspeople, those who know how to run consensus-based decision making and those who know how to maintain a community's health and heal its sick. It needs those who can offer genuine spiritual guidance, and those who can mediate the conflicts that inevitably arise. It needs people who are willing to battle a corporation in the courts, and those who are willing to clandestinely defend themselves from their attacks – with every ounce of their might – wherever they are weakest. It needs the energy of the young and the wisdom of the elders. It needs all of these people severing their allegiance to The Machine and instead offering their unique gifts and talents in a cohesive service to Life, to whom our allegiance in the future must lie.

A resistance movement will need us all bringing our own gifts and passions, stories and qualities, laughter and rage into the mix. There is no right or wrong way to participate. The Machine wants to do what every empire does and divide movements for change, hoping that we channel our energies against each other and not it. But we must resist this and instead unite, against a force that will otherwise destroy everything that makes life meaningful and joyful. It will need pacifists and revolutionaries giving their all, each following their calling, and each supporting the other in doing so. As civil rights leader Howard Thurman once said:

> Don't ask what the world needs. Ask what makes you come alive, and go do it. Because what the world needs is people who have come alive.[209]

It is when we are most alive, serving Life, that we are at our most dignified.

Likewise, do not mindlessly limit yourself to a set of civilised ethics that have themselves been shaped by the protagonists of a politico-economic system intent on converting the remaining few square inches of life into money, quantifying the unquantifiable. Do what needs to be done to protect the Great Web of Life.

For doing whatever needs to be done, in a way that feels dignified to you, is the most loving thing you can do.

CHAPTER SEVEN
THE ANTIBODIES

It's time for a warrior society to rise up out of the Earth and throw itself in front of the juggernaut of destruction, to be antibodies against the human pox that's ravaging this precious beautiful planet.

Dave Foreman

THERE ARE FEW EARTHLY PLEASURES more heavenly than finding yourself laid back in a meadow of vibrant wildflowers, cloaked by oak and ash and weeping willow all enlivened by a pink-skied sunset, watching a flight of swallows toss and turn and toy with each other at breathtaking speed. But wherever joy reveals herself, reminding us of the divine in the mundane, a beautiful sadness is, in these times, never too far away. So it goes with watching birds. Witnessing them at play, and the way they effortlessly embody the quality of freedom many of us crave, provokes both an oddly content feeling of envy, and an attendant sense of primal loss, within the nooks and crannies of my soul.

And with good reason. Such feelings do not arise merely from the fact that the bird's way of being allows them to follow the natural rhythms of the Earth, spending the summer months on the rugged west coast of Ireland where they have their young, before adventuring to more exotic shores for the winter. Nor is it necessarily caused by the swallow's obvious freedom from mortgages and rent, wage slavery, Justin Bieber, bosses, relentless bills, the synthetic pressures of consumerist culture, industrial addictions and their resultant physical and psychological diseases; though freedom from these would all be worth fighting for in themselves. What I long for most when I observe birds – or any wild animal for that matter – is the freedom from the abstract moral chains that we civilised folk are forced to construct and wrap around our necks, just so that we can live our crowded, unnatural lives without acting out our unmet needs in toxic ways that would hurt those living in closest proximity.

The intense overcrowding of humans, an insufferable curse inflicted upon us by The Machine's need for operatives and consumers to be efficiently bunched together in its industrial and commercial centres, is one of the most underestimated problems of our time. Even many prominent environmentalists are now well-intentionally calling for people to be kept inside the walls of the castle – in order to protect the lands outside from its impact – as if there would be no consequences for Nature from separating people from the Great Web of Life in such a forced way. There are consequences, and many of them at that. Not just for Nature, but for humans too.

Ethologist John B. Calhoun conducted some fascinating research on over-population in rat populations, leading him to coin the term 'behavioural sink' to describe the deterioration in behaviour that came about as a result of overcrowding, research which went on to become an animal model of human societal collapse.

His experiment, and findings, went something like this. The rats he used were allowed to eat and reproduce until their hearts were content, but the space they were given to live in was kept constant. Once population levels inevitably started to rise within these increasingly cramped spaces, the rats began to exhibit new behaviours. The rodent version of the alpha male soon started physically abusing other rats. There was also a dramatic rise in violence amongst the overall population. The levels in rape of both females and males rose too, especially homosexual rapes. Females having miscarriages and dying during pregnancy increased, some ate their new-borns (despite the abundance of food), whilst others stopped nursing their offspring and nesting. Many of the rats showed signs of depression because of their new situation, and subsequently became disconnected from those around them. Carl Sagan, with perhaps a hint of sarcasm, summed up the experiment when he remarked that:

> *If there were no differences between rats and people, we might conclude that among the consequences of crowding humans into cities – other things being equal – would be more outbreaks of street violence and domestic violence, child abuse and neglect, soaring infant and maternal mortality, gang rape, psychosis, increased homosexuality and hypersexuality, gay bashing, alienation, social disorientation and rootlessness, and a decline in traditional domestic skills. It's suggestive, surely. But people are not rats.*[210]

Wild creatures, like the rat, do not voluntarily choose to overcrowd themselves, and as such don't need to construct elaborate systems of ethics. Take the robin, who follows me around the garden every day as I'm tending to the vegetable patch. While opportunistically thieving valuable earthworms from 'my' land, he hasn't the slightest notion of private property or theft, less still any abstract ideas about the taking of the worm's life being a bad thing. He has no commandment instructing him that he must not do to others what he would not have done unto himself, nor an external God or guru telling him that he must strive to do no harm to any living creature. He will defend his nest and territory aggressively, not bothering himself with philosophical discussions over whether to do so using violent or nonviolent means. He doesn't have to choose from 50 varieties of his favourite food at the supermarket, many brandishing their own mix of often competing values: organic versus fair-trade versus local versus cooperatively owned, to name a few. The robin made simplicity his gateway to freedom. By not domesticating his life, his needs are naturally met in the most holistically healthy way possible, without him even having to think about ethics, let alone construct some.

Likewise, I suspect the robin does not experience any of the feelings of holier-than-thou smugness that environmentalists seem to exhibit on the rare occasion they shit in the woods, and I'd hazard a guess that he does not care whether or not he is a good bird for living his localised, low-impact lifestyle. The robin just is; he does what he does, living in accordance with his indomitable nature. By living a wild, amoral life, one unburdened by civilisation-induced ethics and where his natural needs have age-old outlets that are life-enhancing to The Whole, the robin paradoxically lives a much more harmonious, liberated, peaceful and sustainable life – one less cruel and violent than those of us locked up in the ethical cage that our disconnected, urbane lives now necessitate.

Of course, we two-leggeds now need codes of ethics and morals to moderate the consequences of living the unhealthy ways we do, otherwise our overcrowded societies would be even more unpleasant than they have already become. Without such ethics we might even wreak more ecological harm in the short term, if such a feat were possible. Because 'the amplification of our lives by technology grants us a power over the natural world which we can no longer afford to use', I, like George Monbiot, have reluctantly accepted 'the need for limitations, for a life of restraint and sublimation'.[211] These intellectual constraints, however, often feel like a profound loss, one which we pay in return for washing machines, light bulbs and other time-saving gadgetry – time we then spend watching soap operas, enjoying some impractical hobby or feeding some addiction or other.

One of the many problems with using ethics as a short-term remedy for the ills of domestication, however, is that the industrial human seems to have a propensity to limit this sense of ethics to the human realm (and to the dominant elements of it, in particular), with the rest of the biotic community not getting much of a consideration – here again we come up against *homo anthropocentro*. This is something Aldo Leopold spent much of his life attempting to ameliorate, and in doing so came up with a 'land ethic'.[212]

Based on what ought to be common sense, he said that 'all ethics so far evolved rest upon a single premise: that the individual is a member of a community of interdependent parts. The land ethic simply enlarges the boundaries of the community to include soils, waters, plants and animals, or collectively the land.' Adopting such a worldview has the potential to transform the existing social contract and base it on a deeper awareness of our place in the Great Web of Life and the interdependency of all things within it, and in doing so replace our current set of anthropocentric morals we enact.

As much as fostering a land ethic would help us live in a healthier relationship with the world around us, the general notion of ethics still self-perpetuates the symptoms they were created to medicate. While many of our ethical constructs act as key short-term coping mechanisms that enable us to live on top of each other as pleasantly as possible (within a culture that prevents our core needs being met in their harmonious ancestral ways), in the long run they are only prolonging the agony of the inevitable. When we artificially synthesise moral and ethical codes to make civilisation tolerable, we ultimately only serve to reinforce the unsustainable domesticated realm to the detriment of all that is Wild and innate, both in our landscapes and ourselves.

We humans, one of the small fraction of species on Earth prone to domestication, have created ways of living for ourselves in which our basic needs and desires no longer have any natural, holistically-healthy outlet. As Monbiot proposes, our out-of-control shopping habits may be a toxic 'expression of the foraging instinct', our 'pursuit of ever more extreme sports ... a response to the absence of dangerous wild animals',[213] and suggests that 'the absence of monsters [from our landscapes] forces us to sublimate and transliterate, to invent quests and challenges, to seek an escape from ecological boredom'.[214]

Because we have created ways of life that are not in accordance with our own nature, we have had to manufacture a complex and often inconsistent sets of rules, ethics, morals and laws to regulate the more destructive ways in which we try to meet these subdued needs. If this was not problematic enough, the consequences for the non-human world are intensified when these rules, ethics, morals and laws are formulated through a distinctly anthropocentric lens. In creating these necessary constraints we wrap ourselves up in all sorts of psychological, emotional and spiritual chains, spending countless hours of our lives pondering what is right and wrong and feeling the inevitable guilt, shame and remorse whenever our actions or instincts contradict our morals.

Aside from cloaking the devil in the garb of a saint, there are many other problems with ethics. For one thing, in the domesticated human realm, we hold a lot of fabricated moral and ethical notions around the ideas of creation and destruction. 'Creation good, destruction bad', seems to be the general mantra we mindlessly chant. Creating jobs, regardless of how damaging their industrial fruits are to life as a whole or how repetitive the work, is generally considered good, and as such is something politicians are always keen to emphasise around election time. In perverse contrast, destroying the headquarters of an institution (perhaps by the act of arson) whose mission statement inevitably results in astronomical levels of ecological, social and individual harm, is considered evil by all but those conveniently deemed eco-terrorists (a term used by us consumer-terrorists while we go about our lives enacting the systemic hyper-violence we ourselves have been cajoled into).

This creation-destruction duality is in part down to the fact that somewhere along our evolutionary path we took a seriously misguided turn – via technologies and techniques such as language, numerical systems, agriculture, private property, money and industrialism – and made the mistake of believing that the processes of life are not in fact circular, but linear.

We created religions based on this ideology of linearity, faiths which tell us that our soul continues on its straight-line trajectory to heaven when we die, while our physical remains are kept from returning to The Whole by way of a coffin.

We devised economic systems based on the same concept, pro-ducing seemingly endless lines of gizmos that have industrial life cycles euphemistically described as 'cradle-to-grave' (the grave usually being enormous landfill sites) instead of the 'cradle-to-cradle' cycle that an eco-logically literate people naturally adopt. We mine minerals and energy from one far-flung place or another, transport them half way across the planet to a factory, where we then combine them into products which, once they become dysfunctional or obsolete, cannot be easily or healthily reintegrated into The Whole. These global processes separate us entirely from the production of all that we consume and so reinforce our linear delusions, in turn fortifying our dualistic notions of creation and destruction and making them appear as two separate processes. All this in the name of 'progress' – itself a linear construct, a straight-line trajectory towards an economic perfection always just out of reach – where we endure all sorts of indignity, inhumanity and humiliation in the pursuit of a contentment which, by definition, is unattainable the very moment we strive for it.

In profound contrast, everything in The Wild exists within a cycle of cradle-to-cradle, where creation and destruction are but two sides of the same coin, a process in which Life gives unto life and in doing so adds to its richness and diversity. Biomes naturally work as closed-loop systems, where nutrients and matter are generally fed back into the landscapes they come from, supporting the enchanting complexity of the Great Web of Life. In the realm of The Wild, creation is not good and destruction is not bad. Instead, one is indistinguishable from the other, two names for what is one ongoing and endless process. Like life and death, decay and growth, one is impossible without the other. One animal's carcass becomes the flesh and bone of another. Plants become shit which becomes soil which becomes plants which become herbivores who shit and feed plants. Round and round it seamlessly goes.

Like everything else in the realm of humanity, our activism has become as tame as our green and pleasant lands. But if life on Earth is to stand any chance of surviving the invasion of the imperialist machine, it is the wild and circular understanding of the world, and not the dualistic foolishness of the domesticated human, that we must reinvigorate our ecological and social activist movements with. If we are going to rewild our physical landscapes – something I argue is crucial for the regeneration of sustainable human and natural habitats – then we need to begin re-wilding the political landscape as a precursor. The time has come for the lesser-spotted activist, known as the Wild Revolutionary, to be reintroduced into the political landscape. In the same way that the wolf can bring life back to the mountains and valleys by killing deer and keeping their numbers to an ecologically harmonious level, the Wild Revolutionary has the potential to help bring harmony back into the human realm by keeping the beast known as The Machine in check. By doing so, this lesser-spotted activist could kickstart the political equivalent of a trophic cascade, leading to a dramatic upsurge in the diversity of our cultural, social and economic terrains.[215]

The result would be a world more captivating than captive, one that is no more ethically complex than the innate knowledge we intuitively understand to be true: that 'a thing is right when it tends to preserve the integrity, stability, and beauty of the biotic community' as Leopold once remarked, and 'wrong when it tends otherwise'.[216]

That 'thing', contrary to popular opinion, may at different times and in different circumstances be what civilised man thinks of as a creative or destructive act. On this basis, rewilding a landscape, creating a permaculture-based garden for a community, or burning down an institution which is pathologically intent on converting the majesty and resplendence of the Earth into money and toxic products, may all be the right things to do if they help preserve the integrity, stability and beauty of the biotic community. On the other hand, destruction (such as the conversion of Life into laptops, cars, internet servers, commercial airliners and synthetic fertilisers) that occurs in a linear process and which undermines and diminishes the strength and diversity of the biotic community, would no longer be seen as right.

When thought of in these wilder and more philosophically-consistent terms, it is the sabotage of draglines and haul trucks at ecologically devastated areas – such as the tar sands in Canada – that would, counterintuitively, be considered right (if all nonviolent options are considered ineffective first), and the act of turning a blind eye to it and walking away which is wrong. These are not abstract moral notions, but a natural underlying principle for any people who want to live in harmonious co-existence with the rest of the biotic community, itself a prerequisite for any human community with a desire for health and longevity.

Yet the delusion is rife even amongst those who are fed up with the status quo. Even within activist movements, destructive (or creative, from a wild perspective) tendencies are described as 'negative' and are weeded out by pacifists and nonviolent practitioners as soon as they detect them, while those who take a more 'positive' approach are celebrated by both activists and the corporate-state coalition alike, a fact that ought to concern the former in their battles against the diseases caused by the latter.

Buoyed by pseudo-wisdoms from people like Buckminster Fuller, who have remarked that 'you never change things by fighting the existing reality. To change something, build a new model that makes the existing model obsolete', we have begun to see acts of intentional destruction towards the existing reality not as a natural part of a creative process, but as something bad and, according to Fuller, even futile.

The problem with Fuller's perspective is that he was primarily an inventor, not a political activist, and while in the world of technological innovation his quote makes sense and accurately describes how technologies 'progress', in the world of politics and social change this is not how things go at all. Simply creating a new model of politico-economic relations, and hoping that people adopt it whilst abandoning the old model, is naïve to an idiotic degree. Many great thinkers have theorised new politico-economic structures that would serve humanity much better than the current form, yet they cannot even find a footing when faced with the machinery of the current order of things. The Establishment will use everything at its disposal – its armies, its police forces, its corporate media, its education system (whose curriculum it controls), its propaganda machine and its own people's taxes – to ensure that people don't know that an alternative to the status quo even exists, let alone allow it to develop to a stage where they may consider adopting it.

So while creating something new to replace the old model is crucial work, to be done by those who feel called to do so, the existing reality must also be fought against and, one way or another, defeated if new ideas and forms are to come to fruition. The political landscape, like the urban landscape, is densely overcrowded by a sophisticated cartel of rich and powerful people. If you want to build a block of apartments in the centre of a packed city, you must first knock down an existing building which, when viewed through a Wild lens, is not an act of destruction but merely another revolution in the great turning of the wheel of creation.

To paraphrase Fuller, drawing up plans for a more beautiful building which would make the existing building obsolete is obviously an essential part in changing the urban landscape for the better, yet whilst the architect has undoubtedly got her role in the whole project, the demolition team has a vital one too.

Yet our indoctrination into nonviolent extremism is so complete that we have somehow come to the preposterous conclusion that only architects and builders have a place in the construction industry, with the demolition crew stigmatised out of a job. As a result, the architect spends her days sitting around her office dreaming up and drawing grand designs, only ever venturing out onto the site to make sure that no one is knocking down the buildings that occupy the spaces her plans are designed to fill. This thought is no less ludicrous in the political world than it is in the construction industry, and therefore until the architect and the demolition crew come together in solidarity, each valuing the other's role and seeing it as two beautiful parts of the creation cycle, our best efforts will be nothing more than political texts gathering dust on a bookshelf labelled 'Missed Opportunities'.

If a dignified and potent resistance to, and revolt against The Machine will require both the constructive and destructive acts that are but two aspects of creation, what form should these take? As always, there are a hundred thousand different responses to the challenges that confront us, and this diversity of reaction is natural, necessary and a sign of vitality. However, if you're looking for inspiration, as always, you need look no further than Nature, whose ways we would do well to mimic.

Our potential response to the ecological, social and personal challenges confronting us could derive its inspiration from two of the keystone life-forms that work on different levels, the macro and the micro, which have been maintaining the balanced health of The Whole for the longest time: antibodies and wolves.

THE ANTIBODIES

Just the thought of defending one's self, people, culture or land against the invasion of The Machine – both its physical manifestations or the forces behind it – can have a paralysing effect on even the most warrior-like of people. Attacking it, in order to diminish its ability to ravage life elsewhere, is an even more disturbing proposition, which is why we so often resort to the reformist half-measures that our hearts know will be futile in the final analysis. After all, industrial civilisation has conveyor belts of factories producing the goods whose sale supplies it with its lifeblood: money.

This money pays for its armed wings, its police forces and armies, along with their countless guns, nuclear weapons and drones, courtrooms and prisons, all ready and willing to be of service to their master. Add to this impressive infantry and arsenal the majority of a civilian population supporting it with their labour, and its resultant taxes, and you have what appears to be an unstoppable juggernaut. It has CCTV on every street corner and, as the National Security Agency leaks made apparent, in every bedroom that has a computer with a webcam or an audio device, along with systems monitoring our emails, internet searches and phone conversations; which, when combined have created a surveillance state so extreme that the only safe place to formulate any plans against it is somewhere out in the wilds with not a trace of mobile technology within listening distance. It has almost the entirety of the world's resources at its disposal, which it can utilise for both defence and attack. The Machine's overwhelming strength is that it is everywhere, in every nook and cranny of our lives, with its greasy spirit infiltrating everything.

One thing life has taught me, however, is that your greatest strength, by its nature, can also be your greatest weakness. For example, men and women are often attracted to each other because of their partner's passion for something, but once in a relationship they can often find that it is precisely that thing they most love about each other that is also the thing they find hardest to live with. A fierce nature may achieve goals in the office, but it may create big problems at home. Conversely, having a laid-back approach to life may make you an ideal housemate, but a frustrating work colleague.

The same goes for The Machine. Prior to writing this book I spent years exploring the critical issues that influence how we face industrialism and its destructive offspring. Unlike Frodo in Tolkien's legendarium, I could not find the one ring any more than I could work out where Mount Doom was, nor any particular evil monster to destroy. The Machine's strength lies in the fact that it is dispersed everywhere: in our shops, our homes, our places of work, our daily habits – its underlying philosophy has even infiltrated our hearts and minds.

My breakthrough came, as any military strategist will attest to, the moment I stopped thinking of its strengths simply as strengths, but also as weaknesses. If its omnipresence seems to be its strength, then perhaps this is also what makes it vulnerable.

Because The Machine has invaded every square inch of the developed world, and is relentlessly sending its troops off to pillage new territories, it is impossible for it to defend all its outposts, all its assets and resources, simultaneously. Despite its best attempts, it has left itself drastically exposed to attack in all but its most important centres. This, incidentally, is one of the many reasons its police forces ask activist movements to inform them, in advance, of the time and location of their demonstrations and protests, and why its propaganda machine has been indoctrinating us with the ideology of nonviolence. The military-industrial complex understands its inherent weakness, and knows that if the people were on revolt en masse using the full spectrum of tactics, its capacity to respond would be overwhelmed.

While its pawns are many, they are completely isolated and almost entirely unarmed and unprepared, meaning that the majority of its apparatus is wide open to guerrilla attacks by a well-oiled resistance movement who can strategically target its bottlenecks and weak points. Whether or not its size, scope and thinly spread nature turns out to be its Achilles heel may depend on whether those who claim outrage at ecological devastation and social injustice are prepared to formulate and enact effective strategies and tactics with these weaknesses in mind, or mindlessly persist with corporate-state endorsed responses that play right into the hands of industry. As army generals unfortunately know all too well, if activists are serious about creating the change they wish to see in society and are prepared to do whatever they can, they are going to have to work out the enemy's weaknesses and hit them hard. Playing into The Machine's hands, doing what its spokespeople tell them to do, is no longer optional for those who are tired of the intolerable systemic abuses that are its blueprints for success.

Another of The Machine's strengths is that it gets to make the laws, all of which are created with its own advantage in mind. Because of this, it has to be seen to play by them to a certain degree, at least on a superficial level, whereas those who endeavour to undermine it do not have to burden themselves with such constraints, unless they find some strategic advantage in doing so. This law making and enforcing capacity is its strength if activists allow it to be, and its weakness if revolutionary movements formulate their strategies and tactics to target it accordingly. To play by the rules that the enemy of Life has formulated is laughable in military terms, something to keep at the forefront of our minds when you remember that, as Naomi Klein has made clear, 'our economy is at war with many forms of life on earth, including human life'.[217] Those who choose to sit on the fence – like the people who walked away from Omelas – will not make the war go away, but simply make themselves feel good by way of a delusional, disconnected and individualistic sense of moral purity.

Taking into consideration the nature of the beast – its astronomical size, the scope of its surveillance, how thinly spread it is – and then drawing up goals and a diversity of strategies and tactics that account for these characteristics, is the only hope that those who profess to want deep change have in counteracting The Machine's many miserable manifestations.

No football team would voluntarily agree to play to their opponents' strengths, or a certain formation that made life easier for them; a tactically astute manager would look to expose the opposition's weaknesses. No nation under attack would agree to fight the fight on its invader's terms; again, it would look for an advantage that would strengthen its own resistance and ability to defend itself. Yet activist movements all over the world, battling in isolation from their allies against the innumerable and horrific consequences of industrialism, do exactly this in their campaigns (although none of these movements identify industrialism and its underlying myths – separation, human supremacy and so on – as the cause). Until they start dictating the play, and reclaiming their power to decide how to respond, the best they can hope for is a marginal and superficial reform to what, if our eyes were wide open, would rightly be perceived as an intolerable system.

One way in which activist movements could begin the long road to harmonious social relations and ecological vitality would be to cease seeing themselves as some sort of pharmaceutical drug whose aim it is to treat symptoms with little or no thought for their root cause. They could instead think of themselves as antibodies, naturally produced by the Earth in defence of itself and the human and non-human life that comprises it, entities whose niche in the Great Web of Life is the protection and maintenance of the health of The Whole.

What is an antibody? In the human body, antibodies are the guerrilla warriors who defend it against attacks from those life-forms that, left to run amok, result in the body becoming ill, diseased or dead. Without these, Paul Hawken reminds us, our bodies 'would perish in a matter of days, like a rotten piece of fruit, devoured by billions of viruses, bacilli, fungi and parasites, to whom we are a juicy lunch wrapped in jeans and T-shirt'.[218]

In biology, antibodies are protein molecules used by our immune systems to identify and neutralise foreign objects, such as bacteria, viruses and chemicals. These molecules, whose uncompromising ways would be considered extremely violent in human terms, are vital to life and the balanced health of the whole human body. Each person has approximately one to two billion antibodies continuously flowing through their body, patrolling day and night, ready to fight infections and diseases in its host – a fairly dedicated bunch, by all accounts.

Antibodies work by recognising a unique part of the foreign target, called an antigen, which they then proceed to attack or neutralise by binding to them. The general structure of all antibodies is very similar, but a small region at the tip of the protein – let's call it 'the calling' – is extremely variable, allowing millions of different types of antibodies with slightly different tip structures, or antigen-binding sites, to exist. This enormous diversity of antibodies enables the immune system to recognise and neutralise an equally wide variety of antigens.

For example, some antibodies, called antitoxins, will bind to a poison and neutralise it by altering its chemical composition. By locking on to some imperialistic microbes, other antibodies can immobilise them and stop them from penetrating the body cells of its host. Even if they can't neutralise the invading microbe by themselves, they can also act as markers, sending signals to other parts of the immune system – such as scavenger cells – who are better placed to ingest the invader.

This is not a book on human biology, however. What scientist James Lovelock has hypothesised with his theory of *Gaia*, and has proven to a reasonable extent, is that the Earth is an organism which works, and regulates itself, in much the same way as the body of one of its animals does. He suggests that all of the organisms on Earth are integrated to form this self-regulating system. The entire biotic community is to the *Gaian* body what antibodies, proteins, bacteria, viruses, molecules and the whole gamut of other cells are to the human body. Through this lens, water could be seen to be *Gaia*'s blood, rivers and streams its arteries and veins, the forests its lungs, with trees themselves as a sort of reverse alveoli, where carbon dioxide and oxygen are exchanged.

This is certainly not to say that all humans are antibodies, and that The Machine is a virus; anything but. At this moment in time it seems that industrial culture has infected humanity and turned us into something resembling more of a pox, or a parasite who wants to consume its hosts, not seeming to care that once it is devoured it will have nothing left to live on.

Yet while many of us within industrial civilisation seem to be putting on the mask of the parasite, it doesn't mean that this is our role on Earth either. Humans can be antibodies or parasites or viruses, as can other species – most often other domesticates, or those transported out of their natural habitat by way of human technologies. Some may, more controversially, argue that even the climate of our biosphere (if even the most conservative predictions by IPCC prove accurate) is itself acting as an antibody, as the rising tide that our warming planet creates threatens to flush the majority of us industrialised folk – many of whom live in coastal cities – off the face of the planet.

When we are living in our natural habitat, and in accordance with our own nature, we may be any one of the many other types of cells that naturally make up a healthy body – platelets, neurons, white blood cells and the like. When the health of the whole has become disrupted by some foreign substance, as it has been by the toxins of The Machine, we may mutate into something that is harmful to the *Gaian* body, such as a cancer, or alternatively act as one of the antibodies that help to restore its health. Humans are, and always will be, both viruses and antibodies, and to pretend otherwise would be akin to denying that both night and day exist. The extent to which we are a virus or an antibody may depend, in part, on the extent to which any one of us humans – one variety of *Gaia*'s many cells – have been penetrated by industrial antigens or other harmful invaders.

Unfortunately for both ourselves and the rest of creation, the dominant culture has forced many of us into a way of life that is parasitic, something that has hurt us as much as it has those whose lives we suck dry. But as Newton's Third Law states, 'For every action there is an equal and opposite reaction'. As the sense of grief, loss and injustice heightens to explosive levels, *Gaia* will react accordingly, and many of us who, unbeknown to ourselves, have been acting out the role of parasites, may be prompted to down our tools and assume the role of Earth's antibodies. For as Newton said, force comes in pairs. Therefore all that is left for us to do is choose, insofar as we have agency in our own decisions, whether we want our lives to be shaped in the mould of a antibody, a virus, a parasite or just a healthy bacterium in its mammoth gut.

Because I subscribe to Lovelock's perspective on the Earth being its own self-regulated organism, I believe that the antibody is an ecologically accurate analogy not just for how the depressed, alienated, enslaved and outraged masses could reawaken their purpose in response to the deluge of systemic abuse and humiliation they endure from The Machine, but for how they might organise themselves, how they could communicate, and how those called towards more revolutionary methods may come together with those who have a natural proclivity towards less combative means.

Many people want much the same thing, after all, even if they do not realise it. Rape is a symptom of a similar quality to ecological devastation or animal abuse, all of which stem from a deluded notion of separation from The Whole. Through understanding the nature of the antibody, and subsequently how we ourselves may best serve Earth and its inhabitants with our gifts, we can begin to unite what were previously considered to be disparate causes, and collectively – though each to their own individual calling – begin the long process of restoring the health and vitality of The Whole and, by interdependency, our communities, bodies, minds and souls. If you can imagine the millions of antibodies in the human body to be the millions of activists and non-profit organisations in the world, or the immune system as an analogy of activist movements as a whole, if you can think of foreign objects to be anything that damages 'the integrity, stability and beauty' of the biotic community, then you can suddenly begin to see how *Gaia* is defending Herself in more or less the same way that the human body does when under attack from a foreign substance.

Central to this book is the understanding that we will only start to see a restoration of *Gaia's* vitality when these human antibodies begin to lock themselves onto the particular antigen (industrialism, human supremacy, patriarchy and so on) that the meta-organism has summoned them to resist or neutralise, all the while respecting the fact that other antibodies are called to bind to other antigens which they aim to neutralise according to their own ability and nature. No one antibody is right because it is neutralising a certain antigen. There is, and probably always will be, millions of varieties of antigens to fight; our task is to know ourselves, know what earthly molecule we were born to be, and to then go and live it to the fullest of our nature.

In terms of how humans could resist and revolt against the invasion of the parasitic machine, the metaphor of the antibody also seems to fit the form of organisation – or lack thereof – that a resistance or revolutionary movement could mimic, and how the individual cells communicate with each other. Considering the ubiquity of the surveillance state, any underground movement of people aiming to fight back against The Machine is going to have to do so clandestinely, and with little or no traceable links between its cells. While these different cells may know of each other, and work in solidarity with one another against a common enemy, it would not be wise or strategically sound for them to be connected in any way that puts them at risk of being exposed to those who would rather see them spend their lives fighting court cases than the viruses afflicting *Gaia*.

One way in which various human antibodies can act as markers and send signals to other parts of the immune system, without communicating with each other in person and exposing themselves to the attendant risks of that, is by sending communiqués explaining their actions (perhaps anonymously signed, *The Antibodies*) and the reasons behind them to the media. If managed thoughtfully, the media could act as a secure and anonymous information dissemination tool for political ideas that their journalists wouldn't have the ideological freedom to publish otherwise. Ted Kaczynski, a.k.a. the Unabomber, employed his own unique take on this approach when he effectively forced *The New York Times* and the *Washington Post* into publishing his 35,000 word manifesto, titled *Industrial Society and Its Future*,[219] by anonymously telling them that he would 'desist from terrorism' if they did so. This is in no way intended to condone Kaczynski's acts – which generally targeted people who, within their own anthropocentric story of the world, were working in what they felt were decent jobs, paying their taxes and so on – but only to highlight what transpired to be an effective strategy for disseminating information (word of warning: it was this published manifesto that eventually got him caught, as his brother David recognised his rather unique style of writing and informed the FBI).

If resistance movements, counterintuitively, formed mutually beneficial partnerships with media outlets – with the former providing the latter with exclusive content in return for their communiqués being printed in full – underground activists could communicate more securely with each other, along with the general public, in much the same way antibodies in the human body do. In reporting these actions, to varying degrees of inaccuracy and bias, media outlets could inadvertently play a role in helping human antibodies send out signals to other parts of the immune system. It's a model that hyper-secure activists such as Wikileaks and Edward Snowden have used, people who fed the likes of the *Guardian*, *The New York Times* and *Der Spiegel* a whole series of press releases and exclusive information. These media understood that their reporting had to be reasonably balanced if they wanted to maintain their semi-exclusive partnerships. In doing so, they unleashed an entire global movement of activists concerned about online and mobile privacy who otherwise would not have been triggered into action. Through the use of a smart media strategy, human antibodies can send markers to other parts of the immune system in a way that may inspire and inform others to defend themselves against the attack of other disease-associated antigens, while minimising their own security risks.

On top of the analogy of the antibody as human activist, I also feel there is a related point to be made. Like a wild animal, an antibody does not concern itself over notions of violence or nonviolence. It is programmed, or perhaps instinctualised is a more accurate word, to attack that which damages the health and vitality of The Whole. If the antibodies and white blood cells arising in the human body were to turn pacifist, we would all be dead. Similarly, intellectuals who, from the comfort of their desks, criticise those who fight back by whatever means necessary, are the equivalent of a neuron criticising an antibody for attacking an antigen, despite the fact that the neuron would undoubtedly perish without its unappreciated protector. George Orwell, himself a revolutionary, summed this sentiment up when he said that, 'People sleep peaceably in their beds at night only because rough men stand ready to do violence on their behalf.'

Those whose natural tendencies and qualities lend themselves towards being healers of one variety or another – doctors, herbalists, shamans – are just as apt to criticise those who commit what they perceive to be acts of violence, assuming that such methods are exactly what are causing so many wounds to begin with. In doing so, these human platelets – themselves an integral part of a healthy society and a resistance movement – often seem incapable of distinguishing between reckless aggression and justifiable force. Neurons and platelets can only bring their gifts into the world because rough antibodies stand ready to protect The Whole, on whose health we all depend.

In an Age where the head rules and the heart is considered to be the folly of the unscientific, neurons are held in far greater esteem than all other cells. It is long past time for the rise of The Antibodies. For them to act to the fullest of their power they must get respect and support for their work – work that will not bring acclaim or fortune but, in all likelihood, great risk, a potential loss of freedom, and vilification from the corporate media, the public, and even friends and family. Work that most of us are often too cowardly to undertake ourselves. This is not to say that neurons and platelets are not important – they're just as important as antibodies – rather that all cells have a role in the Great Web of Life.

This is a sentiment Tolkien relayed through the character Lord Aragorn in *Lord of the Rings*, who at the beginning of the first volume was known to the simple folk of Bree and the Shire as a ranger called Strider, a roughly-clad man by appearance and one mocked by those who had no idea that their lives were protected by him and his kind on a daily basis. At one point Aragorn echoes Orwell's words, when he says:

> *And yet less thanks have we than you. Travellers scowl at us, and countrymen give us scornful names. 'Strider' I am to one fat man who lives within a day's march of foes that would freeze his heart or lay his little town in ruin, if he were not guarded ceaselessly. Yet we would not have it otherwise. If simple folk are free from care and fear, simple they will be, and we must be secret to keep them so. That has been the task of my kindred, while the years have lengthened and the grass has grown.*

The surge of industrialised antigens attacking *Gaia* today is overwhelming. The scale and deep-rootedness of the problems can leave us feeling a mixture of grief, despair and an unacknowledged remorse for our part in it all. However, it also means we live in an exciting time, one that is crying out for a new epoch of humanity which is crammed full of new solutions, ones that are not based on the same kind of thinking that got us into this ecological, social and cultural mess to begin with. In doing so, women and men from across the world have an opportunity to imbue their lives with a renewed sense of purpose, some rising out of the Earth to critique the issues (neurons), others to start the long process of healing industrialism's many wounds (platelets), while those of a different nature continue to defend the whole organism against attacks from foreign substances (antibodies).

As Tolkien knew well, there is a place for everyone in the healing of our societies and lands, for within his Fellowship of the Ring – those tasked with destroying Sauron the Industrialist – were the spiritual elves, the simple hobbits of the Shire, warriors from Gondor and Rohan, a wise old wizard, and just as importantly, Nature as represented by the ents. Only within such a wilder, more diverse approach to change may lie the first steps towards the Age of Reunion.

The good news is that the real world's hobbits, ents and elves are finally responding to The Machine's toxins. Paul Hawken writes that, 'the shared activity of hundreds of thousands of non-profit organisations can be seen as humanity's immune response to toxins like political corruption, economic disease and ecological degradation.' And while, when confronted with an honest assessment of the scale and depth of our problems, it can seem that we need a miracle, the even better news is that such miracles happen every day in the human body. For reasons not well understood by biologists, it is often when we sit on death's doorstep that our 'immune network',[220] battered and dysfunctional from an overload of chemicals, stress or infection, suddenly finds strength out of nowhere and somehow manages to overcome its attackers, eventually enabling the body to heal and regenerate.[221]

Our mission then, if we dare to accept it, is to do everything that is becoming of us – and I mean everything – to ensure we give Life every excuse to produce one more of Her miracles.

CHAPTER EIGHT

In those days we had never heard of passing up a chance to kill a wolf. In a second we were pumping lead into the pack, but with more excitement than accuracy: how to aim a steep downhill shot is always confusing. When our rifles were empty, the old wolf was down, and a pup was dragging a leg into impassable slide-rocks. We reached the old wolf in time to watch a fierce green fire dying in her eyes. I realized then, and have known ever since, that there was something new to me in those eyes – something known only to her and to the mountain. I was young then, and full of trigger-itch; I thought that because fewer wolves meant more deer, that no wolves would mean hunters' paradise. But after seeing the green fire die, I sensed that neither the wolf nor the mountain agreed with such a view.

Aldo Leopold

W E TWO-LEGGEDS ARE BECOMING too well acquainted with the inevitable heart pangs of progress. Which of us hasn't felt a deep sadness when we've returned to our home town, after some time away, only to find that the little patch of woodland we played in as a child has been mutilated by a supermarket car-park, or dissected by some godforsaken road intended to connect us to everything other than that which lies beneath it.

Though we may not have set foot in it for a decade or more, we still experience a profound sense of loss on such occasions, as if the blades which dismembered its many limbs, and shredded its unwritten stories, simultaneously lacerated a fragment of our sense of self in the process. It is well for us then – in the short term, that is – that we seem to be acutely susceptible to what fisheries scientist Daniel Pauly calls 'Shifting Baseline Syndrome'.[222] For as I will explain, without such tendencies we would likely open up a 'world of wounds'[223] which would threaten to render our manufactured realm of plastic-coated mediocrity thoroughly unbearable.

In *Feral*, George Monbiot describes Shifting Baseline Syndrome as a sort of ecological amnesia, where 'the people of every generation perceive the state of the ecosystems they encounter in their childhood as normal'. Because of this, whenever the life in our oceans or terrestrial landscapes is denuded or perceptively depleted from what ecologists, conservationists and activists understand to have been the 'natural' state around their own childhood years, such well-intentioned people usually campaign for them to be restored to the condition they remember them to have been when they were young – what is, in effect, their own ecological baseline.[224]

Therefore when we see a quarry, inhabited by hydraulic hammers and haulage trucks instead of magpies and badgers, we regret the loss of the grassy hillside we mischievously chased sheep around when we were kids. Our parents, in their time, may themselves have lamented the disappearance of the oats that once grew around those exact same slopes before our communicidal fascination with globalisation made local grain production financially infeasible, and thus massacred the livelihoods that went with it. The generations before them are likely to have, at some point, witnessed the deforestation of those hills – and the eviction of the wildlife which, until then, had dwelt within its mossy woods – in order to cultivate the grains that would feed the rapidly increasing populations of people that industrialism was breeding. To those generations, the sheep-infested grassy hillside their great grandchildren mourned may itself have seemed like a travesty. Who knows, their forbears might even have, in a silent contemplative moment, come to regret the extirpation of the wolf from what would once have been a Wild landscape, though such a perspective may only have dawned on them – if it did at all – many years after they had imagined it to be an intelligent idea to eradicate a species which their generation knew only as a foe.

This same idea could apply to our sense of society too. Communities whose ancestors once survived entirely through a non-monetary economic model that anthropologists refer to as 'gift culture' may have recently come to consider the sharing of an electric drill as their communal baseline. Others may bemoan the lack of a friendly morning hello on lands in Washington D.C. where tribes once had such a sense of interdependency and connection that their people believed that if one person in their community was ill, the entire community was ill.

While this bad case of ecological and social amnesia helps to limit our sense of loss to more emotionally manageable levels, the full extent of the cumulative tragedies that have afflicted generation after generation eventually find their way past our best defences and subconscious coping mechanisms. We may read from some literature or scientific study about how our rivers were once so densely filled with sturgeon and salmon that canoeists could catch 600 in a day with simple hooks; how the light of the sun would at times be blocked out by the sheer abundance of migratory birds; how our lands were covered in so much native woodland that a red squirrel could travel from coast to coast without ever touching the soil; or how certain indigenous peoples were so connected to their land that the act of ploughing it would feel no less violent than running the sharp edge of a knife along the scalp of their mother. Our ecological state is so impoverished in the early 21st century that we can scarcely believe what seem to be the far-fetched stories of only a century or so ago.

The depth of our ecological and cultural loss has other ways of making itself known to us more potent than the written word; more often than not it pierces our protective layers through felt experience. The realisation that our own childhoods were not some golden age of ecological health may dawn on us through exposure, by discovery on our travels, to that rare wild landscape so unspoiled by human ambition that our own ecological baseline begins to feel painfully mediocre – leaving us with the feeling of having been robbed of something we hadn't even realised we had ever possessed. Or we may experience a sort of 'genetic memory' when we stumble upon a dead doe and find that, not only do we instinctively know how to pick her up, but that she fits around our neck and back as if she were tailored for us.[225] Our intrigue with the ways of our ancestors may tempt a few of us into a psychedelic experience of one sort or another, where we journey into realms previously outside of our awareness and encounter aspects of our timeless selves which our conscious mind was attempting to protect us from. One way or another, most of us at some point in our lives come eye to eye with a world we have never known and, if we allow ourselves to, we experience the grief that goes hand in hand with such primal loss.

Whatever the stimuli, when the veil of separation is dropped, and we understand our interdependency on a world whose fabric has been ripped into rags, the only reaction that doesn't seem excruciatingly naïve is despair. But while hope, however unsubstantiated, continues to receive all the platitudes – despite its cyclical disintegration under the weight of its own ineffectiveness, and the inevitable cynicism and fatigue that follows – despair somehow continues to get bad press. Hope is positive, we are told, and despair is negative.

Flying in the face of conventional wisdom, it is perhaps despair and not hope which we urgently must feel today. Hope, like reformism, can have the unintended effect of making what ought to be intolerable more tolerable. After all, we are told that any tribulation can be endured as long as there is hope, and it can seem to help us through many a dark hour. But while everyone claims to need this mysterious feeling, it's actually a peculiar thing to desire.

Hope is a sort of admittance of powerlessness, and it can be a strange source of much inaction. At a talk Derrick Jensen once gave, someone in the audience asked him to define hope and, not having a readily-prepared answer, he asked the audience to collectively come up with one. After much discussion, they decided that 'hope is a longing for a future condition over which you have no agency'. To qualify this, he added:

> *Think about it. I'm not, for example, going to say I hope I eat something tomorrow. I'll just do it. I don't hope to take another breath right now, nor that I finish writing this sentence. I just do them. On the other hand, I hope that the next time I get on a plane, it doesn't crash. To hope for some result means you have no agency concerning it. So many people say they hope the dominant culture stops destroying the world. By saying that, they've guaranteed at least its short-term continuation, and given it a power it doesn't have. They've also stepped away from their own power.*[226]

The need for hope is understandable, of course. We all want to feel like something better is on the horizon even if, for whatever reasons, we're not particularly motivated to do anything to make it happen. Who amongst us would strive for despair after all, and only the most dangerously arrogant and deluded people would believe that they have complete agency over the whole world's problems.

Where I differ ever so slightly with Jensen is in my belief that it is possible to do everything within one's power to weaken industrialism's death grip on The Whole, whilst retaining a very human hope that these actions are effective and are not hijacked or scuppered by forces over which we, individually, have little or no agency. Be that as it may, the admirable brand of hope that beautifully accompanies one's best efforts is sadly joining those it aims to defend on the endangered species list, whilst the kind of hope that has become a toxic substitute for action is spreading like an invasive species across the political terrain that activists once dared to travail.

This desire for the latter, more pathetic brand of hope is a powerful influence on the publishing industry, which by way of a chicken-and-egg loop goes on to feed the appetite for a hope that asks nothing of people. Publishers, keen on sales, and therefore editing with them in mind, almost never want to produce books related to social change that don't finish on a positive and optimistic note.

Instead, they prefer to offer the reader some desperately unrealistic

or ill-thought-out future scenario or solution that is palatable to their delicate sensibilities, where as long as we do x, y and z, things will magically
work out fine, despite the fact that x, y and z have no basis in ecological,
social, political or economic reality. Publishers want their authors to go
out on a fist-pumping, 'we can do this' high, leaving the reader inspired
and feeling good, as if the mere reading of their words was enough to
bring about radical change in and of itself.

The fact that this book (which is a rallying cry for more difficult but
realistic action instead of the usually unrealistic but easy hope) has been
published at all is a testament to the courage of my publishers, rather
than an indicator of the industry's integrity in presenting an objective
portrayal of the threats facing the Great Web of Life – an approach which
would, by way of its honesty, equip and prepare us better for what we're
facing. Although hope has an even better track record than J.K. Rowling
for selling paperbacks, unrealistically hopeful endings are more often
than not counterproductive in terms of creating the social change that the
authors of many non-fiction books may claim to want to effect. This lack
of honesty is problematic, considering the power of the written word to
influence us, individually and collectively.

I would love to sit here and tell you how bright our future is looking
if we do this or that, but I can't, at least not in terms that most people
would consider bright. The human experiment has gone badly wrong. We
have messed things up far too much for far too long, and to think we can
undo the phenomenal complexity and extremity of the destructiveness of
our culture by tweaking our consumption and waste habits, or by growing
a handful of peas and herbs in our tiny urban gardens, is ludicrous. Any
author who tells you that minor reforms (or even major reforms) to the
military-media-industrial complex will suffice is only doing so because
either he or she is not looking honestly at the gravity of the industrial
conundrum, is grossly misinformed, or because they want to sell lots of
copies of their book.

An overly optimistic approach, where people jump on the bandwagon
of some unrealistic hope that has no foundation in politico-economic
reality, will not only fail its adherents, but once reality hits home hard, will
inevitably lead to despair, cynicism and the potential recuperation of a
movement by The Machine. The sixties are a testament to this, where those
who sang songs, made daisy chains and joined hands for peace (convinced

by Lennon et al. that this would stop the War on Everything) eventually became so disillusioned by the failure of their blatantly ineffective actions that they were recuperated by the corporate world, whose business models and products demanded they go to War on Life. If Lennon had penned a tune called 'Give Full-Spectrum Resistance and Revolt a Chance' instead of 'Give Peace a Chance', such a scale of a movement may have had the potential to create genuine systemic change. Unfortunately such brutal honesty is rarely fashionable or catchy and so it probably wouldn't have made it to number one in the charts, or been sung by those nonviolent cadres who seemed to think The Establishment would be shaken by peaceful protest alone (peaceful, that is, towards the purveyors of systemic violence, but not towards the inevitable victims of ineffective protest).

That said, the future is bright, but in a way almost the entirety of our species are unable to see yet. There is hope, just not as we know it. Our hope lies, rather ironically, in giving up on hope – to start with – and embracing despair, as it is from this more honest position that the potential for an appropriate response lies. From this low point we can really feel the fullness of what we've lost, to the extent that we will need to if there is to be 'an equal and opposite reaction' to the forces that caused it. Despair can become a springboard from which people resolve to deal with the institutions and culture which controls our lives, in a manner that is befitting of what's before us.

It is often the case that those with alcoholism, or other addictions, have to fully understand that they've lost absolutely everything they value – the partner, the children, the job, the house, the car – before they can start the long journey back to living in a way that is healthy for them. It's what I call the bouncing ball effect, as we often need to hit rock bottom in order to bounce back up again. Hope, despite its best of intentions, cushions the floor and gives us a soft landing, meaning we don't bounce back with the vigour we invariably need. Once we sit with despair for as long as it serves us, we can move forward better equipped to deal with our situation as it really is. As renowned organisational behaviourist Margaret Wheatley suggested, 'The cure for despair is not hope. It's discovering what we want to do about something we care about.'[227]

We would be wise to cease putting all our eggs in the inactive hope basket, and start acting upon whatever ideas and strategies we believe will give us our best shot at defending our communities and lands from those institutionalised forces that want to monetise and mechanise them even further. I believe that one of our best chances of success in restoring the ecological health of the planet, and the human and non-human communities that comprise it, lies with the return of the wolf – literally, symbolically and metaphorically.

On a literal level, the return of the wolf – a species whom I use to symbolise the whole range of keystone species which we have eradicated from our subdued, monocultural landscapes out of an irrational fear of all things Wild – is absolutely essential if we are to begin the long road back to ecological diversity and health. Keystone species are animals, plants and other forms of life that have a disproportionately large effect on their surrounding landscape relative to their population level or abundance, and who play an essential role in maintaining the health and structure of a particular biome.

In the Yellowstone National Park, ecologists found that by introducing one particular keystone species, the grey wolf, 70 years after they had been exterminated, dramatic changes happened to the park. When they first brought them back in 1995, 'many of the streamsides and riversides were almost bare, closely cropped by the high population of red deer'. With the return of the wolf, this began to change. Not only did the wolves keep the number of deer down to healthy population levels, 'they altered their prey's behaviour'. As ecologists soon found out, the presence of the wolf ensured that 'the deer avoided the places – particularly the valleys and gorges – where they could be caught most easily'.

Because of this, trees (free from the browsing of too many deer) returned to the riverbanks and grew larger, which in turn shaded the rivers, providing cool habitat for fish and other species who soon returned. Beavers came back, whose habits created the conditions for otters, muskrats, reptiles and much else to follow suit. The 'bare valleys began reverting to aspen, willow and cottonwood forest', and these healthy new conditions persuaded bison to come home again. As the trees grew without the threat of deer, the rate of erosion was reduced, leading to more stable banks of streams and, as another beneficial knock-on effect, 'a greater diversity of pools and riffles'. By hunting coyotes, the wolves helped 'the populations of smaller mammals – such as rabbits and mice – to rise, providing prey for hawks, weasels, foxes and badgers', while 'eagles and ravens fed on the remains of the deer the wolves killed'.[228]

The list of changes goes on and on, hand-in-hand with a dramatic upsurge in biodiversity and the health of the land.

When you consider the denuded, monocultural landscapes of industrial nations such as England with this in mind, you begin to understand how the absence of natural predators such as the wolf is something much greater to fear than the creatures themselves. For as Aldo Leopold once said:

> *I now suspect that just as a deer herd lives in mortal fear of its wolves, so does a mountain live in mortal fear of its deer. And perhaps with better cause, for while a buck pulled down by wolves can be replaced within two or three years, a range pulled down by too many deer may fail of replacement in as many decades ... hence we have dustbowls, and rivers washing the future into the sea.*[229]

The experience of rewilded areas the world over is similar to Yellowstone. And they are telling us the same thing: that we would be wise to move beyond our myth-based fears of the mega-fauna and apex predators who once roamed our lands and kept the sublime fabric of The Whole, which they once helped weave, inexplicably intact. Not only that, they are telling us that if we are to fear anything, it ought to be our arrogance, that unfortunate quality of the scientific human who believes that not only can he comprehend and quantify the unimaginable complexity of the Great Web of Life, but that he can somehow manage it with fence posts, synthetic pesticides and official 10 year plans.

Protecting and allowing wilderness to simply *be* is valuable on its own terms, as every species on Earth has the same right to live in accordance with its own nature as humans do. But even if the anthropocentric lies we've incrementally convinced ourselves of over millennia were true, and that Nature's worth can only be calculated by its value to a humanity whose lives are somehow more sacred than all others, allowing The Wild back into our world is of utmost importance even from a narrow-minded selfish perspective.

We humans depend on healthy ecosystems, with niches packed full of creatures great and small, to physically survive and thrive. For one, we need landscapes rich with an abundance of Life – away from the sterile urban centres that dominate our mental terrain as much as our geographical maps – to help us keep some semblance of sanity, and to retain outlets which our primitive selves subconsciously crave. We need to renew a deeper spiritual connection to Life if we are to have any chance of desisting from treating Her like some limitless filling station, and instead start treating Her as part of our own flesh and bones. Until we understand such things, in our hearts as much as our heads, we will never defend Life with the same vitality and ferocity with which we would rightfully defend our own bodies.

Wild Nature's value to us doesn't stop there. Wild animals keep us in touch with the rhythms of Life and our immediate surroundings. To live within or traverse an area where predators such as wolves live, you need to develop a keen eye for its tracks, a good nose for its smells, and a sound understanding of the season and time of day, so you are aware of when it will be protective of its young, or when and where it will be out looking for food. The threat of death, ironically, can sometimes keep us fully alive. Take it away, and we end up going for mid-afternoon strolls in the country, oblivious to the qualities and lives of the myriad species which together make up the ecosystems on whose health ours depends. If we don't even pay attention to the wondrous details of the animate, living breathing world around us, we certainly won't lose any sleep in killing most of it. Worse still, we end up where we are now, living mediocre lives and suffering from potentially fatal levels of 'ecological boredom',[230] medicated to barely manageable levels by anti-depressants, celebrity news and retail therapy.

While there are no end of things for environmental and social justice campaigners to be *against*, the rewilding of the Earth is a cause that we all could unite in solidarity *for*. For once Life is released from its human shackles and allowed to run wild and free once again, the long road back to social, ecological and personal health can begin in earnest. All that it requires is for us to turn our energy away from pursuits laced with death and destruction and into the path of great healing, using whatever gifts we ourselves have been given. For that to happen we must blow to pieces a politico-economic system whose dark forces are intent on convincing and forcing us to continue using our intelligence and skills to convert our ecological and cultural commons into numbers.

While the return of the wolf, and the many keystone species it symbolises, is critical to the future of Life in a literal sense, metaphorically speaking its return is just as important to our political and activist landscapes. The landscape of activism today is, like the forests of England and Ireland, dominated by the deer. I love the doe in particular, and the gentleness and grace she exudes and symbolises, and her place in The Whole is as sacred as all others. However, our monocultural political terrain is in as much need of a ferocious predator as our monocultural forests are. New, fragile saplings sprout out of our politico-economic lands every day, brimming with a desire to take root, grow and bring life back to the planet, but are browsed to death before they can make any significant impact on their surroundings.

This isn't due to the corporate-state coalition wiping out all opposition to their regime – neoliberal regimes need a façade of freedom of speech (though not freedom of action), remember – but more down to the fact that, like in the wilderness, they and their ideological partners have simply endeavoured to wipe out one keystone species, the Wild Revolutionary, while permitting a hand-picked selection of domesticated animals – reformists, pacifists and the like – to browse within carefully demarcated fence posts.

There will always be comfortable people who want to eradicate the wolf from the ecological and political terrains, and so there must always be people willing to put their lives on the line to ensure that the wolf is a constant presence, lurking in the shadows, waiting for us to enter realms in which we have no right to go without respect for what is there already.

In Yellowstone National Park, ecologists and environmentalists didn't have to raid Noah's Ark and reintroduce every species that ever lived there by themselves. All that was required was a little humility, coupled with an ability to understand one simple truth: that we have a lot more to fear from trying to micro-manage the complexity of Life than we have from allowing it to find its own harmonious balance. All it took at Yellowstone was the introduction of one ferocious creature in order for biodiversity and health to return. And so it goes with the national parks of our political landscapes. The fierceness of the wolf has its own unique place alongside the gentleness of the doe, the beaver's enterprise, the salmon's indomitable will, the heron's grace, the fox's cunning, the male Mandarin duck's beauty – all of whom, when allowed to live in accordance with their own nature, keep each other in check and the integrity of The Whole intact and strong. The doe strangely needs the wolf as much as the wolf needs the doe, and we all need them both.

If the day comes when we accept that both fierceness and gentleness have their appropriate time and place within our struggles in defence of Life, we may once again earn the chance to experience the only real peace there has ever been: the peace of The Wild.

ACKNOWLEDGEMENTS

Despite what the front cover might fool you into believing, the words in this book do not really belong to me. They're an accumulation of all that has come before them: my ancestry; the conversations I've had; the blunders I've made; the books I've read; the ale I've drunk; the forests I've camped in; the films I've watched; the challenges I've faced; the love and kindness I've received and, for better or worse, the culture I was born into. Considering the complexity of our lives, it would be impossible to thank every one and every thing that, without knowing it, contributed to this book.

That said, there are people whom I would love to convey my most heartfelt gratitude towards. Firstly, to those directly involved in bringing this book into the world. To Kirsty Alston, for visually encapsulating the ideas in the book so beautifully on the cover and, most importantly of all, for wanting to share and explore life with me, the mere thought of which warms the cockles of my heart. To Jess Pasteiner for her literary guidance and years of loving support, Tom Smith for his invaluable feedback, Paul Kingsnorth for putting his little red pen to rigorous use, Fergus Drennan for his musings and illegible notes, and Leigh Pearson for his subtle but important refining. To Benji for breaking up the monotony of editing by insisting I take him out for walks, giving me fresh perspective. To them all for their generosity and friendship over the years.

I want to say a special thanks to the inspirational Maddy and Tim Harland (along with Tony, Rozie, John, Emma and the rest of the fantastic team) at Permanent Publications for their integrity, courage and enthusiasm, and to everyone at New Society Publishers for their exceptional efforts releasing this book in the United States. I'm always indebted to my agent Sallyanne Sweeney at Mulcahy Associates, who somehow manages to get my work out to far more people than I ever would have imagined.

There are many others who had no direct involvement in the book, but who have contributed greatly to my life and work in many other ways.

To mam and dad, for your relentless support and the love you continue to give me. I couldn't imagine better parents. There are too many wonderful friends to list, but people like Shaun Chamberlin, Brian Merrifield, Mari Rapeli, Emily Skinner, Chris Adams, Martin Gallagher, Stephen Ward and Gerard Ferguson stand out by way of longevity, a quality I really value. To my community, both near and far, thank you all for your friendship over the years.

ENDNOTES

1. Figures according to UNESCO.
2. Figures according to Oxfam.
3. Fanon, Frantz (2001). *The Wretched of the Earth*. Penguin.
4. Best, Steven and Nocella II, Anthony J. (2006). *Igniting a Revolution: Voices in Defence of the Earth*. AK Press.
5. www.telegraph.co.uk/news/uknews/1468011/Glaxo-chief-animal-rights-cowards-are-terrorising-us.html
6. Jensen, Derrick (2006). *Endgame Volume 1: The Problem of Civilisation*. Seven Stories Press.
7. Potter, Will (2011). *Green is the New Red: An Insider's Account of a Social Movement Under Siege*. City Lights Books. p.41.
8. Boyle, Mark (2012). *The Moneyless Manifesto*. Permanent Publications.
9. Hallas, Duncan (1973). 'Controversy: Do We Support Reformist Demands?' *International Socialism* (1st series), No.54.
10. www.sheldrake.org/research/morphic-resonance/introduction
11. Thoreau, Henry David (2008). *Walden*. Oxford's World Classics.
12. Lorde, Audre (2013). 'The Master's Tools Will Never Dismantle the Master's House'. In *Sister Outsider: Essays and Speeches*. Ten Speed Press; Reprint edition.
13. Churchill, Ward and Ryan, Mike (2007). *Pacifism as Pathology: Reflections on the Role of Armed Struggle in North America*. AK Press. p.103.
14. wwf.panda.org/about_our_earth/biodiversity/biodiversity/
15. Manes, Christopher (1990). *Green Rage: Radical Environmentalism and the Unmaking of Civilisation*. Little, Brown. p.xi.
16. Eisenstein, Charles (2007). *The Ascent of Humanity*. Panenthea.
17. Žižek, Slavoj (2009). *Violence: Six Sideways Reflections*. Profile Books. p.174.
18. Thoreau, Henry David (1860). 'A Plea for Captain John Brown'. In Redpath, James, *Echos' for Harpers Ferry*. Thayer and Eldridge.
19. Churchill, Ward and Ryan, Mike (2007). *Pacifism as Pathology: Reflections on the Role of Armed Struggle in North America*. AK Press. p.20.

20. Nietzsche, Friedrich (1886). *Beyond Good and Evil*. Penguin Classics; Revised edition.

21. Guevara, Ernesto 'Che' (1965). *From Algiers, for Marcha: The Cuban Revolution Today*. Marcha.

22. Blake, William (1810). 'And Did Those Feet in Ancient Time'. Preface to *Milton a Poem*.

23. Heidegger, Martin (1977). *The Question Concerning Technology: And Other Essays*. Harper Perennial.

24. Nick Dearden is the director of the World Development Movement.

25. Evernden, Neil (1999). *The Natural Alien: Humankind and Environment*. University of Toronto Press. p.10.

26. Watts, Alan (1975). *Psychotherapy East and West*. Vintage.

27. Eisenstein, Charles (2007). *The Ascent of Humanity*. Panenthea.

28. Monbiot, George (2013). *Feral: Searching for Enchantment on the Frontiers of Rewilding*. Allen Lane. p.69.

29. Leopold, Aldo (1968). *A Sand County Almanac and Sketches Here and There*. OUP USA; Enlarged edition.

30. www.theguardian.com/global-development/poverty-matters/2013/nov/27/price-nature-markets-natural-capital

31. www.monbiot.com/2014/04/22/reframing-the-planet/

32. www.theguardian.com/global-development/poverty-matters/2013/nov/27/price-nature-markets-natural-capital

33. Evernden, Neil (1999). *The Natural Alien: Humankind and Environment*. University of Toronto Press. p.10.

34. www.theguardian.com/environment/2014/jan/13/shale-gas-fracking-cameron-all-out

35. Jones, Pattrice (2006). 'Stomping with the Elephants: Feminist Principles for Radical Solidarity'. In Steven Best and Anthony J. Nocella (eds), *Igniting a Revolution: Voices in Defence of the Earth*. AK Press. pp.319-329.

36. Jones, Pattrice (2006). 'Stomping with the Elephants: Feminist Principles for Radical Solidarity'. In Steven Best and Anthony J. Nocella (eds), *Igniting a Revolution: Voices in Defence of the Earth*. AK Press. pp.319-329.

37. www.theguardian.com/commentisfree/2014/apr/07/climate-change-violence-occupy-earth

38. Žižek, Slavoj (2009). *Violence: Six Sideways Reflections*. Profile Books. pp.99-100.

39. Potter, Will (2011). *Green is the New Red: An Insider's Account of a Social Movement Under Siege*. City Lights Books. pp.40-43.

40. Weber, Max (1970). 'Politics as a Vocation'. In H. H. Gerth and C. W. Mills (eds), *From Max Weber*. Routledge. p.70.

41. Garver, Newton (1968). 'What Violence Is'. In Vittorio Bufacchi (ed), *Violence: A Philosophical Anthology*. Palgrave Macmillan. p.170.

42. Monbiot, George (2013). *Feral: Searching for Enchantment on the Frontiers of Rewilding*. Allen Lane. p.9.

43. www.bbc.co.uk/news/uk-england-25622644

44. Bufacchi, Vittorio (2009). *Violence: A Philosophical Anthology*. Palgrave Macmillan. p.207.

45. Garver, Newton (1968). 'What Violence Is'. In Vittorio Bufacchi (ed), *Violence: A Philosophical Anthology*. Palgrave Macmillan. p.171.

46. Gelderloos, Peter (2013). *The Failure of Nonviolence: From the Arab Spring to Occupy*. Left Bank Books. p.20.

47. Gelderloos, Peter (2013). *The Failure of Nonviolence: From the Arab Spring to Occupy*. Left Bank Books. p.17.

48. Ryan, Mike (2007). 'On Ward Churchill's "Pacifism as Pathology": Toward a Revolutionary Practice'. In Churchill, Ward and Ryan, Mike, *Pacifism as Pathology: Reflections on the Role of Armed Struggle in North America*. AK Press. p.126.

49. Jensen, Derrick (2007). Preface to Churchill, Ward and Ryan, Mike, *Pacifism as Pathology: Reflections on the Role of Armed Struggle in North America*. AK Press. p.4.

50. Kuhn, Gabriel (2014). *Turning Money into Rebellion: The Unlikely Story of Denmark's Revolutionary Bank Robbers*. PM Press. p.86.

51. Kumar, Satish (2005). *The Buddha and The Terrorist*. Green Books.

52. Keynes, John Maynard (1965). *The General Theory of Employment, Interest, and Money*. Mariner Books.

53. Plumwood, Val (1993). *Feminism and the Mastery of Nature*. Routledge.

54. Singer, Peter (1995). *Animal Liberation*. Pimlico; 2nd edition.

55. www.sciencemag.org/content/162/3859/1243.full

56. www.monbiot.com/1994/01/01/the-tragedy-of-enclosure/

57. Leopold, Aldo (1968). *A Sand County Almanac and Sketches Here and There*. OUP USA; Enlarged edition.

58. Underwood Spencer, Paula (1983). *Who Speaks for Wolf*. Tribe of Two Press.

59. www.theguardian.com/environment/2014/nov/29/animal-rights-group-sounds-alarm-over-40m-farm-deaths

60. Illich, Ivan (1974). *Medical Nemesis: The Expropriation of Health*. Marion Boyars.

61. Barnet, Robert (2003). 'Ivan Illich and the Nemesis of Medicine'. *Medicine, Health Care and Philosophy* 6 (3): 273–286. Kluwer Academic Publishers.

62. Wolff, Robert Paul (1969). 'On Violence'. In Vittorio Bufacchi (ed), *Violence: A Philosophical Anthology*. Palgrave Macmillan. p.59.

63. Gelderloos, Peter (2013). *The Failure of Nonviolence: From the Arab Spring to Occupy*. Left Bank Books. p.139.

64. Jensen, Derrick (2007). Preface to Churchill, Ward and Ryan, Mike, *Pacifism as Pathology: Reflections on the Role of Armed Struggle in North America*. AK Press. p.11.

65. Lemkin, Raphael (1944). *Axis Rule in Occupied Europe*. The Lawbook Exchange, Ltd.; 2nd edition.

66. Higgins, Polly (2010). *Eradicating Ecocide: Laws and Governance to Stop the Destruction of the Planet*. Shepheard-Walwyn.

67. http://eradicatingecocide.com/overview/ecocide-act/

68. www.reuters.com/article/2012/09/25/climate-inaction-idINDEE88O0HH20120925

69. Schumacher, E.F. (1988). *Small is Beautiful: A Study of Economics as if People Mattered*. Abacus.

70. Mitchell, Alana (2008). *Seasick: The Hidden Ecological Crises of the Global Ocean*. Oneworld. p.8.

71. Worm, Boris et al. (2006). 'Impacts of Biodiversity Loss on Ocean Ecosystem Services'. *Science* 314 (5800). p.787.

72. Davies, R.W.D. (2009). *Defining and Estimating Global Marine Fisheries Bycatch*. Marine Policy.

73. Mitchell, Alana (2008). *Seasick: The Hidden Ecological Crises of the Global Ocean*. Oneworld. p.83.

74. http://sawfish.saveourseas.com/threats/climate

75. Mitchell, Alana (2008). *Seasick: The Hidden Ecological Crises of the Global Ocean*. Oneworld. p.84.

76. Pimm, S.L. et al. (1995). 'The Future of Biodiversity'. *Science* 269. pp.347–350.

77. www.occupyforanimals.net/animal-kill-counter.html

78. McBay, Aric (2011). *Deep Green Resistance: Strategy to Save the Planet*. Seven Stories Press. p.239.

79. McBay, Aric (2011). *Deep Green Resistance: Strategy to Save the Planet*. Seven Stories Press. p.243.

80. Jensen, Derrick (2006). *Endgame Volume 1: The Problem of Civilisation*. Seven Stories Press.

81. Ellul, Jacques and Merton, Robert K. (1964). *The Technological Society*.

Vintage Books. p.vi.

82. Eisenstein, Charles (2007). *The Ascent of Humanity*. Panenthea. p.206.

83. Eisenstein, Charles (2011). *Sacred Economics: Money, Gift and Society in the Age of Transition*. Evolver Editions.

84. http://discovermagazine.com/1987/may/02-the-worst-mistake-in-the-history-of-the-human-race

85. Ellul, Jacques (1964). *The Technological Society*. Vintage Books. p.5.

86. Engels, Frederick and Marx, Karl (1859). *Economic and Philosophic Manuscripts of 1844*. Progress Publishers.

87. Hawken, Paul (2008). *Blessed Unrest: How the Largest Social Movement in History Is Restoring Grace, Justice, and Beauty to the World*. Penguin. p.102.

88. Reuleaux, Franz (1876). *The Kinematics of Machinery: Outlines of a Theory of Machines*. Kessinger Publishing.

89. Mumford, Lewis (1971). *Technics and Human Development: The Myth of the Machine Volume 1*. Harcourt Publishers Ltd. p.191.

90. www.egs.edu/faculty/slavoj-zizek/articles/the-structure-of-domination-today-a-lacanian-view/

91. Olson, Miles (2012). *Unlearn, Rewild*. New Society Publishers.

92. Hancox, Dan (2013). *The Village Against the World*. Verso.

93. Mumford, Lewis (1971). *Technics and Human Development: The Myth of the Machine Volume 1*. Harcourt Publishers Ltd. p.294.

94. Fasching, Darrell J. (1981). *The Thought of Jacques Ellul: A Systematic Exposition*. Vintage Books. p.17.

95. www.theguardian.com/news/2013/nov/20/mental-health-antidepressants-global-trends

96. www.reuters.com/article/2013/10/31/us-usa-poll-crime-idUSBRE99U11Z20131031

97. May, Rollo (1991). *The Cry for Myth*. W. W. Norton & Company.

98. Brown Jr., Tom (1999). *The Science and Art of Tracking*. G P Putnam's Sons; Berkley Trade Paperback edition.

99. Thoreau, Henry David (2008). *Walden*. Oxford's World Classics.

100. Zinn, Howard (2009). *The Zinn Reader: Writings on Disobedience and Democracy*. Seven Stories Press.

101. Rumi, Jelaluddin (2008). *The Essential Rumi*. Harper Collins. p.16.

102. Churchill, Ward (1999). *Fantasies of the Master Race: Literature, Cinema and the Colonization of American Indians*. City Lights Books.

103. Caygill, Howard (2013). *On Resistance: A Philosophy of Defiance*. Bloomsbury. p.10.

104. Gelderloos, Peter (2007). *How Nonviolence Protects the State*. South End Press. p.21.

105. http://discovermagazine.com/2013/may/05-how-ant-slaves-overthrow-their-masters

106. Churchill, Ward and Ryan, Mike (2007). *Pacifism as Pathology: Reflections on the Role of Armed Struggle in North America*. AK Press. p.57.

107. Eagleton, Terry (2012). *Why Marx Was Right*. Yale University Press.

108. Goldman, Emma (1911). *Anarchism and Other Essays*. Mother Earth Publishing Association.

109. This is a term that was widely used to describe various related movements that developed in several societies in the former Soviet Union, the Balkans and the Middle East, encompassing everything from the People Power Revolution (also know as the 'Yellow' revolution) in the Philippines to the 'Jasmine' revolution in Tunisia.

110. Farnish, Keith (2013). *Underminers: A Guide to Subverting the Machine*. New Society Publishers.

111. Hancox, Dan (2013). *The Village Against the World*. Verso.

112. www.theguardian.com/books/2013/oct/10/village-against-world-dan-hancox-review

113. www.theguardian.com/world/2013/oct/20/marinaleda-spanish-communist-village-utopia

114. Pickering, Leslie James (2006). *Earth Liberation Front: 1997-2002*. Arissa Media Group.

115. Holmgren, David (2013). *Crash on Demand*. http://holmgren.com.au/crash-demand/

116. Gift culture is a complex subject I have previously explored in depth in *The Moneyless Manifesto*, but in short it is an anthropological term which refers to a social system where goods and services are not sold, but given without any explicit agreement for immediate or future rewards.

117. https://youtu.be/0v33cxzPcps

118. This refers to the Social Democratic Party of Germany, or the *Sozialdemokratische Partei Deutschlands*.

119. Luxemburg, Rosa (1900). *Reform or Revolution*.

120. Caygill, Howard (2013). *On Resistance: A Philosophy of Defiance*. Bloomsbury. p.209.

121. Caygill, Howard (2013). *On Resistance: A Philosophy of Defiance*. Bloomsbury. p.210.

122. Gelderloos, Peter (2013). *The Failure of Nonviolence: From the Arab Spring to Occupy*. Left Bank Books. pp.36-38.

123. Gelderloos, Peter (2013). *The Failure of Nonviolence: From the Arab Spring to Occupy*. Left Bank Books. pp.36-38.

124. Jensen, Derrick (2006). *Endgame Volume 1: The Problem of Civilisation*. Seven Stories Press.

125. Pickering, Leslie James (2006). *Earth Liberation Front: 1997-2002*. Arissa Media Group.

126. Gelderloos, Peter (2013). *The Failure of Nonviolence: From the Arab Spring to Occupy*. Left Bank Books. p.12.

127. Mandela, Nelson (1995). *Long Walk To Freedom*. Abacus.

128. Alinsky, Saul (1971). *Rules for Radicals: A Pragmatic Primer for Realistic Radicals*. Vintage Books. p.24.

129. Bondaroff, Teale Phelps (2009). *Bitter Green: An Examination of the Strategy of Ecotage*. Undergraduate Honours Thesis. University of Calgary.

130. Kuhn, Gabriel (2014). *Turning Money into Rebellion: The Unlikely Story of Denmark's Revolutionary Bank Robbers*. PM Press. p.83.

131. Abbey, Edward (1984). *Beyond the Wall: Essays from the Outside*. Henry Holt & Company Inc.

132. Dewey, John (1934). *Art as Experience*. Perigee Books. p.59.

133. Watts, Alan (1960). *The Nature of Consciousness*. https://youtu.be/jX8PqznN0ao

134. Calaprice, Alice (2005). *The New Quotable Einstein*. Princeton University Press. p.206.

135. Jensen, Derrick (2004). *A Language Older Than Words*. Souvenir Press Ltd. pp.33-34.

136. Eisenstein, Charles (2007). *The Ascent of Humanity*. Panenthea.

137. Foreman, Dave & Haywood, Bill (2002). *Ecodefense: A Field Guide to Monkeywrenching*. Abbzug Press. p.3.

138. Jensen, Derrick (2007). Preface to Churchill, Ward and Ryan, Mike, *Pacifism as Pathology: Reflections on the Role of Armed Struggle in North America*. AK Press. p.11.

139. Leopold, Aldo (1968). *A Sand County Almanac and Sketches Here and There*. OUP USA; Enlarged edition.

140. Jensen, Derrick (2006). *Endgame Volume 1: The Problem of Civilisation*. Seven Stories Press.

141. Eisenstein, Charles (2007). *The Ascent of Humanity*. Panenthea.

142. Ryan, Mike (2007). 'On Ward Churchill's "Pacifism as Pathology": Toward a Revolutionary Practice'. In Churchill, Ward and Ryan, Mike, *Pacifism as Pathology: Reflections on the Role of Armed Struggle in North America*. AK Press. p.148.

143. This is a tactic used by activists to temporarily hamper the progress of The Machine, usually involving one or more people locking themselves to equipment or fellow activists, using various means (such as bike locks), in such a way as to make it very difficult for police or security forces to move them quickly without injuring them.

144. Biko, Steve (1987). *I Write What I Like: A Selection of Writings*. Heinemann.

145. Garver, Newton (1968). 'What Violence Is'. In Vittorio Bufacchi (ed), *Violence: A Philosophical Anthology*. Palgrave Macmillan. p.170.

146. Garver, Newton (1968). 'What Violence Is'. In Vittorio Bufacchi (ed), *Violence: A Philosophical Anthology*. Palgrave Macmillan. p.170.

147. www.thedailybeast.com/articles/2013/12/09/nelson-mandela-demanded-justice-before-forgiving-white-south-africans.html

148. Ongerth, Steve (2010). *Redwood Uprising*. www.judibari.info/book

149. Churchill, Ward and Ryan, Mike (2007). *Pacifism as Pathology: Reflections on the Role of Armed Struggle in North America*. AK Press. p.71.

150. Goldman, Emma (1911). *Anarchism and Other Essays*. Mother Earth Publishing Association.

151. Gelderloos, Peter (2007). *How Nonviolence Protects the State*. South End Press. pp.108-117.

152. Potter, Will (2011). *Green is the New Red: An Insider's Account of a Social Movement Under Siege*. City Lights Books. p.41.

153. www.greenisthenewred.com/blog/green-scare/#13972952879481&action=collapse_widget&id=3021786

154. McBay, Aric (2011). *Deep Green Resistance: Strategy to Save the Planet*. Seven Stories Press. p.243.

155. Foreman, Dave & Haywood, Bill (2002). *Ecodefense: A Field Guide to Monkeywrenching*. Abbzug Press. p.9.

156. The Luddites were a movement of working class artisans who correctly feared that 'labour-saving' machines would annihilate both their livelihood, their skills and their place in their world.

157. Manes, Christopher (1990). Interview with Bill Devall, Grand Canyon, Ariz., July 10, 1987. In *Green Rage: Radical Environmentalism and the Unmaking of Civilisation*. Little, Brown. p.176.

158. www.historyplace.com/speeches/mandela.htm

159. Marx, Karl (1990). *Capital: Critique of Political Economy v.1*. Penguin Classics.

160. Manes, Christopher (1990). Interview with Bill Devall, Grand Canyon, Ariz., July 10, 1987. In *Green Rage: Radical Environmentalism and the Unmaking of Civilisation*. Little, Brown. p.176.

161. A distributed denial-of-service (DDoS) attack is an attempt by two or more persons to make a machine or network unavailable to its users, and generally comprises efforts to indefinitely interrupt services of a host connected to the Internet.

162. Potter, Will (2011). *Green is the New Red: An Insider's Account of a Social Movement Under Siege.* City Lights Books. p.45.

163. To be considered domestic terrorism in the U.S., an act must fulfil the following criteria: (a) Involve acts dangerous to human life that violate federal or state law; (b) Appear intended (i) to intimidate or coerce a civilian population; (ii) to influence the policy of a government by intimidation or coercion; or (iii) to affect the conduct of a government by mass destruction, assassination, or kidnapping; and (c) Occur primarily within the territorial jurisdiction of the U.S. (see: www.fbi.gov/about-us/ investigate/terrorism/terrorism-definition).

164. Potter, Will (2011). *Green is the New Red: An Insider's Account of a Social Movement Under Siege.* City Lights Books. pp.41-43.

165. *Gaia* theory, a term coined by scientist James Lovelock and named after the primordial Earth goddess from ancient Greek mythology, propounds that all organisms and their inorganic surroundings on Earth are integrated to form a self-regulating system.

166. www.fbi.gov/about-us/investigate/terrorism/terrorism-definition

167. Potter, Will (2011). *Green is the New Red: An Insider's Account of a Social Movement Under Siege.* City Lights Books. p.48.

168. Manes, Christopher (1990). *Green Rage: Radical Environmentalism and the Unmaking of Civilisation.* Little, Brown. p.11.

169. Potter, Will (2011). *Green is the New Red: An Insider's Account of a Social Movement Under Siege.* City Lights Books. p.50.

170. www.fbi.gov/news/testimony/the-threat-of-eco-terrorism

171. Dowie, Mark (1996). *Losing Ground: American Environmentalism at the Close of the Twentieth Century.* MIT Press.

172. www.greenisthenewred.com/blog/wp-content/Images/Other/ DHSflyermemo1.htm

173. From an interview in *If A Tree Falls: A Story of the Earth Liberation Front.* Dir. Marshall Curry. Dogwoof, 2012. DVD.

174. Foreman, Dave (1991). *Confessions of an Eco-warrior.* Crown Trade Paperbacks.

175. Manes, Christopher (1990). *Green Rage: Radical Environmentalism and the Unmaking of Civilisation.* Little, Brown. pp.9-10.

176. www.academia.edu/238985/Bitter_Green_The_Strategy_of_Ecotage

177. http://personalityspirituality.net/2010/08/19/successful-psychopaths/

178. Board, Belinda Jane and Frizon, Katarina (2005). 'Disordered Personalities at Work'. *Psychology, Crime & Law*, Volume 11, Issue 1. pp.17-32.

179. Babiak, Paul and Hare, Robert D. (2007). *Snakes in Suits: When Psychopaths Go to Work*. Harper Business.

180. www.monbiot.com/2011/11/07/the-self-attribution-fallacy/

181. Brand, Russell (2014). *Do Rich People Deserve To Be Rich?* The Trews (E223): http://youtu.be/z-_Mei4-uhI

182. Potter, Will (2011). *Green is the New Red: An Insider's Account of a Social Movement Under Siege*. City Lights Books. p.245.

183. Amritsar, the spiritual centre for the Sikh religion, was the site of the Jallianwala Bagh massacre, where British soldiers slaughtered hundreds of innocent civilians on one of their holiest days.

184. Gelderloos, Peter (2007). *How Nonviolence Protects the State*. South End Press. p.7.

185. Gelderloos, Peter (2007). *How Nonviolence Protects the State*. South End Press. pp.7-9.

186. Gelderloos, Peter (2007). *How Nonviolence Protects the State*. South End Press. pp.7-9.

187. www.tribuneindia.com/2001/20010321/edit.htm#6

188. Gelderloos, Peter (2007). *How Nonviolence Protects the State*. South End Press. pp.7-9.

189. www.pbs.org/hueypnewton/people/people_hoover.html

190. X, Malcolm (1963). *Message to the Grassroots*. 10th November, King Solomon Baptist Church, Detroit, Michigan.

191. Ryan, Mike (2007). 'On Ward Churchill's "Pacifism as Pathology": Toward a Revolutionary Practice'. In Churchill, Ward and Ryan, Mike, *Pacifism as Pathology: Reflections on the Role of Armed Struggle in North America*. AK Press. p.141.

192. Churchill, Ward and Ryan, Mike (2007). *Pacifism as Pathology: Reflections on the Role of Armed Struggle in North America*. AK Press. p.46.

193. Churchill, Ward and Ryan, Mike (2007). *Pacifism as Pathology: Reflections on the Role of Armed Struggle in North America*. AK Press. p.61

194. From an interview in *If A Tree Falls: A Story of the Earth Liberation Front*. Dir. Marshall Curry. Dogwoof, 2012. DVD.

195. Manes, Christopher (1990). *Green Rage: Radical Environmentalism and the Unmaking of Civilisation*. Little, Brown. p.9.

196. Gelderloos, Peter (2013). *The Failure of Nonviolence: From the Arab Spring to Occupy*. Left Bank Books. pp.191-192.

197. Dorney, John (2013). *Peace After the Final Battle: The Story of the Irish Revolution 1912-1924*. New Island Books. pp.22-24.

198. X, Malcolm (1964). *The Ballot or the Bullet*. 3rd April, Cory Methodist Church, Cleveland, Ohio.

199. Scott, James C. (1990). *Domination and the Arts of Resistance: Hidden Transcripts*. Yale University Press.

200. Marcos, Subcomandante Insurgente (2001). *Our Word is Our Weapon: Selected Writings*. Seven Stories Press. p.418.

201. Marcos, Subcomandante Insurgente (2004). *Ya Basta! Ten Years of the Zapatista Uprising*. AK Press.

202. Marcos, Subcomandante Insurgente (2001). *Our Word is Our Weapon: Selected Writings*. Seven Stories Press.

203. Marcos, Subcomandante Insurgente (2001). *Our Word is Our Weapon: Selected Writings*. Seven Stories Press. p.420.

204. Marcos, Subcomandante Insurgente (2001). *Our Word is Our Weapon: Selected Writings*. Seven Stories Press. p.17.

205. Foreman, Dave (1991). *Confessions of an Eco-warrior*. Crown Trade Paperbacks. p.23.

206. Manes, Christopher (1990). *Green Rage: Radical Environmentalism and the Unmaking of Civilisation*. Little, Brown. p.187.

207. Jensen, Derrick (2007). Preface to Churchill, Ward and Ryan, Mike, *Pacifism as Pathology: Reflections on the Role of Armed Struggle in North America*. AK Press. p.13.

208. McBay, Aric (2011). *Deep Green Resistance: Strategy to Save the Planet*. Seven Stories Press. p.244.

209. Bailie, Gil (1996). *Violence Unveiled: Humanity at the Crossroads*. Crossroad Publishing. p.xv.

210. Sagan, Carl (1992). *Shadows of Forgotten Ancestors: A Search for Who We Are*. Random House Inc.

211. Monbiot, George (2013). *Feral: Searching for Enchantment on the Frontiers of Rewilding*. Allen Lane. p.7.

212. Leopold, Aldo (1968). *A Sand County Almanac and Sketches Here and There*. OUP USA; Enlarged edition.

213. Monbiot, George (2013). *Feral: Searching for Enchantment on the Frontiers of Rewilding*. Allen Lane. p.48.

214. Monbiot, George (2013). *Feral: Searching for Enchantment on the Frontiers of Rewilding*. Allen Lane. p.139.

215. See *How Wolves Change Rivers*: http://youtu.be/ysa5OBhXz-Q and *How Whales Change Climate*: http://youtu.be/M18HxXve3CM

216. Leopold, Aldo (1968). *A Sand County Almanac and Sketches Here and There*. OUP USA; Enlarged edition. p.262.

217. Klein, Naomi (2014). *This Changes Everything: Capitalism vs. the Climate*. Allen Lane.

218. Hawken, Paul (2008). *Blessed Unrest: How the Largest Social Movement in History Is Restoring Grace, Justice, and Beauty to the World*. Penguin. p.142.

219. Kaczynski, Theodore (2010). *Technological Slavery: The Collected Writings of Theodore J. Kaczynski, a.k.a. "The Unabomber"*. Feral House.

220. Capra, Fritjof (1997). *The Web of Life: A New Synthesis of Mind and Matter*. Flamingo. p.279.

221. Hawken, Paul (2008). *Blessed Unrest: How the Largest Social Movement in History Is Restoring Grace, Justice, and Beauty to the World*. Penguin. pp.141-142.

222. Pauly, Daniel (1995). 'Anecdotes and the Shifting Baseline Syndrome of Fisheries'. *Trends in Ecology and Evolution*, Vol.10, no.10, doi:10.1016/So169-5347(00)89171-5.

223. Leopold, Aldo (1968). *A Sand County Almanac and Sketches Here and There*. OUP USA; Enlarged edition.

224. Monbiot, George (2013). *Feral: Searching for Enchantment on the Frontiers of Rewilding*. Allen Lane. p.69.

225. Monbiot, George (2013). *Feral: Searching for Enchantment on the Frontiers of Rewilding*. Allen Lane. p.35.

226. Jensen, Derrick (2006). *Endgame Volume 1: The Problem of Civilisation*. Seven Stories Press.

227. Wheatley, Margaret (2002). *Turning to One Another: Simple Conversations to Restore Hope to the Future*. Berrett-Koehler. p.19.

228. Monbiot, George (2013). *Feral: Searching for Enchantment on the Frontiers of Rewilding*. Allen Lane. pp.84-86.

229. Leopold, Aldo (1968). *A Sand County Almanac and Sketches Here and There*. OUP USA; Enlarged edition.

230. Monbiot, George (2013). *Feral: Searching for Enchantment on the Frontiers of Rewilding*. Allen Lane.

INDEX